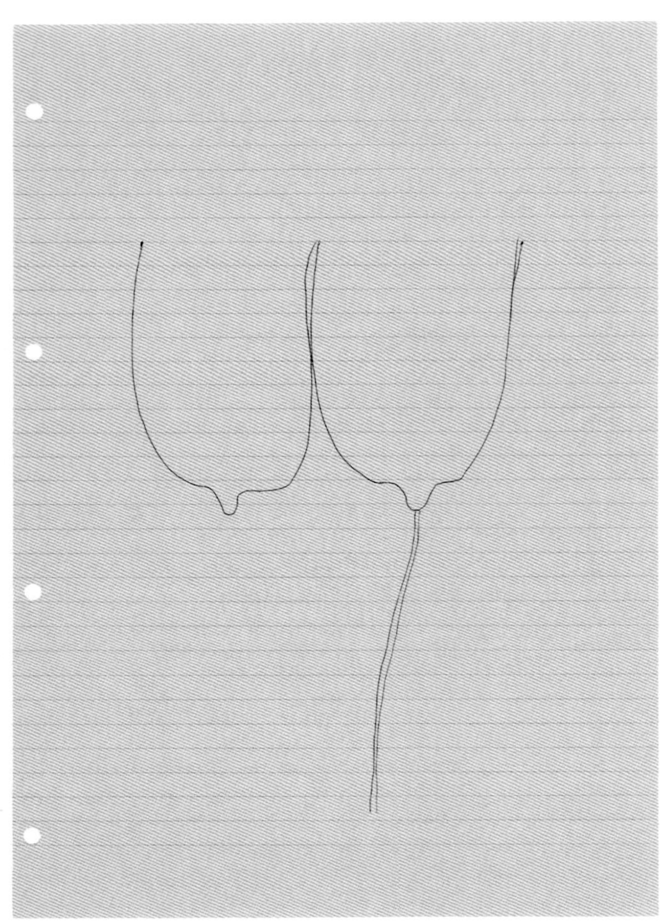

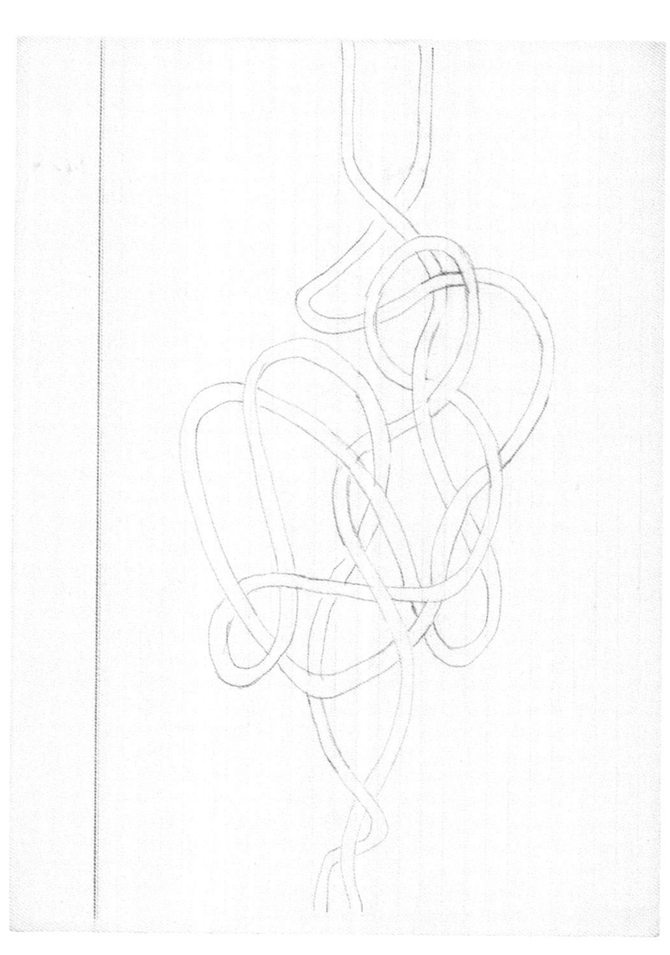

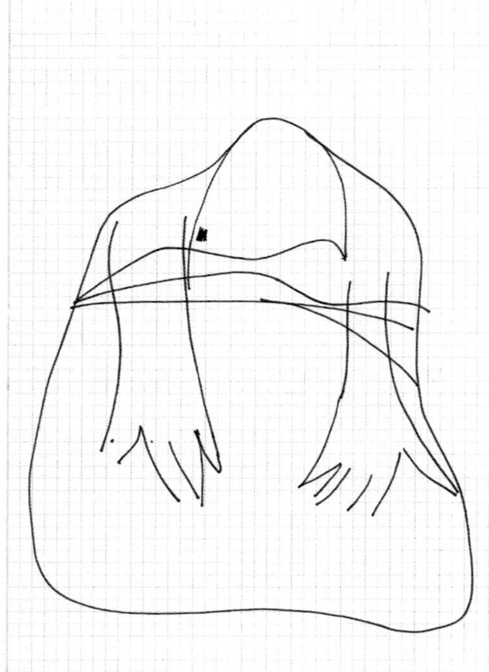

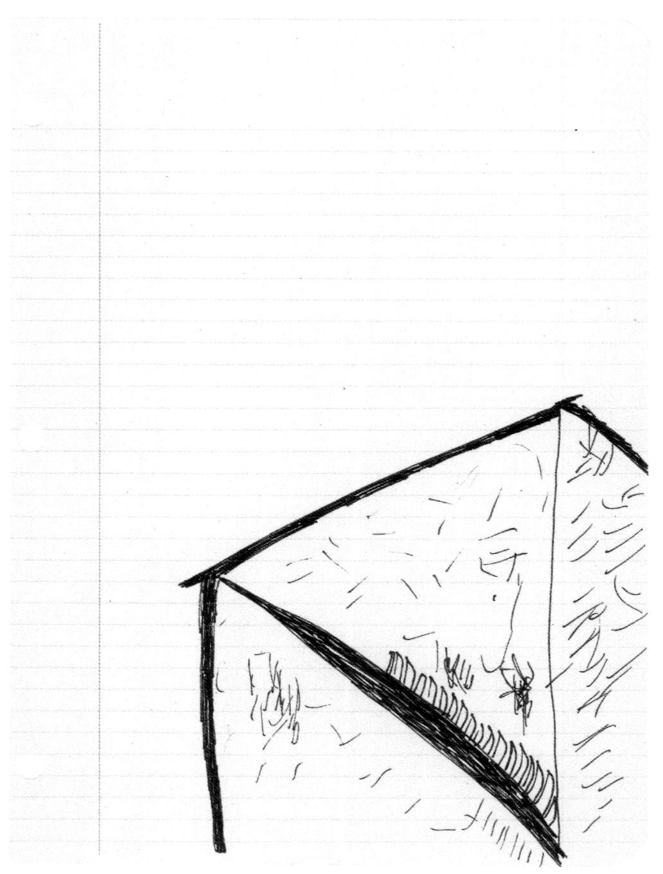

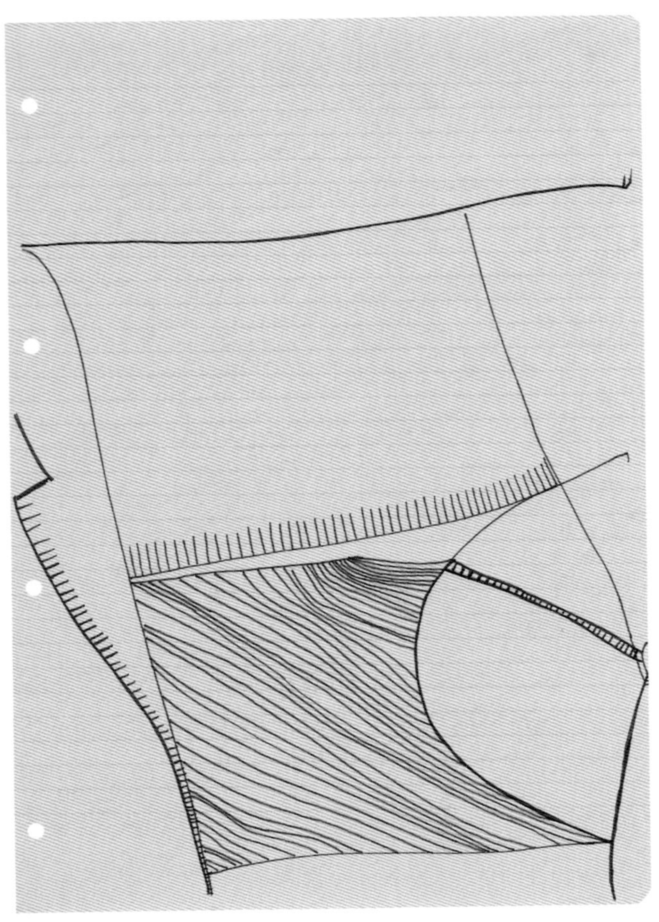

shelf documents: art library as practice

drawings by
Heide Hinrichs

edited by
Heide Hinrichs
Jo-ey Tang
Elizabeth Haines

Contents

listening

the body

Preface

I lived in Brooklyn from 1988 to 2004, and in times of transition or deprivation, the many branches of the New York Public Library served as my adjunct studio. I loved working at its flagship location on 42nd Street. I could read and write and sketch. The Mid-Manhattan library branch across the street holds a picture library—pages culled from deaccessioned books—that supplied images for my journals and zines. I didn't have funds to pay studio rent but I could still make art in fellowship with other workers, whatever their pursuits. The library provided a form of refuge that resonated with my needs and sensibilities as an artist. Solitude is an essential element of artistic practice, but I rebel against the fantasy of the artist toiling in isolation from the world, this ideological freight of a conservatory model of art education. In the library, you are always reminded that your work is tethered to the social.

I carried my attachment to the library as studio into my teaching at Ohio University. When I bring studio art classes to the library, I ask students: if we think of the library as a repository of knowledge, what does our library know? Why is this book in the collection and not another? I want them to understand the hierarchical nature of the space so that they can find the information they need but also understand the political costs of access, how this determines what's on the shelf. Choice is bound up in privilege and it's instructive to understand how institutional accessibility is determined by this calculus. As an antidote, I emphasize the potentials of chance in research. I want students to see the radical possibilities of the chance encounter and how these moments open up lateral fields of disruption and connection. Grab a volume because you like the color of the binding. Check out a novel that your crush is reading. Serendipity and desire as search engines rooted in the experience of the subjective body.

For a foundations course in studio concepts, I assign a project where the students produce a site-specific work in the university's library. I encourage the students to use the resources at hand when responding to the site rather than introducing conventional art materials. In a haunting performance, Nick, a graphic design student, directed his peers to wander the stacks. At his cue, everyone stopped and grabbed a book from the shelf. Each student was then asked to begin reading aloud from their book in a whisper while slowly walking up and down the aisles. The participants had to balance several states at once—quiet recitation while pacing, calibrating the route of their bodies and the volume of their voices in accordance with the group. They hummed—absorbed in their sentient experience and attuned to the collective.

second shelf begins with the inescapable fact that women, queer, and BIPOC artists are systemically excluded from the institutions that shape the art world: schools archives, publishing, granting foundations, non-profit and commercial venues. It's disheartening if familiar news that underrepresentation will remain a battle for liberatory practices. At its heart, Heide Hinrichs' collaborative project extends beyond the necessary act of corrective and pivots towards the radical possibilities that are governed by chance. Like all hierarchical structures, the library is a vulnerable site, ready to be pierced, dismantled, and rebuilt. I imagine a student encountering this collection of works. Does it feel like a gift? A secret society? How can the experience of disorientation open up new paths of inquiry? *second shelf* speaks to the pleasures of promiscuous discovery and the transformative power of communion in the library.

Laura Larson
Columbus, Ohio, October 2020

shelf documents:
art library as practice
an introduction

Heide Hinrichs
Jo-ey Tang
Elizabeth Haines

We are holding this book. It fits in our hands, and in our jacket pockets and in our bags. It doesn't fit very well on the shelf in the art library. It's too small, it gets lost between and behind monographs that stick out of the shelves. We also don't know where to put it. It isn't a reader, it isn't an artist's book, it isn't documentation of a project or a catalogue. It might recall a pamphlet, a roadmap, or a recipe book, but it doesn't really tell you where to go or what to do.

But we like this size. We want to stake a claim in a tradition of books that don't quite fit, that gently destabilise the parameters of a library and the design of the bookshelves as much as the process of indexing. We want a book that gets mis-shelved all the time.

When we're hunting for this book we get to notice gaps on the shelves, and those contours in the library's mass and weight take on a sculptural quality, and confer a particular landscape of origins, languages, labour, processes, transactions that make these books possible. We start to map that landscape more closely, but also to think about the journeys in that landscape. How do we travel from one book to another? Who are the guides? What gestures produce echoes and ripples as we learn from the books and each other?

second shelf

We, the editors of *shelf documents,* Heide Hinrichs, Jo-ey Tang and Elizabeth Haines, ask these questions as members of the project *second shelf.* This research project carried out between 2018 and 2020 involved the practice of thinking not just *about* but *from* and *in* the library. As artists, teachers, writers, scholars, and curators, our individual practices form a collective practice that maps our personal stake in institutions as living organisms that we shape collaboratively. The conversations and reflections we are sharing with you here come from a slow, iterative, discursive practice that unfolded with the other contributors to this volume, with our students, with our colleagues, with librarians and with public audiences.

Over two years of discussion and conversation, we convened – with Marisa C. Sánchez and Susanne Weiß – to identify 243 titles of books by and about those who identify as queer, as women, as Black, Indigenous, people of colour (BIPOC); those who have often been left out – the words, images, and bodies of the artists who are silenced, erased, and made invisible. These books would enter the collections of the libraries of the Royal Academy of Fine Arts Antwerp Belgium, and Packard Library at Columbus College of Art & Design, USA. These books do many things: they fill gaps, amplify voices, hold and make spaces, seek out the self-initiated and the overlooked, and reveal that the library and the institution are porous works in progress that demand our continual attention and involvement.[1] We found, to our surprise, that buying books, and inserting them into the library holdings, the library space, was sometimes a more complicated act than we had imagined. In our stumbling through bureaucracy, we got into conversations with colleagues, re-learned our institutions, negotiated existing protocols and policies, defined new ones, and produced new institutional memories.

The substance, hope and disappointment of such efforts will be well-known to many readers, especially librarians who hold this book in their hands. For decades, projects in radical librarianship have attempted to diversify library holdings and users, to repair persistent historical structural inequalities that have excluded and alienated writers and readers that institutions identified as minorities. Here our aim is to embrace the questions of belonging, inclusion and representation in the art library in the important ex(in)clusionary structural inequalities that are visible in book acquisition, cataloguing, hiring, and in patterns of library use. We want to destabilise the parameters of the library as an architecture. We see the art library as a hybrid space for the practices of librarians, readers, artists, art students, researchers, educators, that blurs the lines between these categories. We see art library practice in acts of reading, rereading, misreading and reproduction. We see art library practice as inclusive of the unseen physical maintenance, like dusting and cleaning, as much as the conversations about and surrounding the books.

In the preface to this book, Laura Larson's biographical reflections demonstrate how library practice is interwoven through different spheres of work, different geographical sites, new institutional relationships. These practices produce what she describes as 'transformative communion' between artists and students, students and teachers, librarians and readers, between researchers and researched, and between readers. How does this work? We have begun to think about the art library as a site where we learn how to *do*, through watching, through visual listening, through imitating, acts of reproduction that Melanie Noel calls 'a species of boomerang, part rose'. The library can substitute for a studio and extend the boundaries of a classroom. We read, we photocopy, we scribble down quotes. Expensive books and lush magazines with elaborate typefaces muddle with pens and papers and cheap notebooks in active moments of artistic process.

It was on a sheet of lined notebook paper, in The Seattle Public Library, that Heide Hinrichs began a drawing based on a drawing by Eva Hesse reproduced in an exhibition catalogue. Just as Hesse's drawing was a sketch that was later realized into an artwork, this process of mimesis activated by Hinrichs led to an ongoing series of work, *Inscriptions,* that now contains 240 drawings. Hinrichs' drawings form a process of personal memory, learning, attention and note-taking which intersects with processes in the larger institutions in which art lives: the acts and structures through which artists' legacies are shared. Those acts of attention blur the line between her learning from peers and predecessors and her role as artist educator. This sense of the library as a site of intersubjectivity has informed our approach. Interspersed within this book are sixty-four of these drawings, a continual process that moves between reproduction and the singular, the collection and the individual, the artwork and the book.

shelf documents

Through two years of trying to *do* things in libraries we have uncovered five scales for thinking about practice in an art library. We'd like to invite you to join us in imagining practice from each one of these five perspectives: the institution, the library, the book, listening and the body.

the institution

We begin with two chapters that address the ways in which art libraries entangle with institutions – an art school, a university, a museum or an art centre.

In *Finding the Core: Our Institutions. Our Selves.* artist and curator Jo-ey Tang maps the connective tissues and fractures between academy, exhibition space and library, and advocates for a greater sense of agility towards departmental and institutional collaborations as pedagogy. These reflections from his previous role as a director of an art gallery situated within an art and design school in the Midwestern US, were enabled by Heide Hinrichs' *second shelf* and through the exhibition of her *Inscriptions* drawing and sculptural intervention at the library.

In *Shelf Shifts*, David Senior, head of library and archives at San Francisco Museum of Modern Art, describes art librarianship as a responsibility towards the visibility of diverse communities and the legacy of their art. The experimentation and accessibility of printed matter from the 1970s to 1990s, by feminist art movements, queer and AIDS activism, and the Black Arts Movement, have shaped contemporary art discourse. Present and future library collections must continue to learn through the tactics of alternative networks and distribution systems of solidarity in order to reflect publishing ecosystems that demonstrate equity and inclusion.

the library

We start to wonder about the corridors and routes that connect the library to the larger space of the institution. These two essays explore the library's role within social infrastructures, patterns of community and readership.

In *Threads from the Labyrinth (About a Library in Beirut)*, Rachel Dedman, Jameel Curator of Contemporary Art from the Middle East at the Victoria and Albert Museum, London, speaks of the library as a refuge and engine. She explores this through the example of the library at Mansion, Beirut. This space emerged as a grassroots necessity for the community, and now physically damaged by the Beirut port explosion, the communal space of the library has taken on even more urgency as a site in the struggle for responsible government in Lebanon.

Elizabeth Haines, historian, considers the physical act of reading as a tool for thinking through the architecture of the library space as gendered. In her essay *Embracing Noise and Other Airborne Risks to the Reading Body*, she asks how different embodied experiences of books, of silent and communal reading practices, are inflected by social identity and what that means for establishing alternative practices.

the book

The book is a container that can travel and act in different spaces. The book infiltrates how and what we talk about, think about, what histories and people are worth remembering, and what ideas we surround ourselves with. The book tells us what is valued and acceptable. The book is a physical manifestation of financial and cultural capital. These three contributions consider books as material objects and as conceptual references within the self-constructed infrastructure of an artist's practice.

In *Not Alone*, Berlin-based curator Susanne Weiß reflects on the role of books in the practices of artists she has collaborated with as a constellation of friendships: Ulf Aminde, Heide Hinrichs, Annette Weisser, Ceija Stojka. Books as text and objects weave in and out of these artists' lives and practices, and find their way into exhibition spaces. She emphasises books as an element of the rich social connectivity that is present in artistic practices, as influences and conceptual relationships shift and change over time.

Pages by Ersi Varveri, an artist based in Antwerp and Athens, are white sheets of paper punctured and marked by cuts, slashes and openings, unmasking the texture of the knitted sweater and the presence of the artist's body that holds them. The rupture, surface and terrain of these pages address the reader in a mutual gaze.

Ghent-based graphic designer Sara De Bondt's working principle is to restore the value of women's contributions to her profession. The typefaces she chose for this book are *Diotima*, designed by Gudrun Zapf von Hesse, and *Lelo*, designed by Katharina Köhler.[2] With this ethic, De Bondt renders visible the design decisions that are often overlooked when thinking about diversity and multiplicity. In *Typography*

Shelf, De Bondt reminds us, through a collage of found text, that histories of inclusion and exclusion, and languages of embodied identity, are inscribed into the printed alphabets we are reading and touching.

listening

We reject the library as a space of silence. The fixity of the printed word is made alive by the spoken word, the sounds where the resonance of the body is present. The spoken word activates our sense of the diversity of vocal tones and embodied experiences that are flattened in print; it refocuses our attention, teaches us to notice differences and to read with empathy, a shared feeling of being understood. Listening as an intersubjective process, internal and external, reaching into oneself and listening to other voices reflecting back. Listening as a dialectic, an active correspondence.

In *Towards a Feminist Practice: Notes on Listening*, art historian and curator Marisa C. Sánchez describes a feminist listening practice, inviting us to reflect upon our own subject position and to what emerges when we start to listen. Grounding the act of hearing in the exchange between beings, she reassociates statements of presence, 'I am here, hear me', with the here and there of participants in dialogue. In discussing artists' interventions into institutions, addressing absences and limitations within art museums and academia, she turns to the work of Indigenous curators and artists in Canada, whose practices are attuned to ways of knowing that reside outside of Western pedagogical structures and encourage an attentiveness to collective, collaborative action.

In *Reading as Activism: the WOCI Reading Group*, London-based artist Samia Malik, in conversation with Elizabeth Haines, offers up her experience as co-founder of the WOCI (Women of Colour Index) reading group. Since 2016 this group has been exploring texts by and about British women artists of colour who were at work in the 1980s and 1990s. Through reading aloud, the group has built knowledge about an important and neglected body of work, as well as gaining understanding about the structural disadvantages those women have faced. Malik reflects on how these readings have changed her perspective on her own career, and also on how difficult hosting inclusive conversations continues to be, thirty years later, in the face of ongoing racial and gender discrimination in the art world.

Heide Hinrichs and Susanne Weiß discuss Hinrichs' art practice and process for *Inscriptions*, in which her embodiment inscribes multiple sites and institutions over time. Shifting the act of looking into a form of listening, Hinrichs traces her sense-making and use of the library as a site for practice. She frames the series of drawings, *Inscriptions* (2006–2020), as both representational and indexical, pointing at and gesturing, the hand as translator.

the body

Listening leads us to a greater awareness of the body, the physical and social limits that separate yet bind us. Although the library is often considered a site primarily for the 'mind', we want to know what kind of learning our bodies do in, and bring to, the library.

The text *Camouflaged for Fire* by Melanie Noel, writer and poet based in Seattle and Reykjavik, maps a landscape of learning to experience ourselves through architectures of gaze, sensation, and of pacing instated by others. She draws on her experience as an audience member of *Feelings* (2019), a performance by Matthew Offenbacher, in which he explored the embodiment of European visual traditions. *Camouflaged for Fire* is to be read aloud, so that its synesthesia can activate the body into motion.

Columbus-based artist Laura Larson's photographic series *All the Women I Know* (2018–ongoing) documents a solidarity of communal looking and being. These tender and defiant portraits of Larson's intimate and social circles are taken from and of the backs of the subjects' heads, who collectively refuse the gaze of the camera.

shelf practice

We see the elements of this book, at these five scales, as part of our practice. *shelf documents* are a call to ourselves and to others to continue imagining the library as a collective site. The book isn't neutral. *It isn't a reader, it isn't an artist's book, it isn't documentation of a project or a catalogue. It might recall a pamphlet, a roadmap, or a recipe book, but it doesn't really tell you where to go or what to do.* It is the result of sustained conversations between a particular group of people, whose working lives and friendships have criss-crossed over time and distance. It reflects both the intimacy and the transience of those relationships as we have navigated changes to our status as migrants, as citizens, as members of institutions. We take our place with gratitude to other practitioners of art libraries – who have consciously and unconsciously been working to acknowledge and change the exclusionary tendencies of those spaces.

This book is part of an ongoing process of negotiation and intervention, as we imagine the invisible lines you, yourself, might draw in the space of the art library, as we imagine how you mobilise your bodies and your listening towards radical change. We imagine art libraries in which artists, writers and readers who identify as queer, as women, as BIPOC have the resources (material, intellectual, practical, communal) to practice and thrive, and in doing so, to transform the institutions themselves.

1 For a list of these books, including photographs documenting the books among their neighbours on the shelves, please see project website second-shelf.org.

2 Köhler's *Lelo* is also the typeface deployed on second-shelf.org.

We wonder how and where
this book might sit on your shelves.

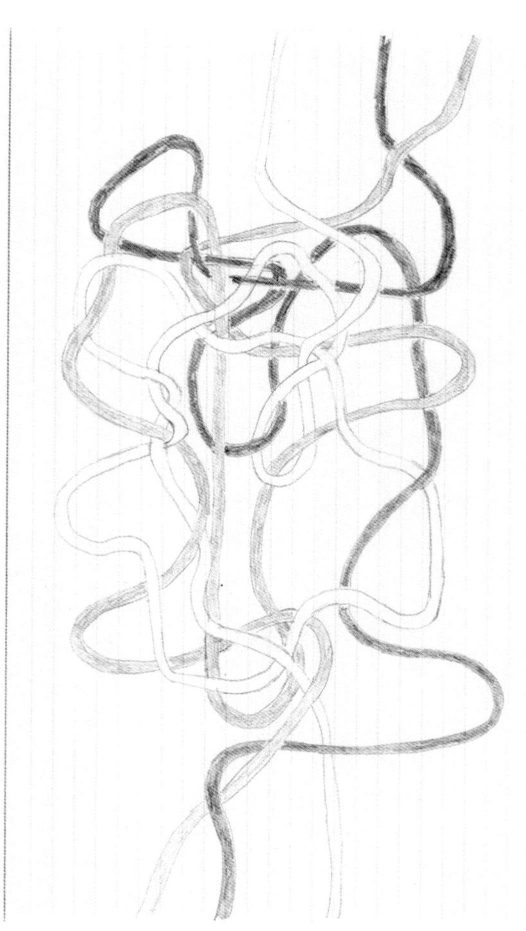

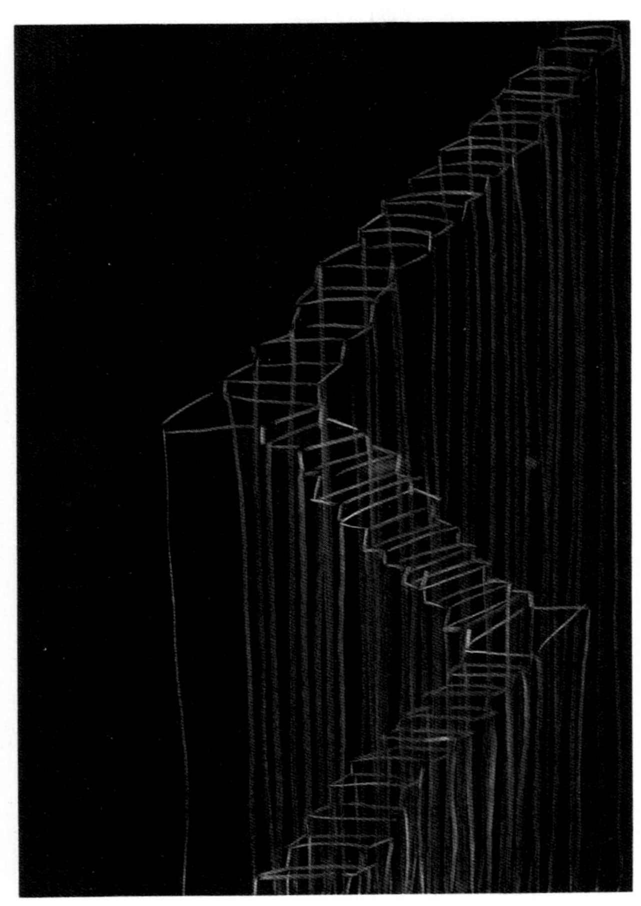

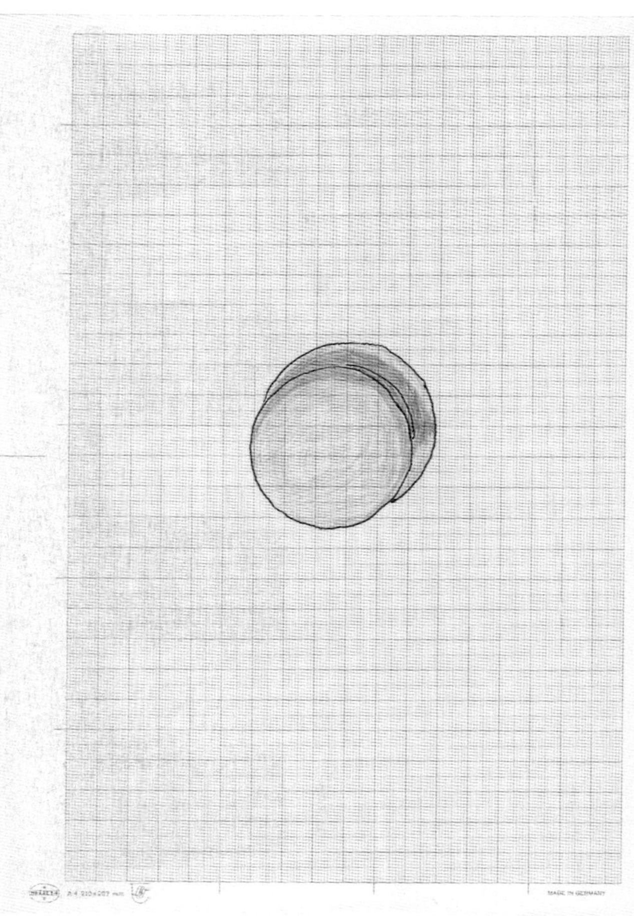

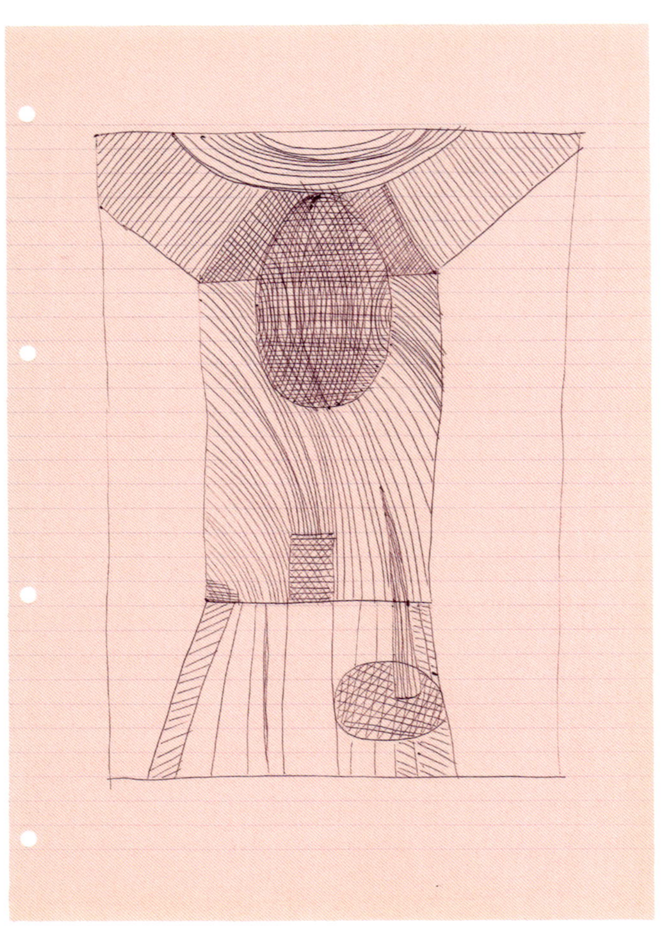

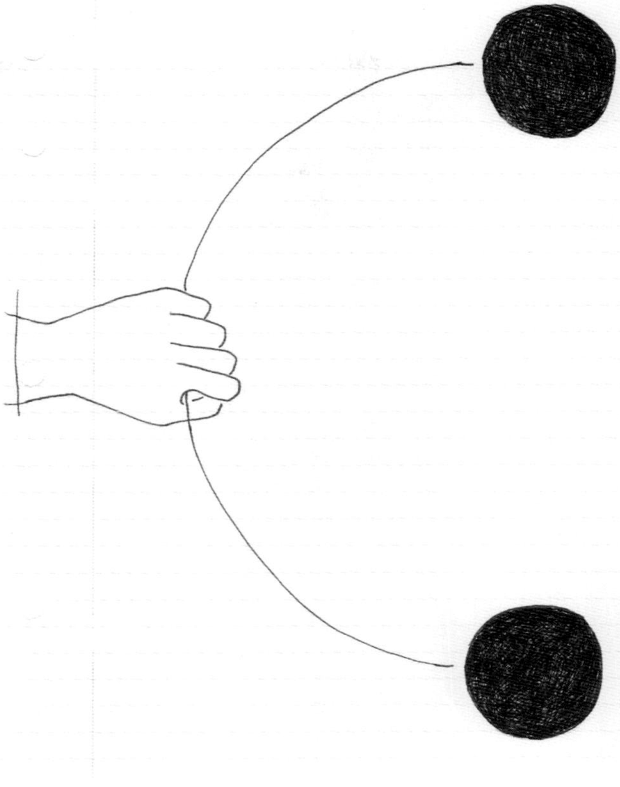

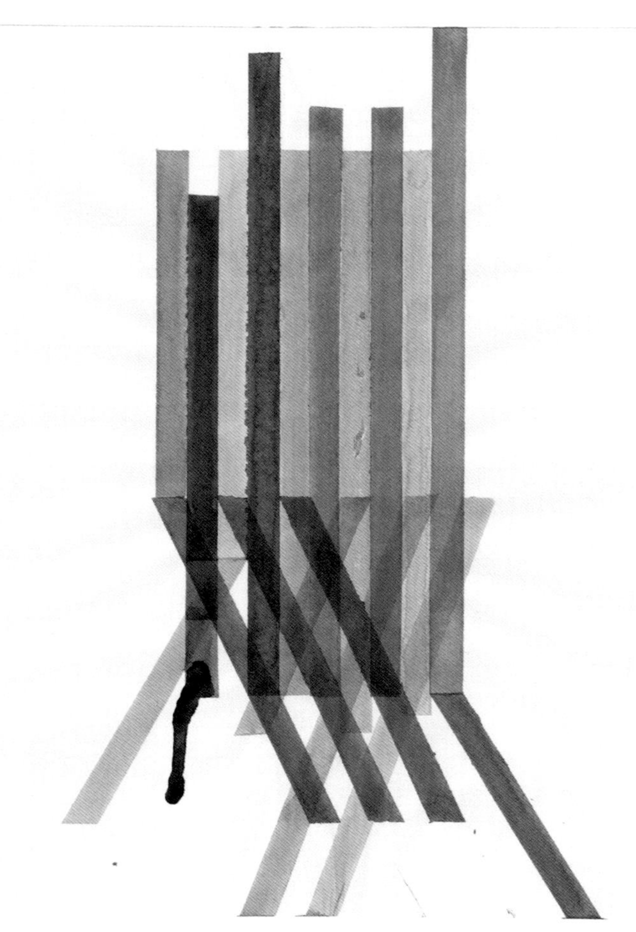

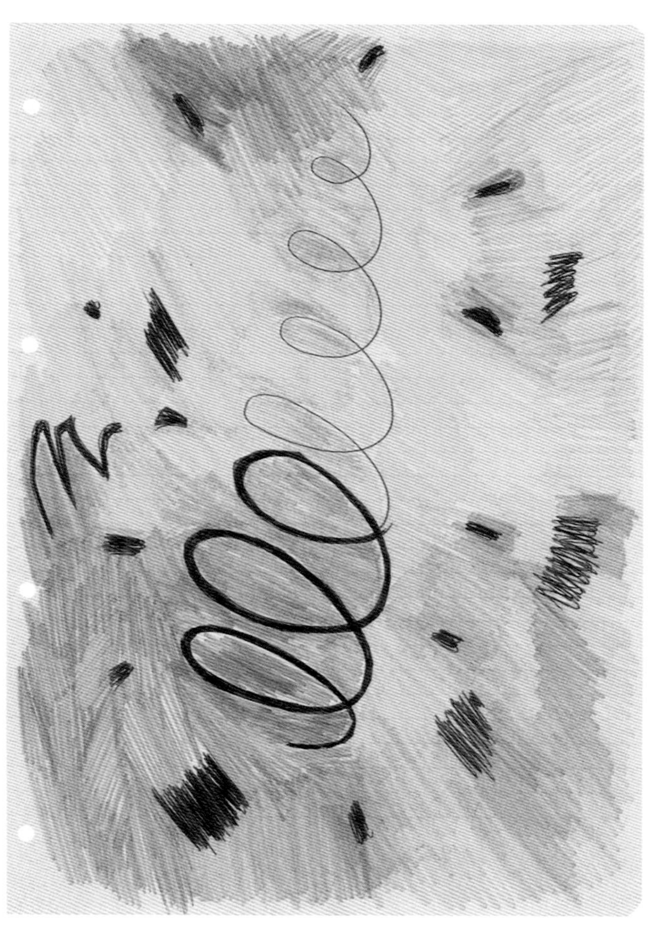

We cannot even imagine how
to be humble.
I can see humility
Delicate and white
It is satisfying
Just by itself

And Trust
absolute trust
a gift
a precious gift

I would rather think of humility than
anything else.

Humility, the beautiful daughter
She cannot do either right or wrong
She does not do anything
All of her ways are emty
Infinitely light and delicate
She treads an even path.
Sweet, smiling uninterrupted, free

the institution

Finding the Core: Our Institutions. Our Selves.

Jo-ey Tang

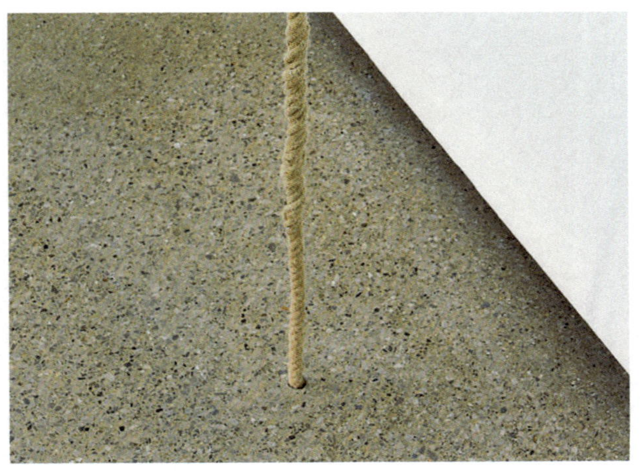

All images: Heide Hinrichs, *untitled*, 2020, as part of *Follow the Mud*, Beeler Gallery at Columbus College of Art & Design and Packard Library. Photos: Stephen Takacs.

I

This rope is a throughline.
A core without a core.
It holds itself and is itself.

A library call number in Dewey decimals would have been assigned to this rope, a sculptural work by Heide Hinrichs.

February 2020. The rope is made up of smaller ropes, themselves made up of strings—all braids and twists. Tied to the ceiling of the gallery, it narrows as it hangs. The change in thickness is imperceptible. At closer inspection, it throws the height of the gallery into question, rendering it both compact and monumental. This rope is solid. It casts a shadow as if burrowing into the wall, as both outside and inside it, a thing and a void. It ripples a shimmering subjectivity. From a hole in the ground it disappears.

Disappearing into the library through a gap between the dropped ceiling, the rope continues. The ceiling panels hide the infrastructure of ductwork, pipes, and wires, creating a void space between the gallery and the library. This rope is flexile. It glides over the Sculpture section, in front of *Nineteenth-century Romantic bronzes: French, English and American bronzes, 1830-1915* / Jeremy Cooper (735.22 c786n) and *19th-Century Sculpture* / H.W. Janson (735.22 J267n), grazing the carpeted floor. Nearby a student reads, unaware of the rope sculpture's presence? It dances a stillness. It quivers.

Amelia Blasio and Akilah-Marie Marshall were Gallery Ambassadors (a title I renamed for the student workers). I was then Director of Exhibitions of the Beeler Gallery at Columbus College of Art & Design where they worked and studied. They spent their shifts writing a description for the rope which, like a book, would be cataloged in the school's Packard Library and could be called upon.

The tuition of 2020–2021 academic year is $37,370. According to *U.S. News & World Report*, 65% of university graduates in the United States borrowed student loans, and the graduating class of 2019 with student loans borrowed $30,062 on average.[1] In 2019, 44 million Americans collectively hold over $1.6 trillion in student debt.[2]

The rope would would have entered the collection of the library after March 15, 2020, when the gallery season *Follow the Mud* concluded. On March 13, the gallery closed to the public due to COVID-19. March 31 was my last day in my position, following the school's decision earlier in the year to shift the gallery focus to student/alumni/faculty projects. I never saw the rope again.

II

The institution is a throughline.
An institution without an institution.
It holds itself and is self.

In the gallery, the rope formed a backdrop for Heide Hinrichs' *Inscriptions* drawings, some connected by other ropes made into suspending structures, a loose net, and a hanging system of cascading ropes that echoed the width of the aisle in the library below. Physically navigating the drawings activates the sinuous motion and porous energy in the lines in the drawings, as gallery and library became a vertical stack.

Inscriptions were part of *Season Two: Follow the Mud* (October 2019–March 2020, which I co-curated with Ian Ruffino and Marla Roddy, assisted by JiaHao Peng and Wei Ling Chang), a six-month process of accumulation by instances. Each instance inscribed an event or an artwork's entry. Hinrichs' presence marked *Instance No. 7.*

Working with and alongside artists in an embodied entanglement, adjacencies, proximities, and contingencies are set into motion, sustained by an ethos I termed "slow programming." Its name is a dig at the pervasiveness in the co-opting of "curation." *Slow programming* co-opts the infusion of the Slow Food Movement in aspects of contemporary life. *Slow programming* is active, and is held together through collective labor and bodies over time. *Slow programming* motivates attentiveness and brings the transformation of awareness into view. *Slow programming* occupies the time and space in between as well as what it envelops. *Slow programming* reorders how time is used and felt, as artists, their works and their publics move through the physical space of the gallery and beyond its confines. *Slow programming* advocates for a flexibility around rigid administration, bureaucracy, budgetary allocation and fiscal projections to take into account how artists work and live in the world. *Slow programming* acknowledges that institutional memories are developed by people and might be short-lived. *Slow programming* reshapes infrastructure to participate in a collective past, present and future, where staff, adjuncts and tenured professors, students and publics live out histories. *Slow programming* embraces the volatile instability of institutions as one that is already found in the world, and as such animates pliability to construct with artists in their temporary residence in institutional structures. *Slow programming* tends to and cares for. *Slow programming* enlivens contradictions. *Slow programming* reckons with the capitalist amassing of student-debt and teacher-debt.

Hinrichs' invitation to be an advisor to *second shelf* in 2017 was an open valve of ideas, resources, and labor. As a gesture of reciprocity, I implemented *second shelf* as a mirror site, housed within the school's library. Ordinarily, books are purchased based on course syllabi and requests from students and teachers, without a protocol beyond the informal acquisition process. Packard Library director Leslie Jankowski agreed to match the advisors' book list within the library's existing budget. A testament to diversity, certain artists and books were already present or well represented. At the same time, any collection presents its own blind spots *and* soft spots. *second shelf* aligns multiple structures, across schools from different continents, and brings together the public-facing entities of the gallery and the library. *second shelf* renders professional endeavors as more than transactional, as more than Memorandums of Understanding as capital. We put our existing and invisible labor into view. Our work *is* the work. The question remains whether underscoring the invisible labor renders null its value and our roles, dispensable in the budget lines.

In 2018, the first batch of books acquired by Packard Library was unveiled in the public thoroughfare at the entrance of the gallery where paths to lecture hall, admission and administration offices intersect. Artist Laëtitia Badaut Haussmann designed a large-scale bookshelf with steel pipe materials she previously built into seating arrangements for a past season. A smaller version of the bookshelf was later on display in the library.

With *Instance No. 7*, local artists Laura Larson and Ryland Wharton joined in the co-mingling. Interpolating ninety-six *Inscriptions* drawings on notebook papers—reproductions of artworks in the acquired books—is a selection of Laura Larson's series *All the Women I Know*, 2018–ongoing (see chapter in this volume on the body, page 234). Defiance and vulnerability in the portraits of the backs of heads of women Larson knows and will get to know, reject our gaze. This community of bodies speak to how access is conditional. Larson and Hinrichs take their act of "looking at" as a "responsibility with."

The *Inscriptions* drawings were installed for viewing in multiple bodily positions: sitting, standing, and lying. They laid low along Michael Stickrod's camping cots in

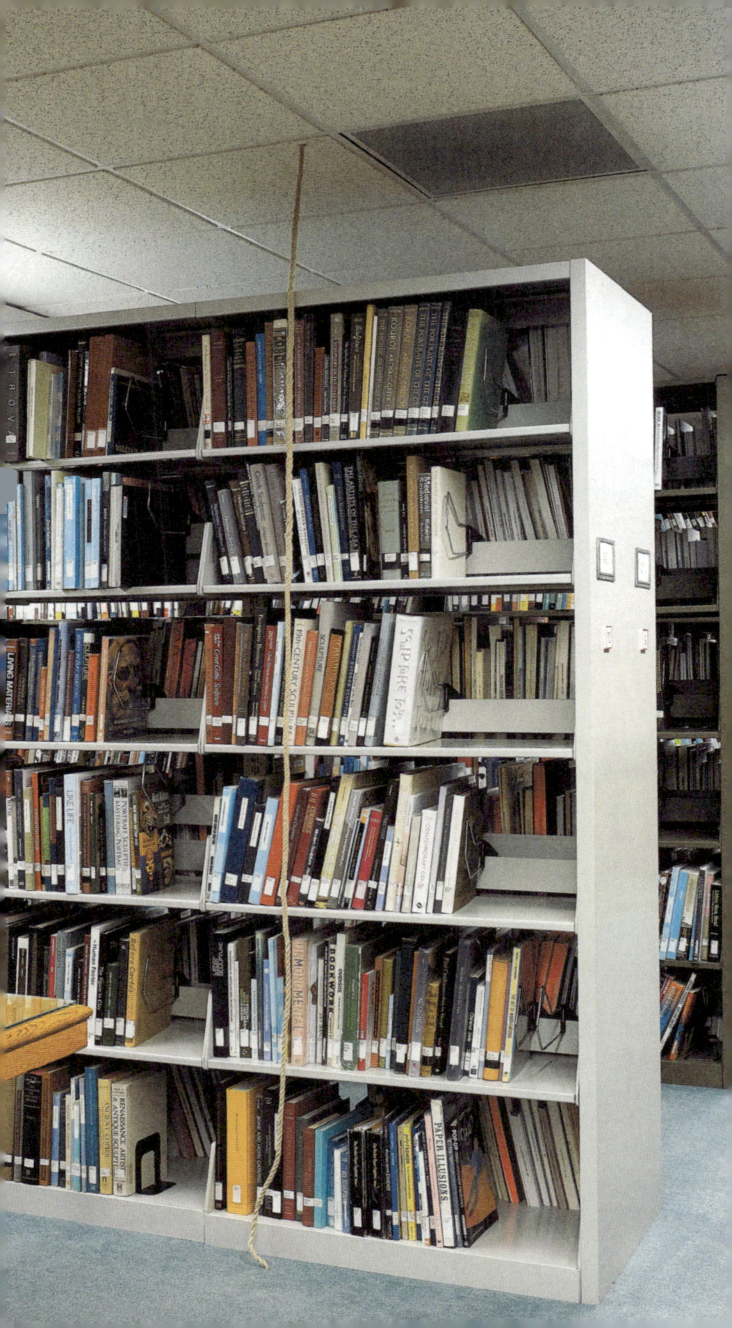

SCULPTURE TODAY
PAPER ILLUSIONS
MONUMENTAL
BOOKWORK
LIVING MATERIALS
19th-CENTURY SCULPTURE
LIKE LIFE
Human Factor
RENAISSANCE ARTISTS & ANTIQUE SCULPTURE
KOUROI ARCHAIC GREEK
THE PORTRAITS OF THE GREEKS
Greek Sculpture

his collaborative installation with Michel Auder's video *May '68 in '78*, and got close to the ground along Laëtitia Badaut Haussmann's floor cushions for the viewing of Julia Trotta's film on her art historian grandmother, *Forget to be afraid: A portrait of Linda Nochlin*. Ryland Wharton conceived a modular seating with a tabletop that held an *Inscription*, after Hilma af Klint (page 264). This piece of furniture was made for the Gallery Ambassadors, who encouraged visitors to take a seat while viewing the drawing of an enigmatic shape of O, filtered through Hinrichs' marks.

Besides C. Spencer Yeh's opening performance on amplified violin that was sampled for a video commission by Stickrod, *Follow the Mud* veered White. Yet this should be taken into account as a continuum of programming, to be rejoined by what occurred and the unrealized. *Season Three: From Fire/Flies to Desirable Body* would comprise two exhibitions. *Fire/Flies*, co-organized with Renee Musai and Valentine Umansky, situates the Midwest as a contested site of power and would include artists such as Sophia Al-Maria, Obayomi Anthony, Epoxy Art Group, The Otolith Group, and Constantina Zavitsanos across four venues in Ohio and Kentucky. *Desirable Body*, inspired by Tunisian writer Hubert Haddad's novel of the same name, by curator Melanie Pocock, would include artists of multiple Asian Diasporas, such as Gina Osterloh, Seulgi Lee, and Renee So. *Season Four: DUST: The Plates of the (Ever) Present* would expand upon the collective photogram archive I co-founded with Thomas Fougeirol that is now in the collection of Centre Pompidou, by 136 artists, including the school's alumni/faculty/staff I had invited. *Season Zero: How well do you behave? IN THE FLAT FIELD.* contained videos by Ephraim Asili and Sable Elyse Smith. *Season One: arms ache avid aeon: Nancy Brooks Brody/Joy Episalla/Zoe Leonard/Carrie Yamaoka: fierce pussy amplified* featured the artists' individual output alongside their work as queer art collective fierce pussy.

was invited to change the installation halfway during the exhibition's run. She chose instead to implement small shifts in the form of care over a month, such as cutting out single beads that weighed down a beaded curtain work, *"Untitled" (Golden)* (1995), in accordance with Gonzalez-Torres' instructions that the beads are to hover just above and never to touch the floor.

At The Notary Public, Bove contributed a handful of bronze cast peanuts and shells, which I accumulated on the fireplace mantel throughout the ten-week exhibition. Nearby, Hinrichs' work *tests for a work regarding a fresh widow* rested on my bookshelf during the first half of the exhibition. In the second half, her work "performed," the stick held under the weight of a book stack dangling the tender sculpture over my desk. Bookshelves, personal, transitional, public, holding time and space for transmission of information and knowledge, and their presence and absence on and off, atop and under their armature, had brought Heide and I together, as artists, as educators, with, through, on, off, atop, under, holding up and hovering over institutions.

Columbus, Ohio, November 2020

1 https://www.usnews.com/education/best-colleges/paying-for-college/articles/see-how-student-loan-borrowing-has-risen-in-10-years. Accessed on November 10, 2020, published June 12, 2020.

2 https://www.cnbc.com/2020/06/12/how-student-debt-became-a-1point6-trillion-crisis.html. Accessed on November 10, 2020, published June 12, 2020.

Shelf Shifts

David Senior

We are walking in a hall of books and the aisles proceed on and on. The shelves are unfathomably tall. We are faced with infinite choices of languages and subjects. There are no tables to sit at and the sheer volume of volumes is crushing to any sense of a clear beginning. We have no pencil to take notes. We have a piece of paper with the correct location of the book we seek, but somehow the call number is obscured or illegible. We are looking at a familiar book but somehow the language cannot be deciphered. We want to ask for help, but there is only a strange person in the stacks that gives confusing answers to our questions.

This is a playful list of potential forms of fever dreams of our intellectual and creative pursuits. In it we characterize how the stacks—the impenetrable library and its mass of books—serve as conceptual personae for a type of impasse in thinking. We are so close to knowing something, but at the same time, fully distant or excluded.

My field of art librarianship is a subset of the larger academic field of librarianship, in my case, it is nestled in the belly of museums that collect and exhibit art. Art librarianship can connect to the history of encyclopedic art museums and their legacies, layered with broad histories of art and regional focuses. Some of us are charged with documenting newer things, modern and contemporary art that bring us into contact with visual, written and performative experiments from the more recent past. When we turn to the task of documenting this art, we must accept the task of tracing actions and gathering materials that can be inscrutable.

The primary documents of art practices that exhibit anti-art tendencies can be a little confounding. We can miss things that are proven essential years later because they were in disguise as something minor. It is okay to miss things, but we need to train ourselves to try not to miss things. This is part of the art of art libraries: to arrive at processes to capture art disguised as ephemera, manuals, posters, advertisements, menus, telephone books, pulp novels, popular magazines and newspapers, etc.

Publishing for artists, designers and art workers allows a swerve from established discourses. Historically, the space of publishing has been another kind of alternative space for the production and display of new art and writing. Manifesto journals of the historical avant-garde and conceptual publications of the 1960s now live in our special collections but would have been on their own second shelf in their time.

In the last fifty years, we have learned from the publications of the feminist art movement, the interventions and activism of the queer arts community around the AIDS crisis, and from the writing and organizing of the Black Arts movement, that little magazines, posters, flyers and books are invaluable tools to document and grow new movements in the arts. For the feminist art movement in the United States in the 1970s, magazines, artists' books and experimental exhibition catalogs were substantial mechanisms for community building, dialogue and information sharing. Magazines such as *HERESIES*, *Chrysalis*, *The Feminist Art Journal* and *Womanspace* show ways that collective groups coalesced around the pages of a periodical publication to document and expand networks of feminist thinking, art and activism. These titles also connected women working in similar fields across different geographical locations, permitting cross-pollination of local scenes with expansive, often international, perspectives on the work of the women's movement and the amplification of women's voices in contemporary art.

Similarly, with artists' books, women like Adrian Piper, Carrie Mae Weems, Laurie Anderson, Suzanne Lacy, Louise Lawler, Martha Wilson, Carolee

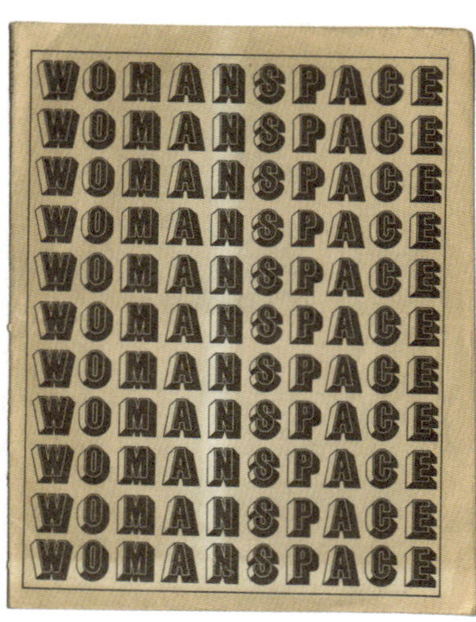

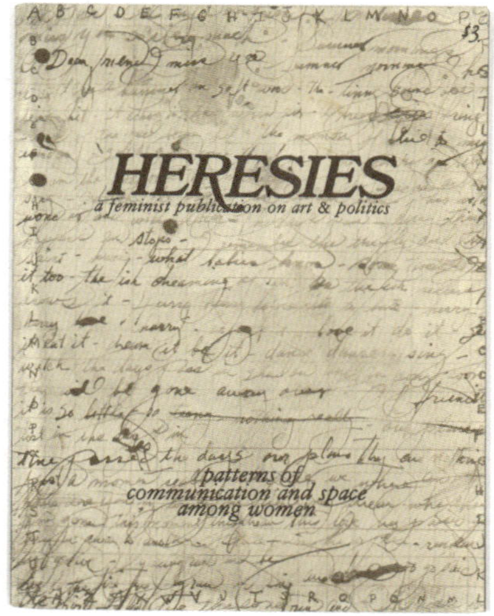

Covers of *Womanspace*, no. 1 (Los Angeles, 1973) and of *HERESIES*, no. 1 (New York City, 1977).

Schneemann, Ida Applebroog, Bernadette Mayer, Athena Tacha, Jenny Holzer, Barbara Kruger, the Guerrilla Girls, and Barbara T. Smith are examples of artists from this period who used books as a way to circulate new work, when other avenues of exhibition and recognition were not afforded to them. Through this space of the artist's book, with its alternative networks and distribution systems, they were able to stage new works.

Martha Wilson's Franklin Furnace, the independent artists' book archive and performance space she founded in New York in 1976, is an extension of this discussion and essential regarding the preservation of artists' books in contemporary art. That collection, which featured all the authors mentioned above, was founded with the intention to support the genre of artists' publishing that many of Wilson's friends and colleagues had adopted, and that had not been recognized yet by institutional collections. The purpose was to create an informal archive and reading room for people to encounter the work.

Other artist-run spaces popped up around this time that had similar intentions: to preserve and document the vibrant bodies of work being created by many artists and art workers under-recognized by institutional collections. Printed Matter in New York, Art Metropole in Toronto, Other Books and So in Amsterdam, Zona Archives in Florence, Artpool in Budapest, and Galeria Foksal's Living Archives in Warsaw are examples, like Franklin Furnace, of places where artists and art workers implemented plans to collect and document the abundance of printed matter being produced by contemporary artists and experimental art spaces. These organizations were changing the terms of how art history could be preserved and are a part of the history of artists' publications and their impact. They created archives of an international movement that mapped the growth and function of artists' publishing and, in the moment they emerged, served as necessary information hubs for artists and art workers who were seeking to engage with this expanding field.

In creating and solidifying networks of artists and art workers, little art publications have connected new interlocutors across geographies and across historical periods. These works changed art and discourse and readjusted expectations about who can participate in this discourse. The participants did not ask for permission to enter their field. They took space with their published work and modeled for others how new paths could be formed and new forms of advocacy and support could be achieved through publishing.

As an art librarian, I am wholly dependent on these models to help me navigate new possibilities for the collections I manage. In our current moment, the pressing urgency of changing our collections to include a greater diversity of voices critically expands on this commitment to a more nuanced attention to artists' and designers' experiments in publishing. The contemporary ethics of collecting mandates a critical inspection of the white imagination and the recognition of malignant biases in our field that alienate potential audiences, particularly related to race and gender.

When I recently encountered *second shelf* and its conveners, I noticed it as a proposal for further, necessary support and advocacy for these important areas of contemporary art practice that should be addressed more fully within the collecting processes of academic and art libraries. The secondness alludes to the perceived alterity of this genre to "regular" academic materials, but it is clear that the topic of the project should be primary in the minds of librarians working in the field. In some ways, the project of librarianship remains somewhat consistent with the prior generations of library work with its cataloging, acquisitions and circulation processes of printed materials. Other elements of the work reflect real questions and challenges to former ways of working and to the structure of collections and their perceived audiences.

I can say frankly that in many ways the answers, to the question of how to find a path in our stacks of books to equity and inclusiveness, are not there, and that it is a failure that should drive change in our field.

For the past fifteen years, this is a question that has confronted me as I thought through collection development strategies in the museums where I have worked—first at The Museum of Modern Art in New York and now at the San Francisco Museum of Modern Art. I work with curators and scholars to learn about new materials and have the responsibility to manage acquisitions budgets for new materials and to prioritize what and how these materials get cataloged. Libraries' annual budgets are devoted to acquiring new materials and we should ask: what commitments should librarians make to apply these budgets towards change?

Often, the lurching force of big institutions, plus the fact of many stakeholders pushing agendas in different directions, makes change seem difficult to achieve. All art and academic institutions are caught in a new cycle of austerity and reduced resources. How are we to rethink our work when we lack the resources and staff to continue with basic services?

These will be common hurdles for most of us in these professions. Staff working in academic settings and libraries are quite accustomed to making do with minimal resources. The types of materials reflected in *second shelf*, and the materials I advocate for, are often intentionally produced as affordable publications, meant to be accessible in this way.

I am proposing that librarians focus more attention on small publishers that are increasingly adjusting their publishing agenda to amplify diverse voices in the visual arts and design and are producing innovative works from a feminist, queer, anti-colonial and anti-racist perspective.

All our problems are surely not solved by this gesture, and there are still clear asymmetries of representation in this publishing field, but this strategy simultaneously supports these small entities and new collection development priorities. The benefit of such a development policy is not only that it supports a richer publishing ecosystem, but also, that it provides new titles to our audiences that complicate how we tell the history of modern and contemporary art. It complicates our usual understanding of our readerships and who can engage with our collections.

As a librarian in a contemporary art museum, it is impossible to do my job well without engaging with the international community of artists, designers and art workers that produce publications with small publishers. These are imprints that are often run and managed by artists, designers and art workers themselves. These publishers work on a small scale, in terms of production and distribution, and rely on things like art book fairs and distribution hubs like Printed Matter and other independent book shops of art, design and theory. They are connected through social media, international fairs and their own unique distribution strategies. Some are designated as non-profit organizations formally, but all are clearly not driven by profits as part of their mission. In this community, there is potential for representation of different voices, of increasing representation of and resistance to political, environmental, social and economic injustice, and the development of new peer networks to broaden conversations around equity and inclusion in contemporary art.

As *second shelf* illuminates, there are mechanisms that need to be introduced formally to collections, to document and amplify voices that have been omitted from our stacks. Alluding to the network of small publishers of artists' books, experimental design and architecture publications, experimental journals and theoretical texts, one clear point of change would be for larger institutions to develop more flexible acquisitions programs to allow them to connect with small publishers and artists that publish directly.

There are often logistical obstacles for academic libraries and art institutions to engage directly with artists and designers who publish. Their system for billing, for instance, only connects to more centralized distribution networks of big publishers and specialized companies that distribute books to libraries and commercial entities. This is a basic point, but one that speaks to the need to find broader ways to support publishers doing the increasingly essential work of changing the composition of our collections.

Questioning the established system of book acquisition for academic and mass market art and art history books does not preclude these types of books from our acquisitions processes, but it does help us think about the type of system of exchange we would prefer to work within, rather than the one most libraries currently depend on for new materials. There are logistical realities that make the mostly automated selection process of new books advantageous for academic and museum libraries. It is a process born out of need for efficiency in accounting and workflow.

I would just nudge the field a little to begin to think about developing additional paths for materials to enter collections and to affirm those paths as essential to balancing efficiency with relevancy in our contemporary context. There is a sense that we can connect what is ethically imperative with an idea that collecting these materials will also serve to make our collections unique and valuable in the future. Other than the admitted pitfalls of cataloging these often strange and mysterious objects, the only risk, from my perspective, lies in ignoring this field of production and ignoring the degree to which our field needs a clearer accounting of our biases and our reliance of the history of the white imagination. We can make a different library and we can directly support artists, designers and art workers in the process.

The techniques that can change our collections are not new, as we see from the examples of past artist-run archives. I had the benefit of working with the Franklin Furnace's artist book collection within its current home at MoMA Library for many years. The clear lessons from this collection of thousands of international artists' books from the 1970s through the 1990s was that committed and consistent engagement with artists, and artists' book publishers, can result in an astounding historical record of artists' work, artists' networks and friendships, and broad geographical reach.

The archive also functioned to chart the intersection of art and activism in this period and was noticeably more inclusive to the voices of women, people of color and, generally, to international voices of radical dissent in contemporary art. In our communities of contemporary art and design publishing now, we can observe such a broad spectrum of materials, content and global participation. There is an open opportunity to follow along and document this work in our institutional collections.

For the last twelve years, I have partnered with Printed Matter to help stage the NY Art Book Fair at MoMA PS1 and have consistently been in awe of the sheer volume of printed production we find at such

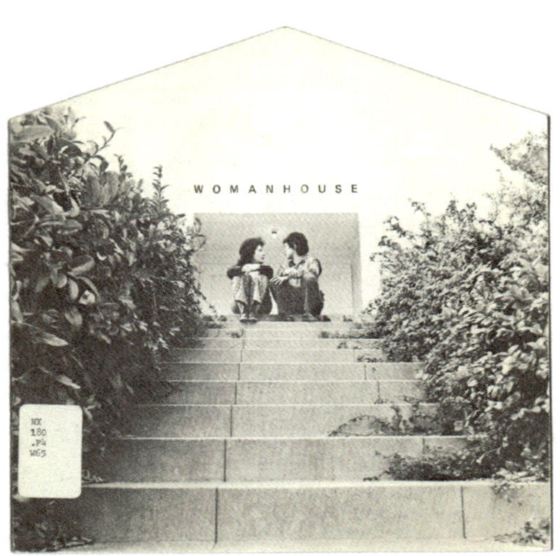

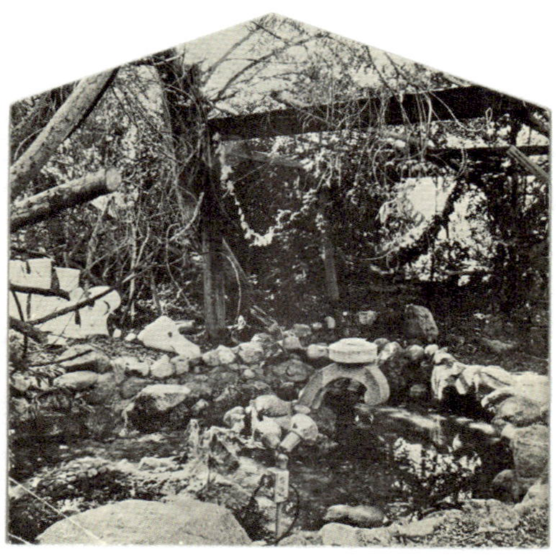

Front and back of *Womanhouse*, an exhibition catalog designed by Sheila Levrant de Bretteville for the inaugural exhibition of the Feminist Art Program at California Institute of the Arts, Los Angeles, 1972.

events. Following the general model of the Printed Matter art book fairs, many international art book fairs have popped up around the world over the past decade. For example, large fairs have been staged in recent years in Los Angeles, San Francisco, Berlin, London, Paris, Vienna, Barcelona, Madrid, Turin, Tokyo, Beijing, Shanghai, Hong Kong, Mexico City, Sao Paolo, and Buenos Aires. At this cross-section of art and design publishing communities, it's possible to witness global shifts in the field, and track the work of new and established publishers in this field like never before. From my vantage point, particularly in the last several years, we have a growing movement of dissent and resistance, a global theme within the printed matter of artists and designers. Demands are being made of our art institutions and our related fields of academic and curatorial practices to think critically about race and gender, equity and representation, and to decolonize and find ways to express affinity for historically marginalized groups in contemporary art and design. This is a main thread from discussions hosted at our recent Printed Matter Book Fairs in New York and Los Angeles and it will continue into our virtual iteration of the Fair in winter 2021.

Libraries in the fields of art and design can support these conversations and actions towards equity and inclusion. The work is being done in the publishing field and we have the opportunity to preserve and amplify this work and invite partnerships with diverse groups of artists, designers and art workers. From my experience, support and expressing affinity for this type of publishing work can take many forms, from direct acquisitions, to hosting discussions, promoting on social media and offering advice about the library field to those publishers new to these types of collections. Outreach with small publishers often involves simply informing them that these institutional collections exist and are interested in documenting their work. These conversations are part of the work of collection development and speak to steps necessary for demystifying the use and function of library collections. If the producers of books need further clarity about the role of libraries in documenting their work, we can imagine their audiences and peers can also use further introduction to the work of contemporary art libraries and their missions.

We cannot predict the future use of library collections, but we can ensure the contemporary materials that depict what we aspire to be in the present are included and preserved for future researchers and students. As academies and institutions rethink their roles and missions in our society, libraries can be a repository of creative work that helps us better imagine the full range of possibilities for positive institutional change and greater access for all.

San Francisco, California, September 2020

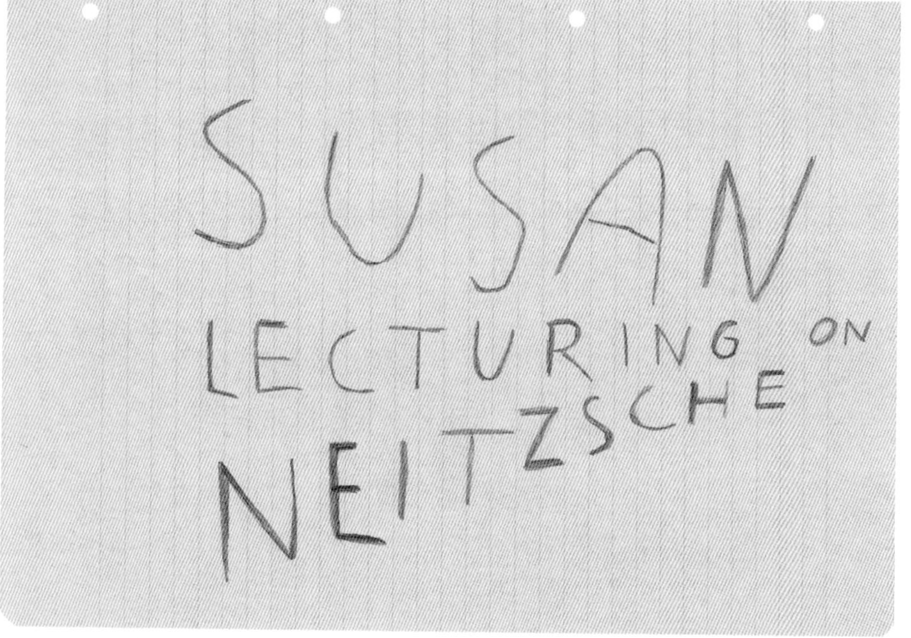
SUSAN
LECTURING ON
NEITZSCHE

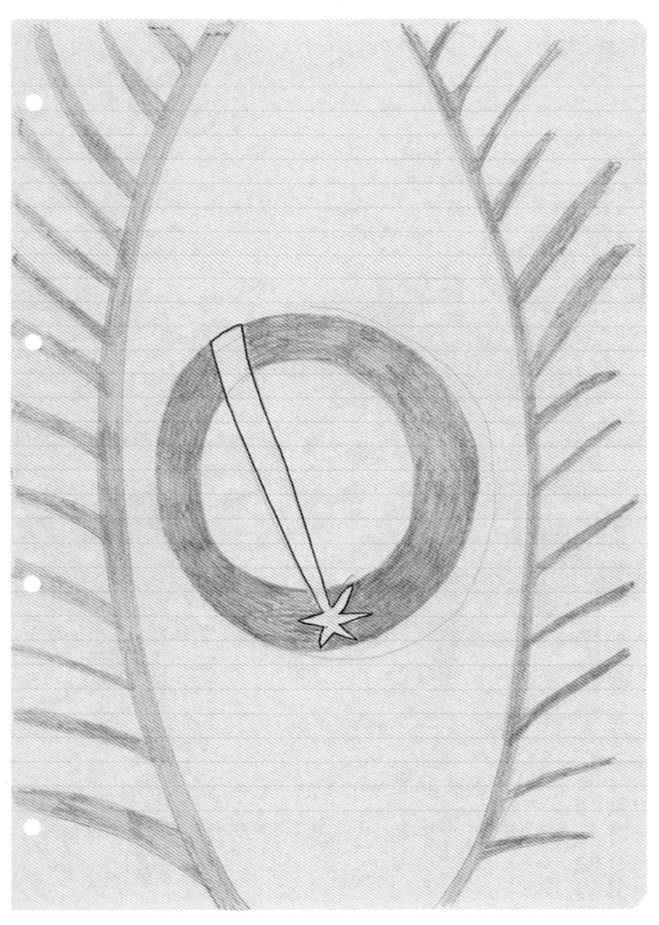

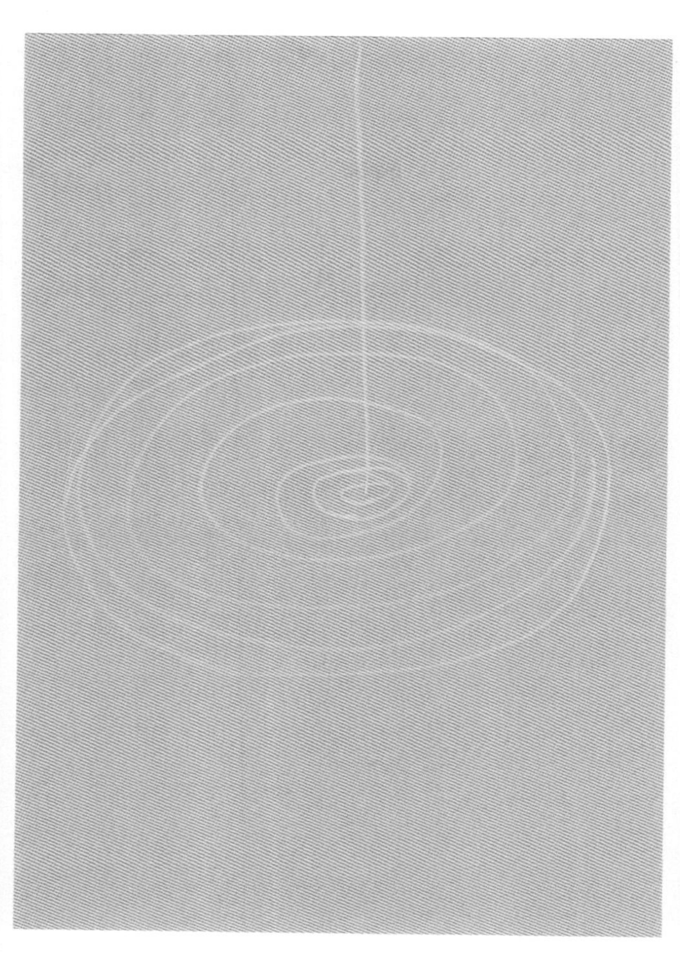

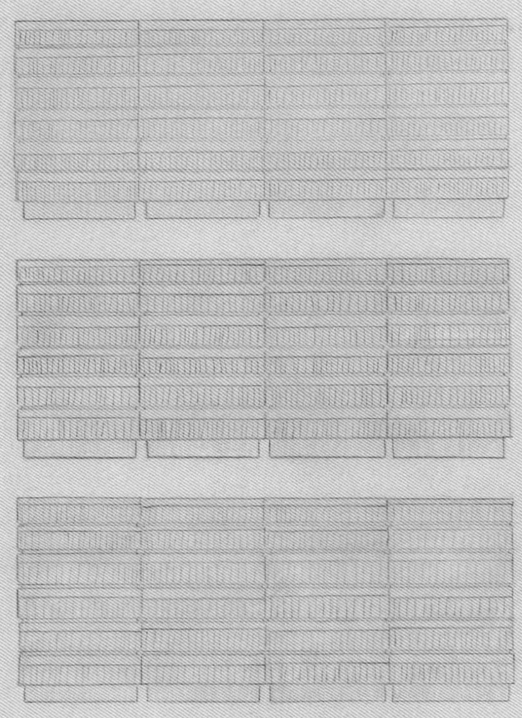

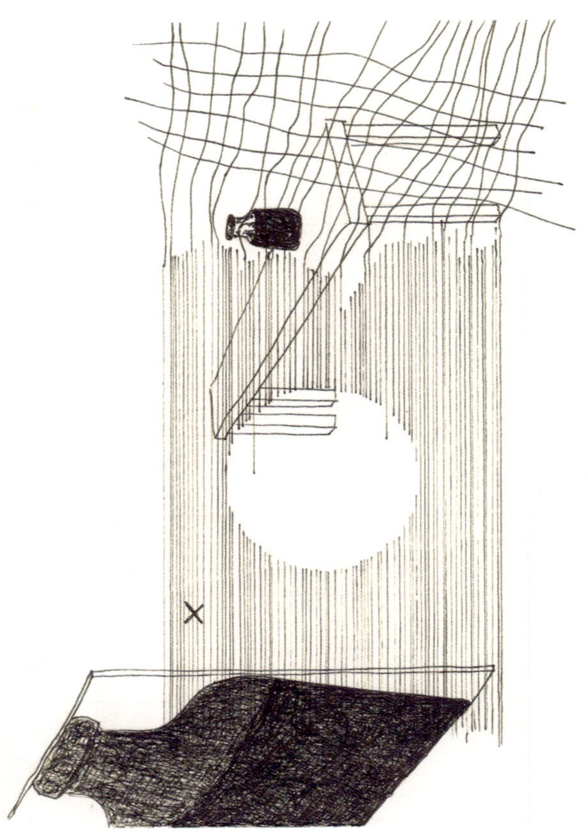

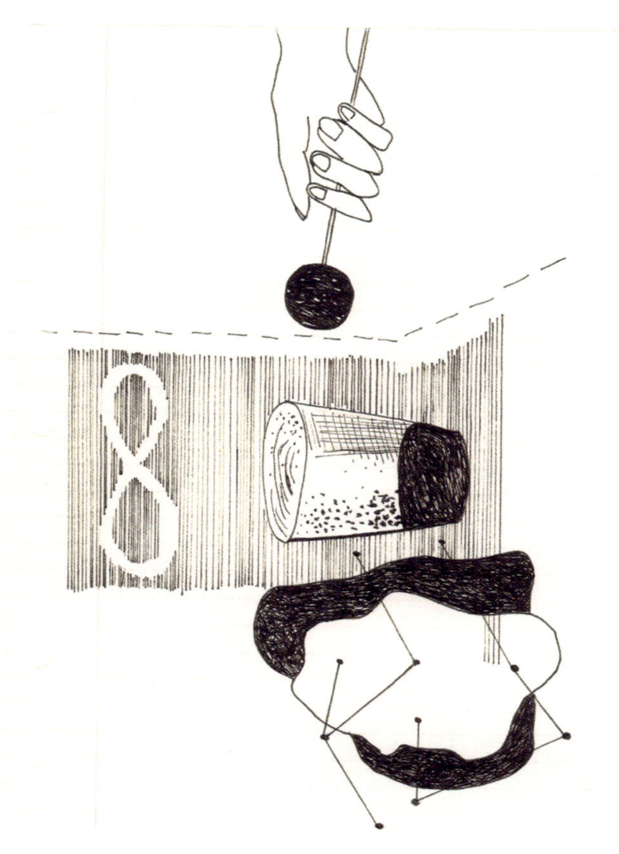

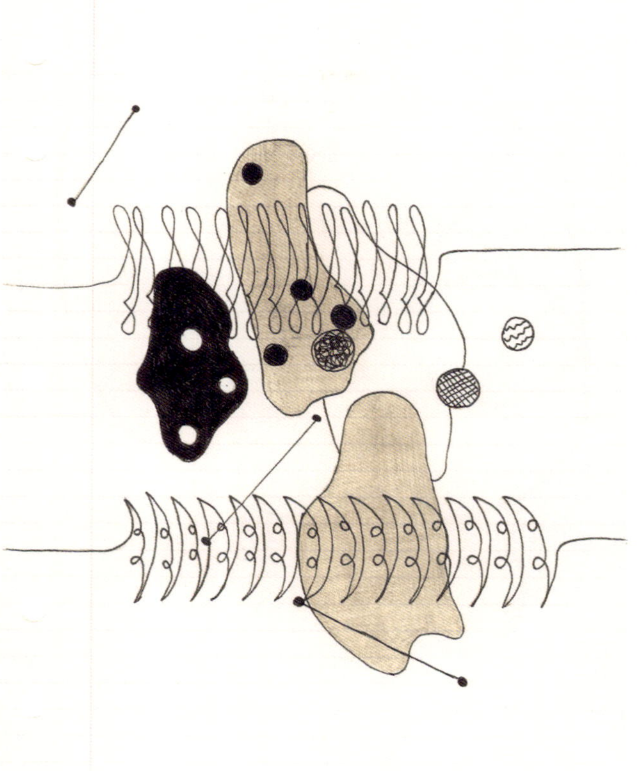

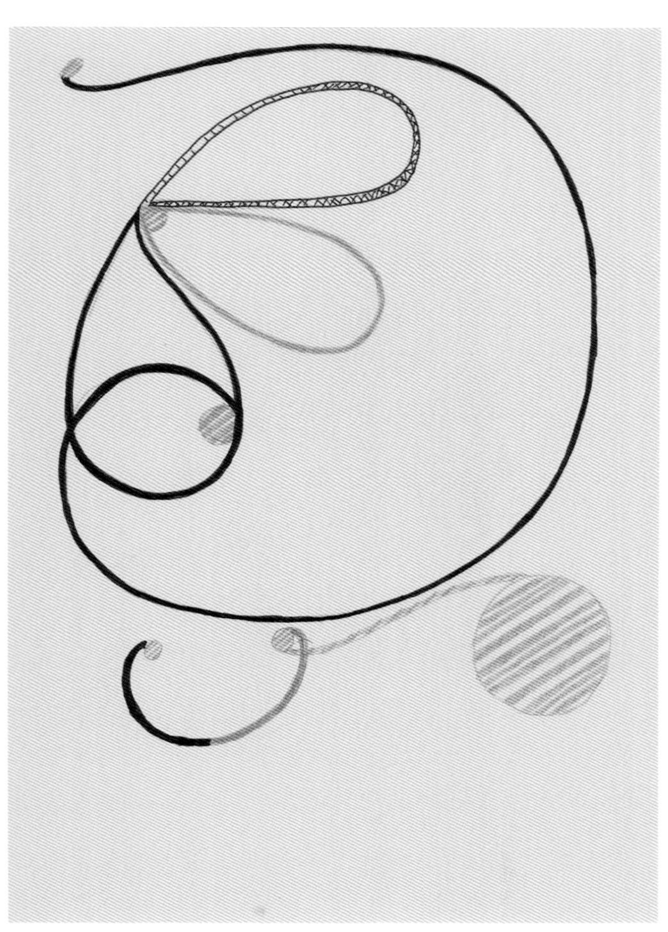

the library

Embracing Noise and Other Airborne Risks to the Reading Body

Elizabeth Haines

Spill

Spill is Lutz Bacher's re-framing of a found photo of a person sweeping a document storage space, a photo which itself has been torn and dribbled on by some staining substance. She draws our focus to the work of keeping a collection safe from physical destruction and dissolution: cleaning, sweeping, organising. Here I take on that focus and celebrate the physical and emotional labour of managing risk to reading bodies in the library. The need to create comfortable space for silent reading bodies, safe from noise and spills might seem obvious and straightforward. However, feminist, queer and critical race theories trouble the idea that there might be simple or singular kinds of reading bodies. They have shown us that gestures, behaviours, and architectures invite some bodies to make themselves comfortable, but disorientate and deter others.

This essay explores what the iconography of reading bodies can tell us about risk and reward in the library. It asks how the activity of reading is choreographed, and whom this benefits. In art school libraries, artists seek inspiration, company, sparring partners as they develop creative practices which often result in social and economic precarity. It seems an obvious place to develop techniques for living with risk with your immediate contemporaries as well as negotiating a relationship with a wider imagined community of artists and with the past.

An iconography of reading bodies

If I asked you to imagine someone reading a book, there's a strong chance that the image your imagination produces has been influenced by a long iconography of the reader in the visual arts of the Global North, as well as by your own personal experience. In this tradition there are probably two main categories of embodied readers. One is the active public reader, perhaps most easily imagined as a statue holding a book on its lap or at arm's

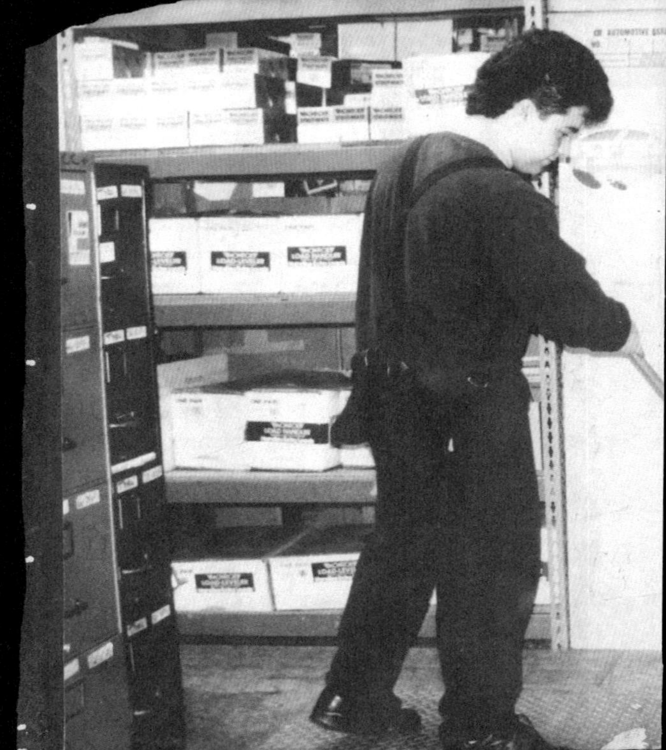

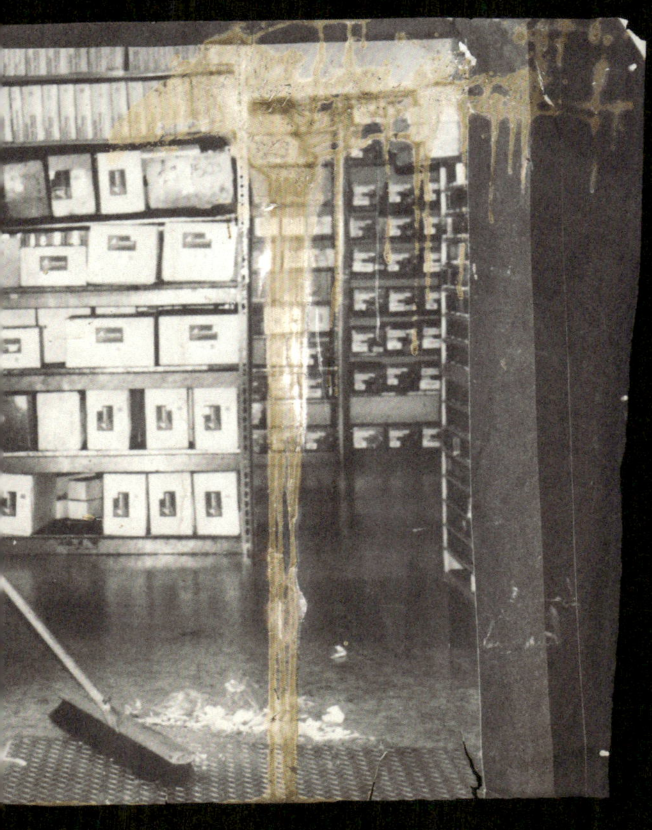

Lutz Bacher, *Spill*, 2008.
Transparency of found photograph with unknown substance, courtesy the Estate of Lutz Bacher, New York.

length. Take the statue of the philosopher David Hume on Edinburgh's Royal Mile for example. I suppose technically speaking he's not actually reading, he's holding the book up at you, while leaning back lazily in a kind of toga, but that's the tradition of the public reader. They are reading *to* you, looking *at* you, wielding the book as an instrument.[1] Maybe it's a book they have written themselves, or a subject they are proselytising (think gospels, politics).[2] The relationship that this kind of reading body has to *you* is that of a teacher. Your body is framed by theirs as less learned, less enlightened, and possibly even illiterate. I've been guiding you towards this in a slightly overhanded way but you'll notice that the public reader is usually coded as masculine.

Women have fairly consistently been denied the opportunity to be active public readers, and to wield books *at* an audience. Women's voices have been derided as too shrill, too sharp, too animal for addressing crowds since ancient Greece.[3] Women have struggled to be accepted as news anchors, as lecturers, and in many religious traditions still don't have the opportunity to incant sacred texts to gatherings of other devotees. Contemporary audio engineering technologies continue to disfavour the typical frequencies of the female voice.[4]

But, in fact, your first conjuring of an imagined reader would more likely have been someone who was in quiet contemplation, a passive, private reader, a consumer of text. This is not so easily gender coded, but there are reasons to align it with the feminine. Images of the female reader whose attention is absorbed in her book, fall neatly in line with other iconographies in which a woman's attention is captured by a task that leaves her 'open' to the male gaze.[5] It is hard to ignore the connection between images of women reading and other images of women in their intimate lives, caught unawares as they wash or brush their hair. The secular tradition of the 'reading woman' seems to have begun in Dutch painting in the sixteenth century, but it has never let up as a minor genre. There is no end to the kitsch images of women reading.[6] The relationship that this kind of reading body has to yours, is that of victim to your voyeuristic gaze. The book she is holding is a pretext for a representation of her body as one that can be spied upon. She does not meet your eye, she is objectified. So, while there has been objectification of men in the iconography of the private reader (some of which I'll address later on), I'm going to keep aligning the private reader to the feminine body.[7]

Accepting that the iconic bodies of the public reader and the private reader exist in dialogical counterpoint to you as an invisible other, prompts us to ask about the spaces in which their bodies and our bodies find themselves. It seems that masculine public readers are reading to an assembly, feminine readers are reading (almost) alone. The relationship of those reading bodies to yours, and the spaces in which these relationships unfold, is a question that is tied up in the cultural history of the binary public/private spaces. However, that binary doesn't do all the work that embodied readers deserve, so alongside thinking about the private/public, I'm also going to invite you to consider 'communal' and 'autonomous' readers ...

Communal readers

Throughout most of history, for most people, communal reading, that is to say reading aloud with others, has been the norm. Books have had audiences rather than readers. The historian Robert Darnton describes how in eighteenth-century France and Germany there were even names for the hour of the early evening when one person would read to other members of their community while they mended their tools and clothes.[8] This collectivity meant that the labour of reading could be shared, one person directly occupied with words while others listened and continued with the material necessities of their lives. In other situations, communal reading has been a means to build solidarity, or to increase access to texts where these were scarce. Eric García-Mayer describes oratorical reading among Cuban literary exiles in the United States in the nineteenth century and Elizabeth McHenry has investigated African American reading societies in the nineteenth and twentieth centuries.[9] The South African historian Archie L. Dick describes how in 1962 Jean-Paul Sartre's short story 'The Wall' was read aloud to new arrivals at the training camp of the uMkhonto we Sizwe (the armed wing of the African National Congress).[10] The architectural paradigm of the histories of these reading bodies is that of communal living, of shared spaces, shared goals, shared risks and shared responsibilities.

Autonomous readers

Jürgen Habermas' influential idea suggests that the emergence of a public sphere in eighteenth-century Europe was accompanied by the parallel emergence of a private sphere: a new separation between the sphere of public activity and economic production and the sphere of private lives and domesticity.[11] The circulation of ideas through books, in a republic of letters, generated imagined communities of like-minded readers.[12] However, the public/private division meant that although reading was uniting the *minds* of a group into an imagined community, in physical terms reading became a solitary activity. The imagined community was constructed through the content of the books rather than around the communal *activity* of reading. The readership of a book was no longer a group gathered together, it became an archipelago of individuals. This was enabled by the increasing number of bourgeois private households in which autonomous reading might take place.

Bourgeois women struggling to be autonomous reading bodies

It is in this context of the architecture of private domestic reading that the more strongly gendered iconography of the reading body seems to emerge. Certainly, in the iconography of the passive feminine reading body mentioned above, she is mostly depicted in the bourgeois home. However, for many women in bourgeois households, occupying the private sphere didn't lead to the possibilities that were *in principle* open to an autonomous reading body.[13] This is made starkly clear in an advice manual for young women from nineteenth-century Bengal.

> ... when you grow up, you won't be able to play, because you won't have time to spare and, as a result, you won't be able to enjoy yourself anymore. But the pleasure of your studies will remain with you your whole life ... There is no one with whom it must be shared. Even mourning for a son has no effect on it.[14]

For most bourgeois women, reading in private was not the same as autonomous reading. It seems that although reading might have offered them a route to joining an imagined community of the mind, in many cases it was just as much an attempt to escape from the emotional and physical demands of the real community with whom they cohabited, from organising food, from organising cleaning, from breastfeeding, childbirth, multigenerational nursing and deathbeds. The kitsch portraits of bourgeois women as pseudo-autonomous readers represent a fantasy about domestic idyll, that did not map onto most women's experiences. Aside from lacking the space and time to read, the whole principle of autonomy was out of the window for women. Historically, and around the world today, the status of women within the household has most commonly been that of property. In looking at portraits of women reading, it is important to remember that the subject's status was (and in some places is) closer to that of her book than to that of her male cohabitants.

More pseudo-autonomous reading bodies

There are others beyond bourgeois women whose lives and experiences don't map neatly along the division of lives into a public/private dichotomy. Those lines have been drawn along the lines of race and class as well as gender. The larger part of literate human beings haven't been able to keep the activities of reading and study separate from their commitments to economic necessities and domestic responsibilities. Those who have no time or space set apart from money-making, dust, dirt, sleep, sickness or even from close physical contact with others. These other pseudo-autonomous readers have had to squeeze reading in and around their acts of sustenance, struggle and survival.

Returning to the iconography of the reading body, the genre of street photography has generated a slightly different kind of objectified reader: a context in which both men's and women's reading bodies fall under external gazes and voyeuristic compulsions. This image of readers on a train is from the series *On Reading* by the Hungarian photographer André Kertész. Kertész's series spans a fifty-year period between 1915 and 1965 and covers a very wide range of reading bodies and architectures. Importantly for us, though, he offers us portraits of 'pseudo-autonomous' reading bodies. These train passengers number among many reading bodies who didn't (don't) have the benefit of a private architecture for reading that allowed for (allows for) solitude. His working-class readers are attempting to participate in an archipelagic imagined community, while sitting on trains, in parks, standing on doorsteps, between duties at work. They are working hard at imitating autonomous reading bodies by actively ignoring the sensory stimuli around them.

Pseudo-autonomous readers and the library

The library then, is an odd kind of space, an architecture designed for the coincidence of pseudo-autonomous reading bodies, the architectural paradigm of the imagined community, a place where people read not *with* or *to* but *alongside* each other. This doesn't happen automatically. For one, it relies on the principle of silent reading. Silent reading doesn't seem to have been common before the medieval period, and was still the exception rather than the norm in the nineteenth century. Even lone readers would vocalise the words that they were reading. In fact, the historical architecture of libraries offers clues about when silent reading emerged. The first side-by-side cubicles for reading in monastic libraries date from the thirteenth century testifying that the practice had taken hold – readers couldn't sit side by side if they were mumbling

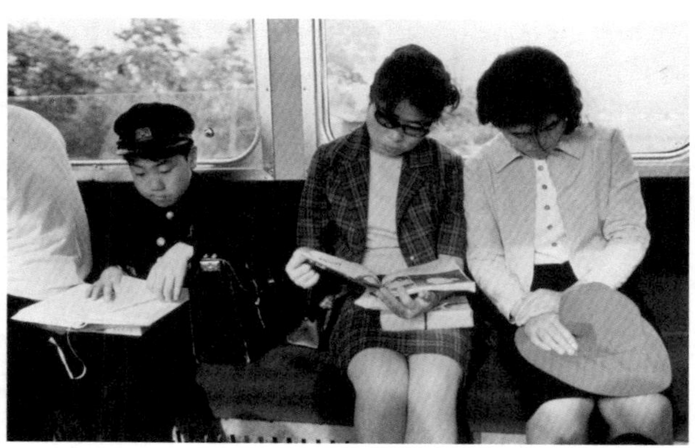

André Kertész, *Untitled*, Japan, circa 1960.
© Estate of André Kertész / courtesy Stephen Bulger Gallery.

and murmuring.[15] We see the gradual emergence of an experience of reading where we act as if we were alone, as if we were separated from each other.

Yet, although we are, in some senses, pretending to be alone in a library, we are being encouraged to be autonomous rather than private readers. We know this because other kinds of behaviour that we would perform in the private realm (sleeping, snoring, eating, or even more bodily intimate activities) are often discouraged in libraries. This paradigm of architecture and behaviour is then enforced by the librarian. To follow Michel Foucault, the widespread emergence of public libraries in Europe and North America in the nineteenth century was part of the process of creating new and modern forms of political subject. Library design very often follows the principle of Jeremy Bentham's panopticon. You can see the librarian, and the librarian could be looking at you at any given moment, so you behave as if they were.[16] The lines of sight in the space generate a certain auto-disciplining of behaviour. The librarian is on hand to prevent behaviours from the private realm that might disturb other readers, ensuring uniform pseudo-autonomy.[17]

To bring libraries into the context of Foucault's larger arguments about the technologies of power in the nineteenth century, it is helpful also to consider technologies and techniques of hygiene, such as sewers and domestic water supplies. It was during the nineteenth century that the circulating library (a library from which books were borrowed rather than one in which valuable books were stored and carefully consulted), really took off. As a result, it was not only readers but also books as objects that passed in and out of libraries' architectural spaces. As books entered the domestic spaces of readers they were at risk of exposure to the bodily fluids produced by the acts of feeding, sleeping, excreting, breathing and sex, all the mechanisms of sustaining life that happened behind closed doors. Circulating books came in direct contact with the domain of activities that were gendered feminine, activities of the body, animal activities, rather than those of the mind. As drains removed waste from residential areas, so library books that circulated into domestic spaces were subjected to special cleansing practices. The risks that one reader's private practices might represent to a subsequent reader were eliminated by steam, heat, acid and beating books in ingenious combinations.[18]

The inherited role of the librarian can be seen, then, as a gatekeeper between the worlds of the body and those of the mind, keeping books clean and bodies quiet. The libraries were to be silent and pristine, designed to allow pseudo-autonomous reading bodies to pursue the project of enlightened self-interest without suffering from any impediments imposed upon them by their colleagues. The librarian's invisible labour is to choreograph books and people into an orderly circulation as books and people travel between the spaces of intellectual production and those of social reproduction. The librarian carries the burden of managing the ways in which the architecture for an imagined community of pseudo-autonomous readers does (and does not) map onto behaviours in the private sphere.[19]

The pseudo-autonomous reader in the twenty-first century library

Access for women, for the working class, and for people of colour into library spaces does not change the socioeconomic patterns that mean that those individuals' lives might fit only very awkwardly (if at all) into the categories of the private and public space that frame and constrain readers into pseudo-autonomy. Those who lack the resources to *live* autonomously (a room of one's own) can use the library if they mimic the behaviours of those who *do* have those resources. Communal reading bodies, groups for whom the activity of reading is not

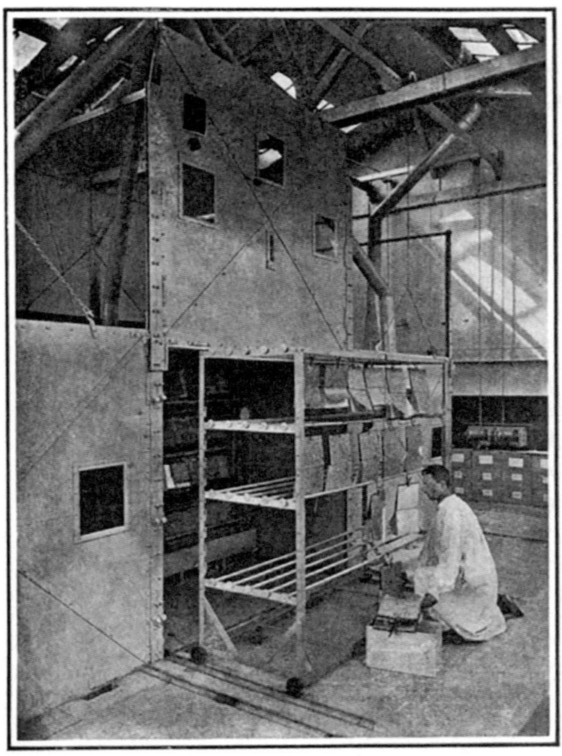

Fig. 1.—Sliding the rack of books into the disinfecting oven.

'The Disinfection of School Books'
Scientific American, no. 101
(July 24, 1909): 60.

separate from their full embodied existences, for whom reading is an activity in which risks and responsibilities are negotiated, would usually have to look elsewhere for architectures that sustained their practice.

Not all libraries have the ambition to eliminate the embodied, communal aspects of their readers' lives from the architectural space. There are plenty of outstanding examples of city libraries, local libraries, even educational libraries, that meet the different needs of their readers by allowing discussion, eating, speaking, reading aloud and sleeping alongside their books. Generally speaking, however, the more serious a library sees itself to be, the less likely it is that these activities will be allowed, and more likely a view of the reading body as solitary and pseudo-autonomous will prevail.[20]

Autonomous reading bodies in contemporary art

Books and archives have assumed an unprecedented importance in contemporary art practice. For a very large part, however, this interest has focused on *ownership* of books as an insight into an individual's biography and cultural influences. This has produced a new kind of iconography in contemporary art—the presentation of artists' private bookshelves. There is an eminent tradition of this kind of fetishism. Probably the most famous of these is Walter Benjamin's essay from 1930 on unpacking his library in a new apartment, in which he is unabashed about the affective experience of private ownership of books.

> The most profound enchantment for the collector is the locking of individual items within a magic circle in which they are fixed as the final thrill, the thrill of acquisition, passes over them.[21]

In the presentation of artists' private bookshelves, the artists' reading bodies have often been eliminated entirely. The books stand in as a proxy for the artists' disembodied minds. This is often, in fact, a celebration of the creative individual as an autonomous reader, a member of an imagined community, *despite* limitations imposed by aspects of their biography. In this vein one can think of the various displays of Martha Rosler's books in contemporary art venues (and online) as representing an imagined feminist community.[22] We could read the work of Fehras Publishing Practices reconstructing the private libraries of intellectuals such as the late Saudi novelist Abd Al-Rahman Munif in a similar way: representing an imagined community that has been destabilised by war and devalued by anglophone scholarship.[23] The display of books in the alternative panopticon of (not the library but) the art gallery, again invites us to participate as silent, autonomous readers – new members of the imagined communities of which the artists were/are part. They implicitly require us to buy into the idea (ideal?) of the autonomous reader.

Communal reading in contemporary art

Communal readers are less common in contemporary art, but they have been granted visibility, their own iconography. In the film *La Lectora* by Yulia Piskuliyska, we see a woman reading to a factory full of cigar-rollers in Cuba, her reading generates care, comedy, affection and aesthetic pleasure in their working lives.[24] Dora García's film *The Joycean Society* documents a group who have met, every week, since 1985 to read James Joyce's *Finnegan's Wake*.[25] There have also been forms of relational practice in which artists have used reading to build bridges with colleagues, to build shared goals and responsibilities as a group, within, around and despite institutional infrastructures. Many of these have taken place in educational sites. Rainer Ganahl has organised collective readings of Marx across Europe and Asia, including within art schools.[26] Kristina Lee Podesva has organized a variety of collective reading practices, including *colourschool,* a free school within art schools, hosted by the University of British Columbia and Emily Carr University of Art + Design (2006–2008).[27] The Women of Colour Index Reading Group have read aloud from papers held at the Women's Art Library in London in schools and educational libraries as a way to bring attention to the absence of opportunity and memory for women of colour in British institutional spaces.[28]

Reading bodies in art school libraries

What might happen if we reclaimed the art school library as a space for different kinds of reading bodies? Recalibrating the relationship of the library to reading bodies beyond the pseudo-autonomous requires more than reclaiming shelf space for books that represent different modes of life. It requires more than re-categorising books. It requires rethinking the architectural paradigm of the library in ways that make space for bodily beings who use the act of reading to share their vulnerability, their hopes, their germs, their fluids and their different tones of voice. It also requires reconfiguring the patterns of the physical and emotional labour that have organised the library around the autonomous reader. What might this mean? Could we imagine architectural paradigms for reading in which the library space was a forum for a living community who cared for books and read *together*?

The sense in which physical labour of care for books can be generative in and of itself is given by the playwright Dario Fo in *The Worker Knows 300 Words, the Boss Knows 1000, That's Why He's the Boss.* The premise of *The Worker Knows* is that the library at the *Casa del Popolo* is being put into boxes, after years of disuse as television had taken a central role in the *Casa*'s cultural activities. As the workers pack up the boxes, they begin to read extracts to each other, until eventually characters from the history of socialism emerge from the books and join in with the conversation. Fo's work gives a sense of the certain charisma or potentiality that books have, a relationship that is physically cemented by contact with them, during the invisible labour that is usually carried out only by the librarian.

What of the emotional labour necessary if the positive potential for risk and social encounter in reading are to be realised? The project *Read-in* was founded in February 2010 in Utrecht, the Netherlands by artist Annette Krauss and theatre maker Hilde Tuinstra. They run an evolving experiment in group reading that began by testing out the process of ringing neighbours' doorbells with a request that the neighbour host a collective reading. *Read-in* transformed their neighbours' living rooms into locations for a discursive encounter with strangers and has produced new spontaneous communities drawn together by the act of reading.

The remarkable series of reading projects by this group dislocates the architecture of libraries, remaps private space into a communal one and generates an entirely new perspective on the civic role of education. It suggests that the potentiality of reading bodies and library architectures lies at an even bigger social scale. Making room for more diverse reading bodies in an art school might mean disrupting the division between the spaces of production, social reproduction and consumption that are writ large in the relationship between the library and the rest of the school's architecture: the studio, the lunch hall, the gallery space. Even if, as Samia Malik of the WOCI Reading Group attests in this volume, the emotional work required to renegotiate identity whilst simultaneously challenging forms of institutional authority and opportunity is significant.

Germs, risk and new architectures for reading bodies

As I write, in September 2020, the prospect of walking in and out of my neighbours' houses, and even of passing books between a group sits in a rather different dimension than it did when I first sketched these ideas out in September 2019. My life and my interactions with other human bodies are regulated by new hygiene regimes that Foucault would have a lot to say about. Layers of plastic and anti-viral chemicals mediate my physical contact with most of the other members of my multiple communities.

This situation also radically changes the way that I will teach this year. I will be using new digital architectures of pedagogy that dictate very different relationships between the body and the mind than that of the classroom or studio. Libraries, around the world, have largely been emptied of people. The digitally-carried human voice has become the basic thread binding communities who cannot share space in embodied ways. There has been a new and astounding blurring of the sites in which we work, study and live our intimate bodily lives: the long-standing division between sites of production and social reproduction.

There is much to dislike and much to fear. We are policed and monitored in new ways. But there is also some hope that this situation might bring more attention to the role of bodies in education. This situation might be an opportunity to acknowledge the practices of more diverse kinds of reading bodies, and to introduce new practices that don't require us to mimic social and economic privileges we don't have. Whatever kind of library architecture and behaviours emerge from a global pandemic, we should demand that while it gives space to silent pseudo-autonomous reading, it also privileges time and space for reading together, and gives space to the communal reading body.

Didcot, September 2020

1 You don't actually have to keep imagining this, do a quick image search. *Statue of David Hume* (1995) by Alexander Stoddart (1959–), Royal Mile, Edinburgh, Scotland.
2 You might also try looking up Harold Knight, *Alfred Munnings Reading Aloud Outside on the Grass,* (c. 1911) or Paul Cézanne, *Portrait of Gustave Geffroy* (1896).
3 Mary Beard, *Women & Power: A Manifesto* (London, UK: Profile Books, 2018).
4 Tina Tallon, "A Century of "Shrill:" How Bias in Technology Has Hurt Women's Voices," *The New Yorker*, September 3, 2019; Aniqah Choudhri, "On My App and at the Mosque, I Want to Hear Women Recite the Quran," alaraby (*The New Arab*, June 1, 2020), https://english.alaraby.co.uk/english/comment/2020/1/6/the-day-i-heard-a-woman-recite-the-quran, accessed September 24, 2020.
5 For example, look up Pierre-Auguste Renoir, *The Reader* (1876), *Student Reading* (1937) by Matvey Manizer, in the metro station *Ploschad Revolyutsii*, Moscow.
6 Try this in your search engine too – 'woman reading painting'– and you will see what I mean.
7 There is a tradition of Christian imagery of masculine private readers, usually monks or saints, particularly St. Jerome, in which the principal 'other' is spiritual, rather than bodily. These are not entirely free from erotic objectification, however, as can be seen in Matthias Stom, *Young Man Reading by Candlelight* (1628–32).
8 In France the veillée, in Germany the Spinnstube. Robert Darnton, "First Steps Toward a History of Reading" in *The Kiss of Lamourette: Reflections in Cultural History* (New York, NY: Norton, 1990).
9 Eric García-Mayer, "Narrating Nation Aloud: Oratory, Embodied Reading Practices, and the Cuban Imaginary in Villaverde and Mariño's El Independiente," *Folklife in Louisiana: Louisiana's Living Traditions*, 2013, http://www.louisianafolklife.org/LT/Articles_Essays/lfmnarrating.html, accessed August 19, 2020; Elizabeth McHenry, *Forgotten Readers Recovering the Lost History of African American Literary Societies* (Durham, NC: Duke University Press, 2002).
10 Archie L. Dick, *The Hidden History of South Africa's Book and Reading Cultures* (Toronto, CA: University of Toronto Press, 2012).
11 Jürgen Habermas, *The Structural Transformation of the Public Sphere: An Inquiry into a Category of Bourgeois Society*, trans. Thomas Burger and Frederick Lawrence (Cambridge, MA: MIT Press, 1989).
12 Although this is not entirely what Benedict Anderson famously referred to as an 'imagined community' it bears some similarities. Benedict Anderson, *Imagined Communities: Reflections on the Origin and Spread of Nationalism* (London, UK: Verso, 1983). But on the ways that readership formed new and dispersed communities with shared values see, for example, Robert Darnton, "Readers Respond to Rousseau: The Fabrication of Romantic Sensitivity," in *The Great Cat Massacre and Other Episodes in French Cultural History* (New York, NY: Vintage Books, 1984).

13 In a more famous expression of the desire for 'a room of one's own' in which to write (rather than read), Virginia Woolf highlights the ways in which the domestic space precluded solitude for women, and the perverse and invisible socio-economic architectures that constrained the participation of bourgeois women in the 'republic of letters' in the early twentieth century. The misfit of women's reading into either the private or public sphere is underlined by the curiously persistent importance of reading groups among women. As Elizabeth Long points out, these groups are neither strictly part of the 'serious' public sphere (the realm of politics, religion or work) or of family life—nonetheless collective activity around books offers empowerment to small spontaneous communities. Elizabeth Long, *Book Clubs: Women and the Uses of Reading in Everyday Life* (Chicago, IL: University of Chicago Press, 2003), 31.

14 Nabinkali Dasi, *Kumari Siksha* (Calcutta, IN: Nabinkali Dasi, 1883) quoted in Swati Moitra, "Reading Together: 'Communitarian Reading' and Women Readers in Colonial Bengal," *Hypatia* 32, no. 3 (2017): 634.

15 Paul Saenger suggests that the spread of the practice of silent reading is demonstrated by the changing architecture of monastic libraries in the thirteenth century, new seating arrangements placed readers next to each other, a layout that was only possible if people had *not* been reading aloud. Paul Saenger, *Space Between Words: The Origins of Silent Reading* (Stanford, CA: Stanford University Press, 1997).

16 For more on the library as a panopticon see Alberto Manguel, *The Library at Night* (New Haven, CT: Yale University Press, 2009); Lewis C. Roberts, "Disciplining and Disinfecting Working-Class Readers in the Victorian Public Library," *Victorian Literature and Culture* 26, no. 1 (1998): 105-32.

17 The tension around the use of libraries by the unhoused, to wash, sleep and keep warm, is indicative of that tension between the library as the site of private reading, and the elimination of other aspects of the private sphere. There is, of course, also illicit private activity in libraries around corners and behind shelf stacks. These non-reading bodies in libraries have their own humorous, suspenseful and erotic iconography in popular culture. Trawling news reports on the internet shows up a number of incidents of pornographic films being made surreptitiously in public and academic libraries. These non-reading bodies in libraries deserve a whole other essay.

18 For those interested in exploring the world of nineteenth-century library hygiene, I recommend Thomas Greenwood, *Public Libraries: a history of the movement and a manual for the organization and management of rate supported libraries* (London, UK: Simpkin, Marshall, Hamilton, Kent & Co, 1890). Available at https://archive.org/stream/publiclibrarieshoogreeiala.

19 The library in this mode has its own iconography evident in the design of the large national libraries of the early twentieth century in neoclassical style. The library as ideally silent and

clean is perhaps most extremely represented in Candida Höfer's series of large format photographs of libraries, in which the embodied reader has been entirely eliminated. See for example, Candida Höfer, *Biblioteca Palafoxiana Puebla II* (2015).

20 Long, *Book Clubs*, 11.

21 Walter Benjamin, *Illuminations* (London, UK: Fontana Press, 1992), 60.

22 Martha Rosler's library was originally on display at e-flux, New York in December 2005–April 2006, and later travelled to the Frankfurter Kunstverein, and MuHKA, Antwerp in 2006. It is available online at http://projects.e-flux.com/library/. I'd argue for the disembodiment of the artist in this practice notwithstanding the material traces of Rosler's life on the book collection, see Elena Filipovic on Rosler's use of toilet roll as bookmark. Elena Filipovic, "If You Read Here… Martha Rosler's Library," *Afterall: A Journal of Art, Context and Enquiry* 15 (2007): 90–95.

23 See their exhibitions *Disappearances. Appearances. Publishing.* hosted by Villa Romana, Italy (2017) and Sharjah Art Foundation, UAE (2018). Kenan Darwich, Omar Nicolas, and Sami Rustom, eds., *When the Library Was Stolen: On the Private Archive of Abd Al-Rahman Munif*, trans. Eyad Houssami (Berlin, DE: Fehras Publishing Practices, 2017).

24 Yulia Piskuliyska, *La Lectora*, 2017. Video, colour, 10 minutes.

25 Dora García, *The Joycean Society*, 2013. Video, colour, 53 minutes.

26 Rainer Ganahl, *Reading Karl Marx*, ed. Craig Martin (London, UK: Book Works, 2001).

27 https://www.on-curating.org/issue-19-reader/kristina-lee-podesva.html, accessed September 10, 2020.

28 See the interview with Samia Malik in this volume, page 172.

Threads from the Labyrinth

(About a Library in Beirut)

Rachel Dedman

Some buildings are more than stone; Mansion is one of those. The house sits up a street off the short dual carriageway that connects West Beirut to East. The main fabric was built during the French Mandate period, in an Ottoman style, but its inner skin holds traces of rough-hewn extensions, improvised renovations, urban shift. It is painted yellow, and from the outside seems small, dwarfed by the high-rise apartment blocks immediately behind it. Inside, it unfolds in layers: the corridor gives onto a double-height hall with arched windows, spills down into a sprawling basement, and leads up a switchback staircase to a warren of rooms and balconies, eventually to the sun-bleached roof. The building was abandoned during the Lebanese Civil War, which ended around 1990. Ghassan Maasri, an architect, spent much of the 2000s exploring Beirut's many empty buildings and inquiring about their ownership, with a view to regenerating one into a creative community space. In 2012, he managed to meet and negotiate with the owner of a building in the neighbourhood of Zoqaq el-Blatt and took custody of the house. Mansion, as it came to be known, has since transformed from a half-derelict building into an active community space, conscientiously animated by its inhabitants and visitors.

Since the end of the war, logics of fast profit have ruthlessly damaged neighbourhood relations in Beirut, and public space is fraught and contested, dominated by local sectarian interests. In a city without green spaces nor public squares for safe congregation, Mansion yearns to be a site of community structure and connection. Ghassan, his partner Sandra Iché, and a community of friends and colleagues evolved Mansion's labyrinth of rooms into offices and studio spaces. These are rented out at a low cost to those who would otherwise struggle to work independently in the city: an elastic collective of artists, researchers, architects, activists, playwrights, bicycle-deliverers and others. Mansion is an experiment in shared dwelling and collective responsibility. The group manages Mansion together (testing different modes of governance as circumstances change), and develops and maintains its public resources: film archive, silk-screen station, sound studio, dance floor, internet connection, kitchen, garden, library. In the main space downstairs, people huddle on sofas around the stove in winter, or spill into the garden for sun and cigarettes. In the summer the air is animated by standing fans, whose dying and resurgence become markers of the municipal cuts in electricity. Discussions, exhibitions, meetings and performances take place in this space; people use Mansion when their event doesn't fit elsewhere, isn't safe elsewhere, or isn't affordable elsewhere. The house is open to anyone who wishes to walk into it, to work, read, rest, or think.

With the formation of Mansion and its community came a library, a collection of a few thousand books and printed ephemera in a small room off the main space, with a gloriously intricate plaster ceiling. On sets of shelves, things that found their way to Mansion had been piled haphazardly over the years. The books were jumbled and inaccessible, dusty and uninviting; the room more storehouse than portal. One summer, Mansioners committed to several renovation projects, and I offered to show some care to the library. The aim was to reanimate its contents, and shift the books from backdrop to foreground.

Most libraries are characterised by order and logic, following international systems of classification. On the surface, the library in Mansion appeared arbitrary, formed by accident. It had started with books inherited with the building, and grew through volumes that Ghassan found in other abandoned houses in the neighbourhood. It was bolstered by printed matter that

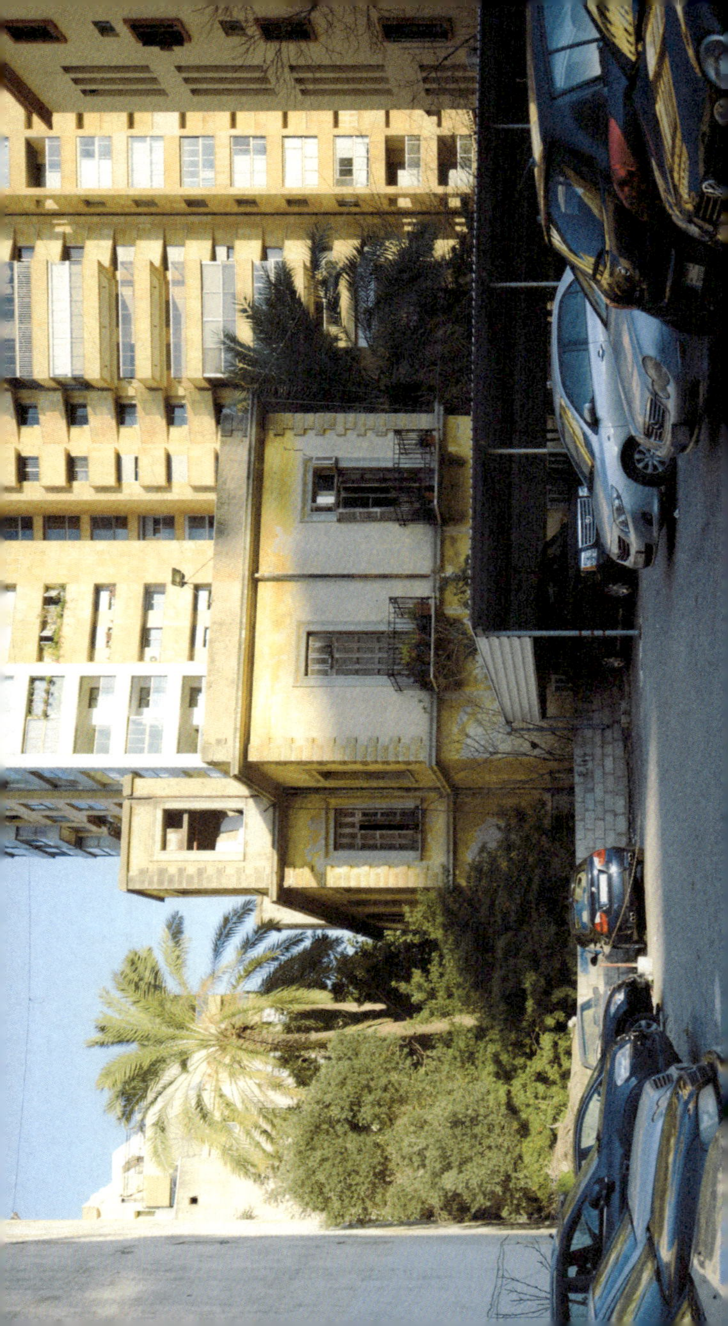

Mansioners came across or donated, or transferred from their studios for public use. When local people cleared out their houses and gave books away, along they came to Mansion. But the eccentricity of its content belied the significance of its formation. Reviewing the collection book by book, the more the library reflected, in an intimate, if largely incidental way, the socio-political and economic history of the local area. A large collection of German philosophy treatises spoke to the influence of the Max Weber Foundation's Orient-Institut just down the street; a diverse range of old-school French fiction mirrored the Francophone and -phile character of Beirut's Christian communities. Esoteric manuals for mid-century machinery attested to the interests of Beirut's middle classes before the war, while shelves of resources on political history in the Arab world, and on global art and architecture, reflect those who use Mansion today. More recent additions – a small but helpful set of maps and guides to Beirut – are traces of the artists and researchers who visit Mansion on residencies.

Exploring Mansion's library, therefore, is like an archaeological tour of this modest corner of the city. It has been shaped both consciously and inadvertently by local events, former inhabitants and current residents. We asked ourselves what value such a library might have beyond its significance as an unusual sort of archive. It seemed pointless to introduce a classification system. There didn't seem a need for a catalogue. This isn't a library where one comes in the hope of finding something specific, but a place you visit to stumble across the unexpected.

One inspiration was the Reanimation Library, initiated by the artist and librarian Andrew Beccone in the United States. It formed in response to the loss of information – particularly visual information – that happens when libraries deaccession books

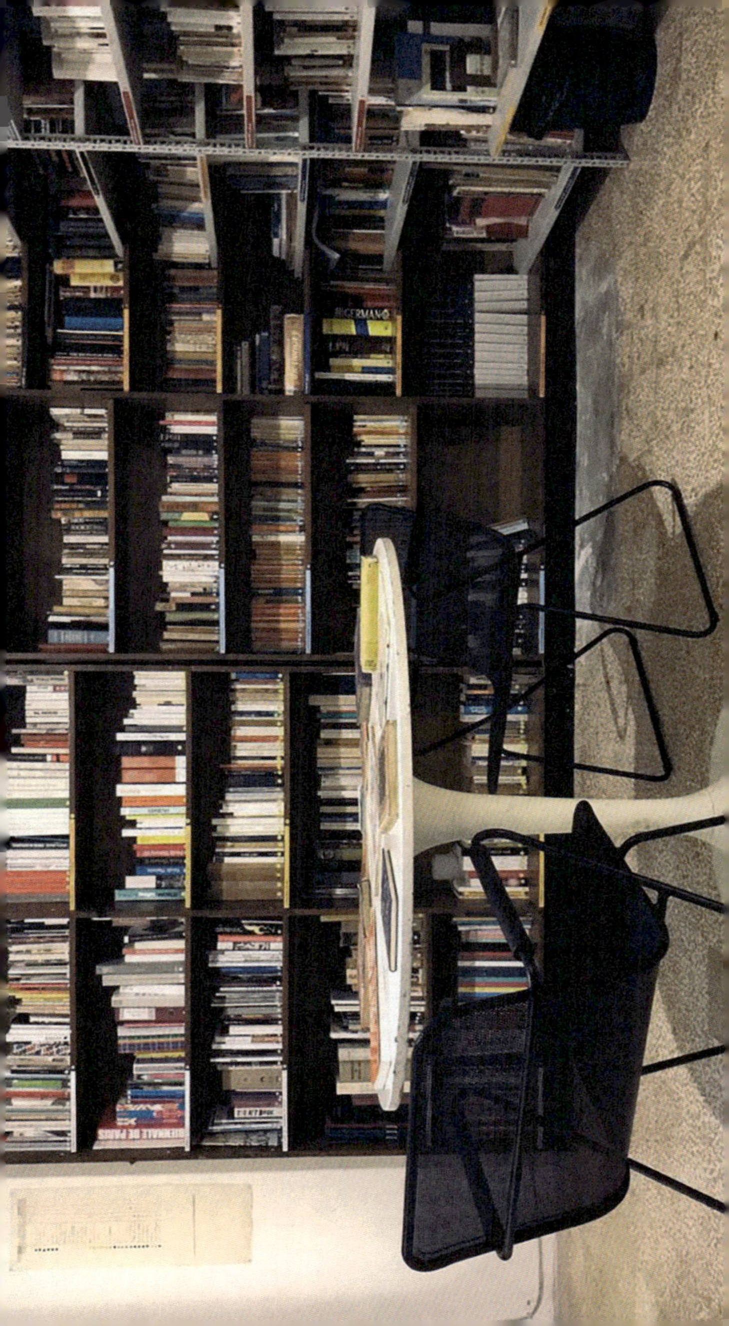

from their collections. Governmental or municipal libraries usually require or aim for their content to be 'correct' or up-to-date; things that seem outmoded or overwritten by newer editions, such as textbooks or manuals for old technologies, tend to be removed to make space for new material. 'This protocol', Beccone writes, 'coupled with the continual production of newer editions, creates a growing fossil record of outdated books – a veritable feast for image archaeologists.'[1] The Reanimation Library posits itself as a kind of ongoing dig, a repository for materials rich in visual information, 'regardless of the currency of their textual content' – a library that values books for images, more than for words.

At Mansion the metaphor of archaeology seemed fitting, in part from the sheer quantity of dust. We cleaned and repainted the room, carrying armfuls of books out of the space, wiping and sifting and initiating some loose and instinctive categorising principles. We grouped books by kind, unless a more elegant or appropriate solution emerged as we went, and colour-coded them. These stickers corresponded to shelves, or bookcases, indicated by a handwritten key on the wall. Materials on art, architecture, design, and cinema, in Arabic and English, were linked by subject in a shared case. Smaller collections of foreign volumes (Italian, Armenian) were clustered for ease; graphic novels, Elizabethan history, and the annual reports of local NGOs sat in independent groups. A section of material on the local area of Zoqaq el-Blatt was grouped together, made up of maps, old census data, and a Mansioner's PhD thesis. A shelf on music contained books, sheet music, and a slightly heat-warped collection of vinyl. The Levantine film archive run by Nadi Lekol Nas, based in Mansion, was accessible on a dedicated computer in one corner, with a central desk for meetings and quiet work. My treasured section

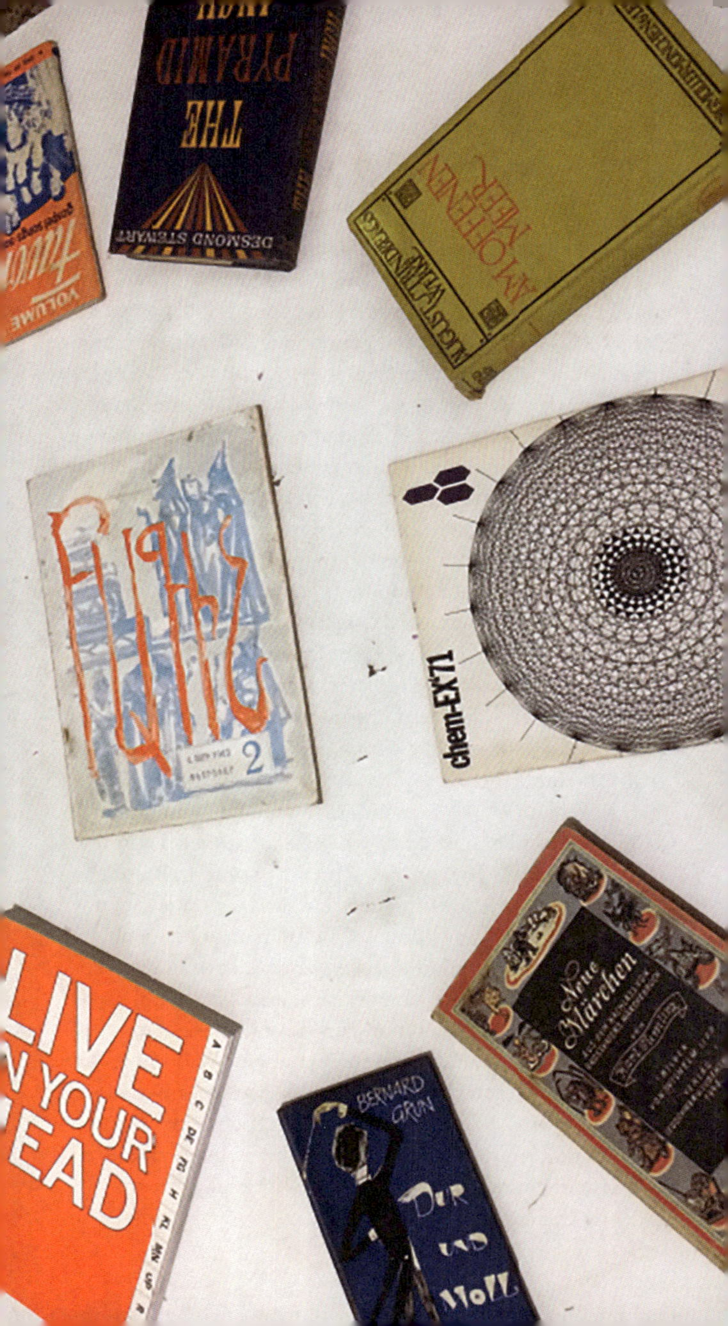
DESMOND STEWART
chem-EX'71
LIVE
N YOUR
EAD
BERNARD
GRUN
DUR
UND
MOLL
Neue
Märchen

was a pile of esoteric ephemera, which included, among many other things, a small book of vivid Ukranian folk patterns, a delicately illustrated encyclopedia of birds, and a plastic album filled with water-damaged photographs. Every stiff and cracking page was full of enigmatic ex-pictures, their contents bleached of colour.

We discarded almost nothing. A library inevitably ascribes value to its collections, and has the privilege of determining what is worth preserving. We considered everything potentially interesting. In Mansion's wood workshop a small set of slanted shelves was built to act as a modest display panel. The idea was that Mansioners would be invited on a rotating basis to spend some time exploring the library, select between five and ten books that spoke to them, and place them on display. They could choose things related to their work or research, of course, but equal value was placed on things for their visual, graphic or sensorial qualities. I fell in love with books for their strange typography or their unusual binding, their scent and texture. Whatever the reason for their selection, each item represented a way into the rest of the library for other visitors: a set of threads peeking from the labyrinth.

I heard about the Reanimation Library in 2014 via the VOLUME project, curated by Sara Giannini and run in collaboration with 98weeks, a project space in Beirut.[2] The project addressed the concept and potential agency of the contemporary library. One of its more morbid inspirations was the Wikipedia entry, 'List of destroyed libraries', which charts the political and accidental circumstances in which libraries have been lost to history. She writes of her feeling that 'public libraries are disappearing today not only as a consequence of the hegemonic role of the Internet in the production and circulation of information and knowledge but also because of the wild and virulent neoliberal practices eroding the commons'.[3]

Never has this seemed more pertinent than in the last few weeks. On the fourth of August, 2020, 2,750 tonnes of ammonium nitrate, which had been stored in the Port of Beirut since 2013, caught fire and exploded. The enormous mushroom cloud and bright red smoke filled the world's social media within hours: extraordinary, barely-comprehensible scenes, looped without end on Instagram, forwarded on WhatsApp, accompanied by expressions of disbelief inadequate to the scale of what was witnessed. The blast was the strongest in human history after Hiroshima and Nagasaki. I write this in late August; people are dead, still missing, injured and displaced. Homes are decimated, historic buildings destroyed – in a country in the grip of popular revolution, full economic collapse, hyper-inflation, mass unemployment, a refugee crisis, poverty, pandemic. A country whose banks have illegally withheld their customers' money for almost a year, while funnelling politicians' wealth offshore; where the army shoots protestors campaigning for everyone's basic rights. The explosion was not a tragic accident. It was a crime of the most epic proportions, enacted by a corrupt and criminally negligent government, who created a disaster waiting to happen, and has been almost entirely absent now that it has.

As Lina Mounzer wrote the day after the blast, 'Growing up in Lebanon taught me that an explosion resonates across time, that the shock reverberates forward into your life, and the pressure reconfigures the landscape of the mind.'[4] The Mansion community is mostly physically fine, grappling with the trauma of the explosion, and how best to organise, rebuild, support others, and channel anger. Mansion's building, already old and unstable, is no longer entirely safe to be in, and there is little money to keep the lights on, let alone repair it. The beautiful Ottoman ceiling of the library lies in large pieces on its floor, the century-old glass blown out of the windows. I think of all the glass in Beirut now mingling in enormous street-side mountains. The incessant grate of it being swept from balconies. Clear cast sand, now shard, returned halfway to dust.

In the face of the death and destruction of human life and endeavour, a library is a small and unimportant thing. But the broader political aims of Mansion resonate all the louder now. The political cancer that caused the August explosion has been metastasizing in Lebanon for decades. At the end of the Civil War, the warlords that had terrorised the country granted themselves amnesty from its crimes and secured a parliamentary system that set in place the corruption, nepotism and absence of accountability that characterises power in Lebanon. Neoliberal violence has unfolded ever since; destruction only fuelled speculation. The market, controlled through collusion between banking and governance, has slowly devastated the city and the lives of its people. In architectural terms, the dominant impulse of Beirut's post-war reconstruction was to refurbish historic buildings into lavish and exclusive 'heritage' sites, or demolish them entirely, and to grant national construction contracts worth millions of dollars to companies owned by politicians. In a gated city of private car parks and empty high-rises, Mansion took custody of a building thought of as 'failed' (abandoned, empty, uncared for) and reclaimed it for practices of habitation, public encounter, and production. Its library sought to reignite interest in and exploration of materials society has deemed no longer useful, and to slow down the ways we find information.

The erosion of the commons that the VOLUME project identified has rarely been so literally enacted. One area of Beirut's harbour is a free port – a privileged

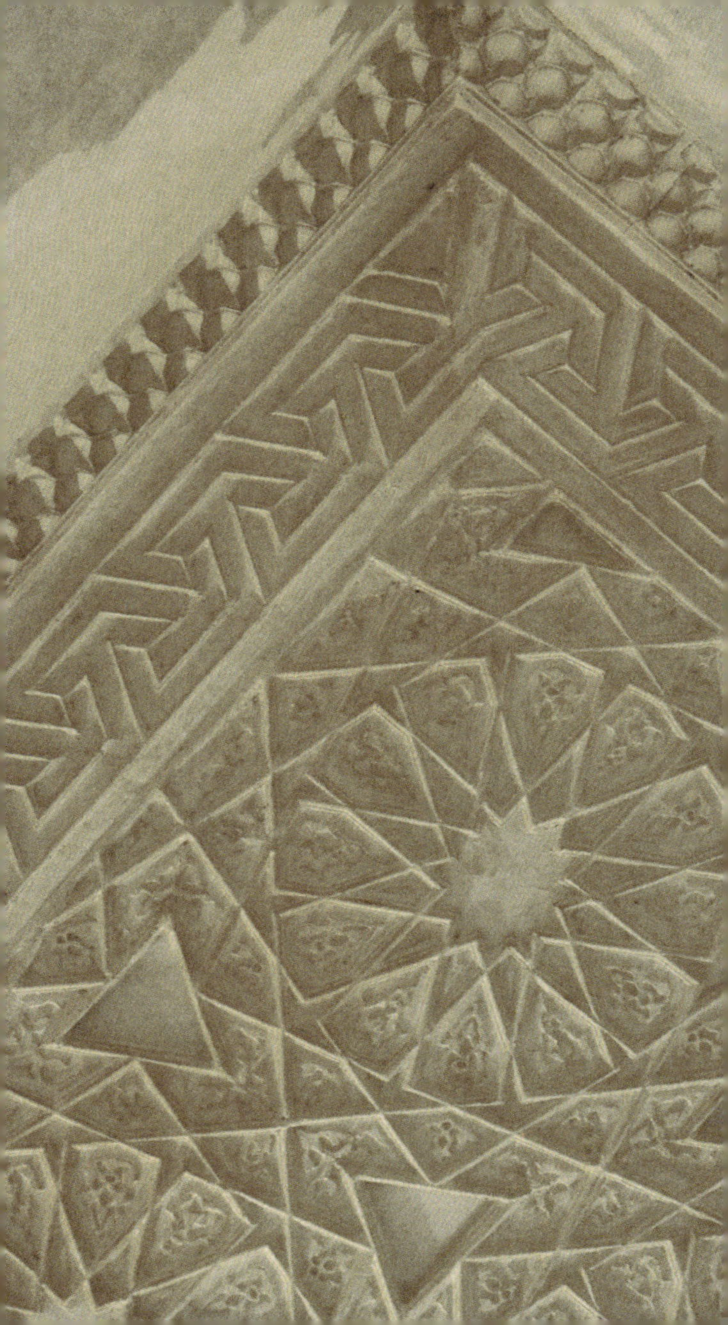

zone that for legal purposes sits outside national borders, enabling the shipment and storage of goods without tax. The most important resident of Beirut's free port is the Lebanese National Library, which has been stored there for decades, awaiting the building of a permanent space. Although for now there is little news of what happened to it in the blast, at least some of its collection of seven million volumes, including historic and rare manuscripts, will have been damaged or destroyed. The prominent architect of the new library, Jean-Marc Bonfils, was killed in the explosion. Assabil, the independent NGO that operates Lebanese public libraries and a book bus in the absence of state infrastructure, is now crowdfunding to rebuild and repair its Beirut outposts.

One branch of the VOLUME project, entitled *Unfold*, invited guest curators to collate online constellations of digital materials, as an alternative to tangible forms of the library. Proposing the digital folder, hyperlink, and drop-down menu as forms for the curator/librarian, *Unfold* takes the shape of a website that unfurls in layers. Texts, commissions, screenshots and scans appear at a click, all available for download and distribution. Exploring the site feels like stumbling around in someone else's hard drive, strangely intimate and labyrinthine, like panning for gold. In an interview with the curators of *Unfold* #2, Giannini asks Anna-Sophie Springer and Etienne Turpin how they imagine their collection being read. They reply, 'We only envision intimacy. Reading is so procedural, always moving from one page to the next, beginning to end. But, in *Unfold*, through the lateral movement, the schizophrenia of the structure, and the possibility for exploration, pleasure, and discovery, the approach might be best described as a becoming-intimate with the lessons and the ruins of zoology.'[5] By the lessons and ruins of zoology, I think they mean the places where classification has failed us.

Mansion library after the 4 August 2020 explosion. Photo: Jad Melki

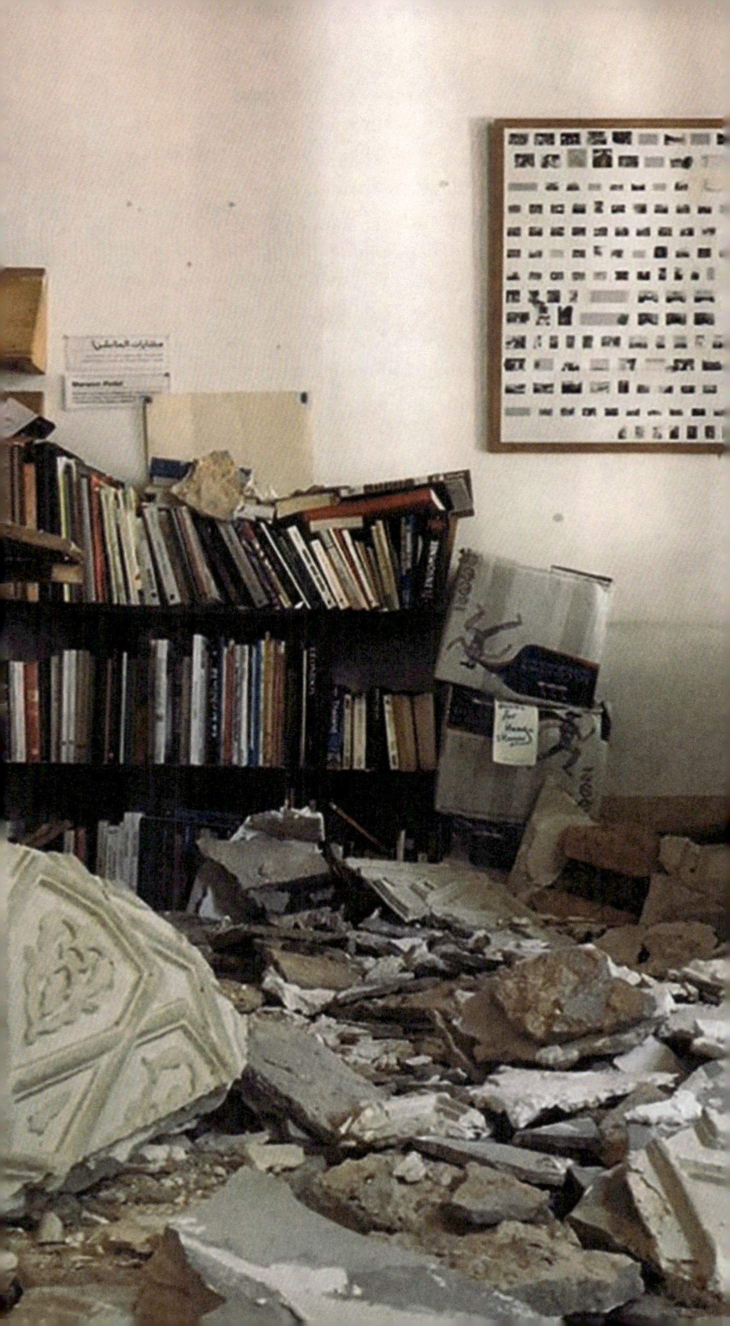

Where the masks of order and logic have slipped, and the ideology of libraries – their colonial formation, their value systems – peek through the chinks of the Dewey Decimal System. Although most libraries aim to educate and inspire, they can also be quietly rigid places, that discard things that do not fit, jettison the unruly, and police worth. A misfit library is no cure for political disaster, but Beirut needs unruly spaces, needs such intimacy and counters to authority: libraries that are more than books, in buildings that are more than stone.

London, August 2020

1 Andrew Beccone, "The Library as Platypus: On the Dual Nature of the Reanimation Library," https://www.libraryasincubatorproject.org/, September 26, 2012, accessed August 2, 2020.

2 The VOLUME project, 2013–14, was curated by Sara Giannini in collaboration with 98weeks, Beirut, and Vision Forum, Stockholm.

3 See *About.html* http://unfold.thevolumeproject.com/, accessed August 12, 2020.

4 Lina Mounzer, "It Sounded Like the World Itself Was Breaking Open," *New York Times*, https://www.nytimes.com/2020/08/05/opinion/beirut-port-explosions.html, August 5, 2020, accessed August 18, 2020.

5 "The Literal Intimacies of Zoology: Reading Through the Folders of Colonial-Science," Sara Giannini in conversation with Anna-Sophie Springer and Etienne Turpin, *Unfold* #2, http://unfold.thevolumeproject.com/, accessed August 20, 2020.

Mansion library after the 4 August 2020 explosion. Photo: Jad Melki

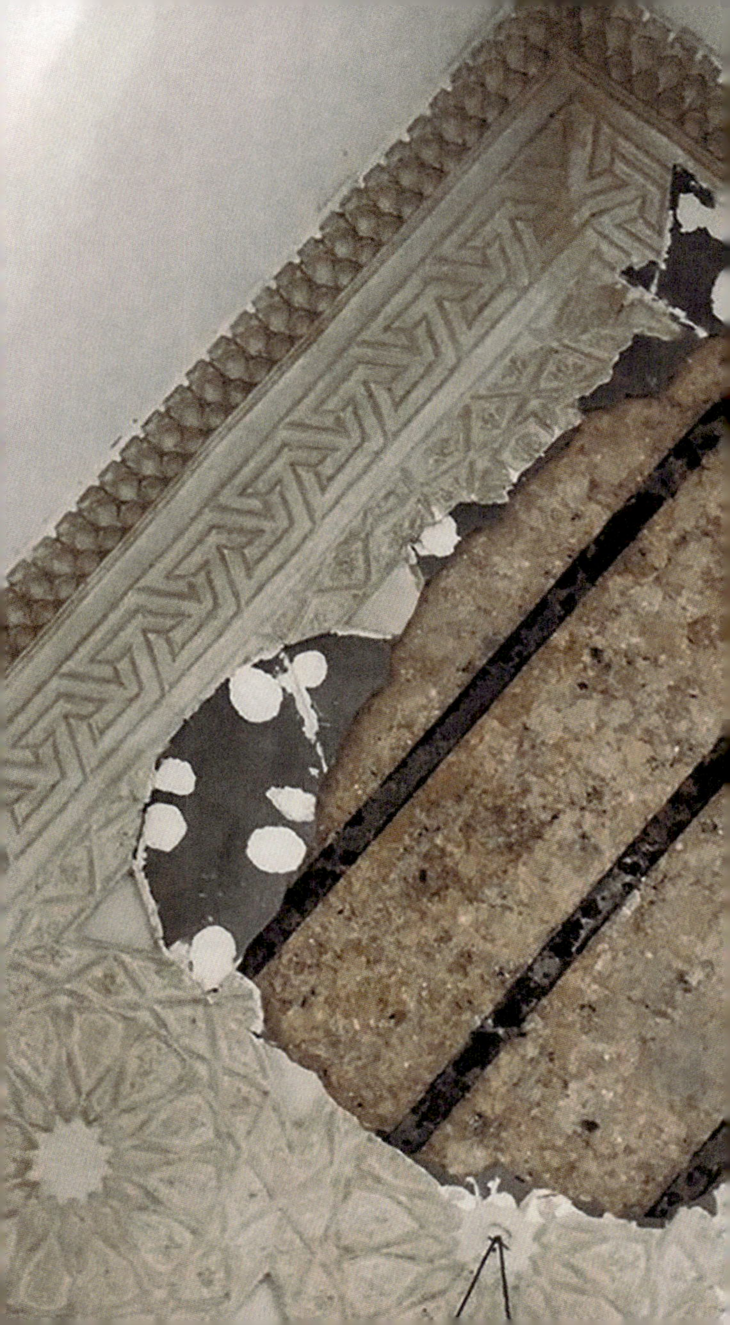

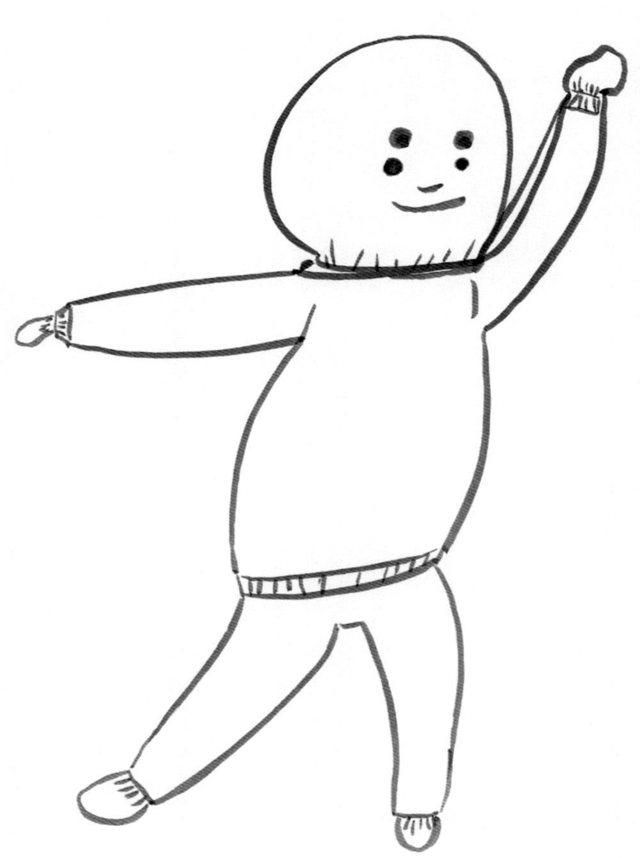

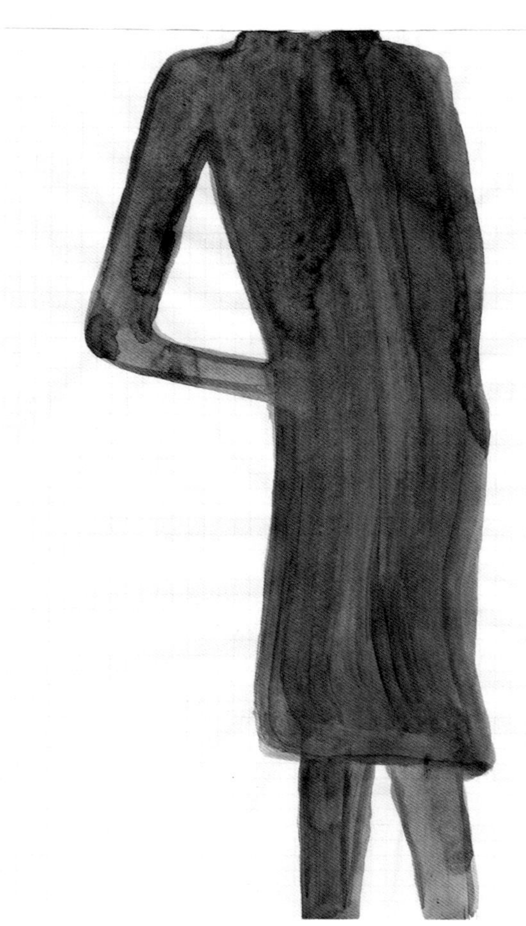

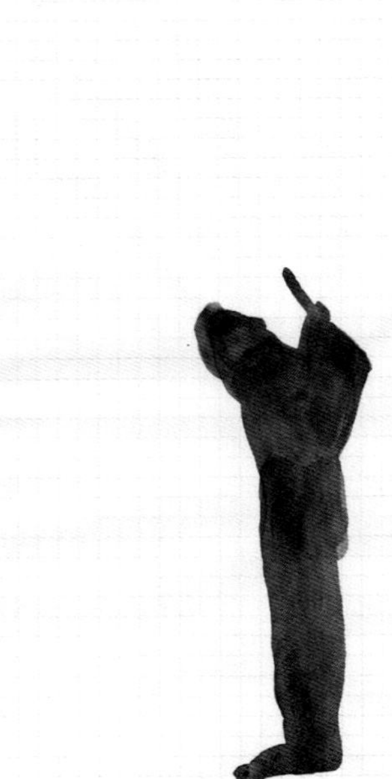

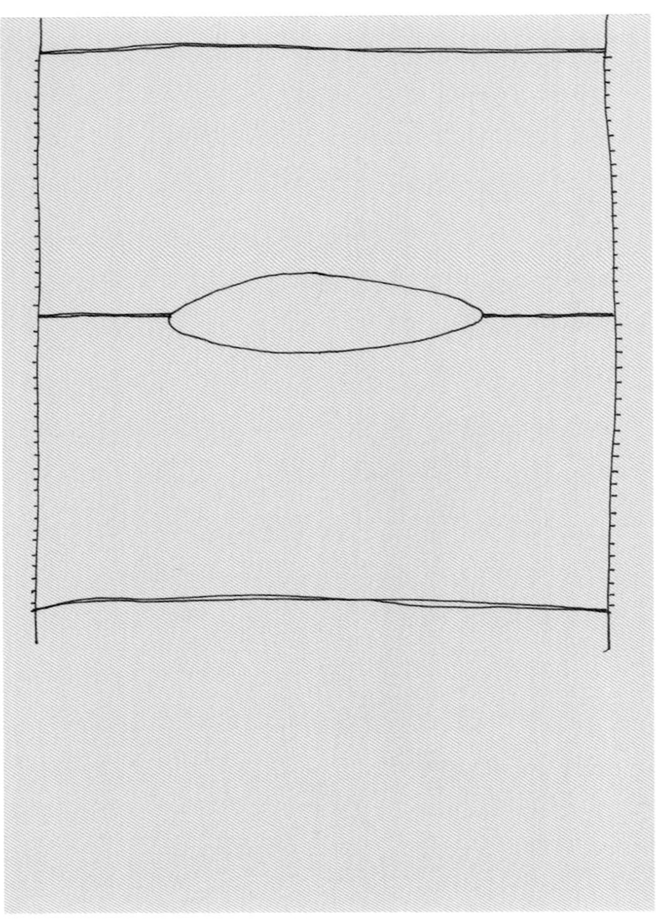

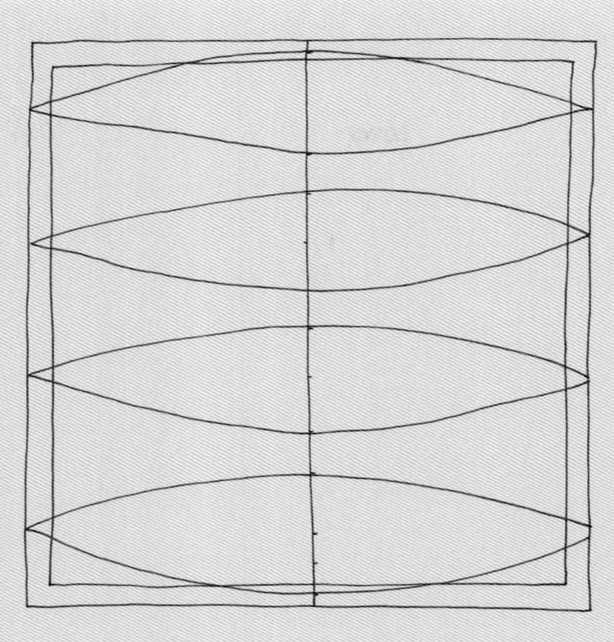

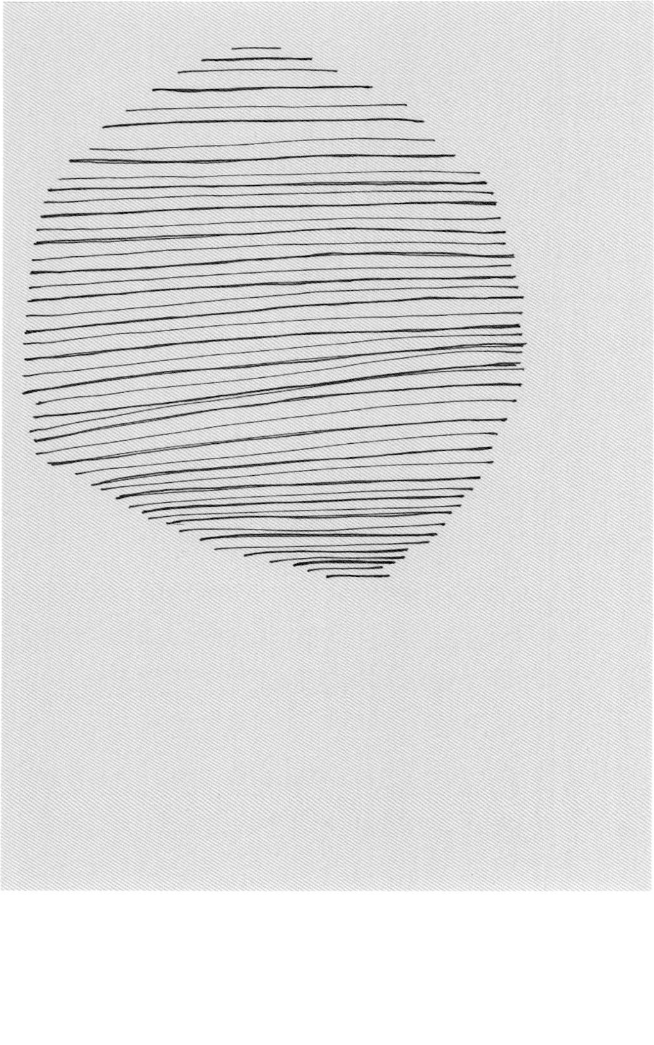

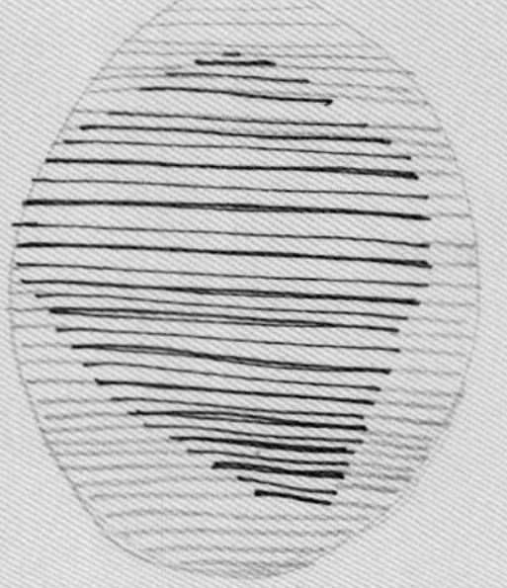
I can never reach the precision
calmness

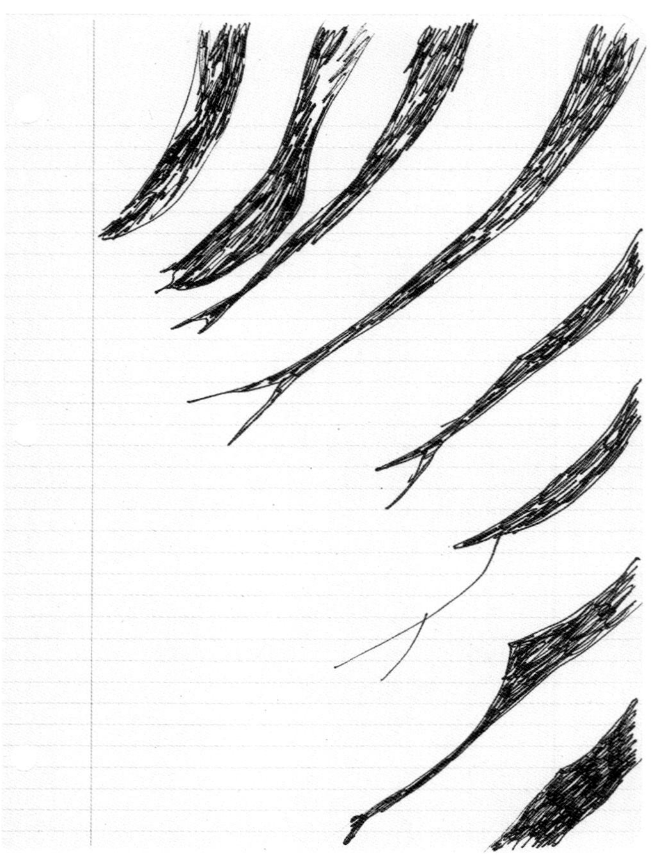

the book

Not Alone

Susanne Weiß

> Sun, moon, mountains and rivers are the writing of being, the literature of what-is. Long before our species was born, the books had been written. The library was here before we were. We live in it.
>
> Robert Bringhurst, *The Tree of Meaning: Language, Mind and Ecology* [1]

Can this mean that we have inherited our relationship to books, and therefore everything that books do to us, they do it epigenetically? What does this mean for our way of looking at things? Do I know things which have been recorded, written down, finalized and discussed intuitively?

I must confess that in lazy periods of my adolescence, I loved my mother's advice to put schoolbooks under my pillow before a test so their contents would flow into me at night. Of course, she meant it as a ritual for finals, and not as a general practice, but there were times when I trusted in this magnificent method. Predictably, the results were not so magnificent. And there were other practices of physical book embodiments in our family: for instance, my grandmother enjoyed teaching us table manners by requiring we put books under our armpits – while eating. My brother and I had to sit upright with our arms pressed tightly to our bodies in order not to drop the books. Luckily, she only used this method to demonstrate table manner methods she experienced when she was a child. Although this took place only two or three times for educational purposes, I can still recall my feeling of concentration trying not to drop the book on the floor. Perhaps sitting upright enhanced my height by a few millimetres, but books definitely helped me to reach things I was not supposed to reach.

Another exercise was walking upright and balancing books on my head to improve my posture. This time I used outdated schoolbooks. Surely my mother appreciated my balancing sessions as they just added to her idea of how book content is transmitted. In fact, this would have been even more efficient since there was no pillow between book and head.

'We live in it'. I totally agree with Robert Bringhurst. On so many levels we do. For me this proves that without books next to me I simply don't feel comfortable. I grab a book because I like the look, or the title. I hold it, I embrace it; eventually we form a relationship and live together.

Thinking about my own curatorial practice and its relationship to libraries and books, it feels apparent to me that books can become some kind of spine to an exhibition, and often appear to be the backbone of the artistic process. When in the artist's studio, I might grab a book that is laying around, and the conversation starts from there. Therefore books in artists' practices seem to me like portals to a normally invisible context, but one that is relevant for diving more deeply into the artists' work. Words, lines, pages, books carry ideas and lead to propositions and different perspectives. They become a trajectory – lead or distract, confuse or enlighten, speaking in different tongues among themselves, talking eventually also to me, as well as the public. The same is the case when the genealogy of an artwork is revealed through the artist, their references, catalogues and literature, contemporary #media and the exhibition itself.

In 1920, Aby Warburg described all movable mediums, like graphics, tapestries, books and manuscripts, as 'automobile image vehicles'. His ambitious studies of influences, back and forth movements, the early implementation of popular culture through antique images and figures, can be seen as his private cosmology. He turned his thoughts into a visual argument, leaving behind much more than a library. In that sense, the book is a vehicle that can move in all directions.

When I started to develop my curatorial programme for the Heidelberger Kunstverein in 2011, I knew I would like to take a closer look at the potential of the so-called solo show, as I find it extremely relevant to unravel and unfold an artistic practice for all parties involved: the artist, curator, mediator and public. The term 'solo show' did not feel right to me, because we think in relations, and we live and work in networks. We remember important knots in our lives that made us stay tied together or become untied. Our thinking, action and styles are shaped by these influences and, for some, it's even an idolatrous tie.

This brought me to the idea for the format of 'solo show: not alone'. In close cooperation with the artists, we found very individual ways of including their references in the exhibition to frame the complexity of each artistic practice. The ideas and outcomes brought the backbone of artistic production to the foreground, mediating between the artwork and the public.

In spring 2012 I opened my programme with visual artist Ulf Aminde. To describe, in brief, a complex artistic practice, his interdisciplinary approach enforces dialogues and embodies conversations in specific social and political contexts. For the concept of his show, Heidelberg's history during the NS-Regime became a relevant starting point: namely, that Heidelberg was one of the first cities to joyfully celebrate – twice in 1933 – the concept of the public book burning (*Bücherverbrennung*) when the Nazis took power.

Heidelberg is divided by its river. On one side, on a little hill, are the remains of its medieval history. This *Heiligenberg* (the holy hill) was the desired destiny of the Nazis, who wanted to build a *Thingstätte* on top, in line with its historic foundations. Within a year – from 1934 to 1935 – they built this open-air theatre with a massive sound system and a stage that could seat 10,000 people, with space for 20,000 more standing. Used primarily for NS propaganda, the Heidelberg theatre made a one-time appearance in 1939. They staged *Die Braut von Messina (The Bride of Messina)*[2] by Friedrich Schiller. The first line of the play is 'Der Noth gehorchend nicht dem eigenen Trieb' (Constrained by bitter need, not by my wish).[3] This striking sentence became the title of the show. As a consequence, the main hall of the Kunstverein developed into a stage with two wooden circus stands. The stands transformed the exhibition space into a performative space: five acts with manifold protagonists expanded the space (artistic and curatorial) throughout the exhibition.

But before we came up with the idea of the stage intervention, we spent a lot of time in dialogue about how to transform the space for a curatorial setting that employs dialogues, discourses and participation, all of which heavily inform Ulf's practice.

The space itself created the question: how do we present an artistic practice that is based on video art in a hall which is full of light and designed for large-scale

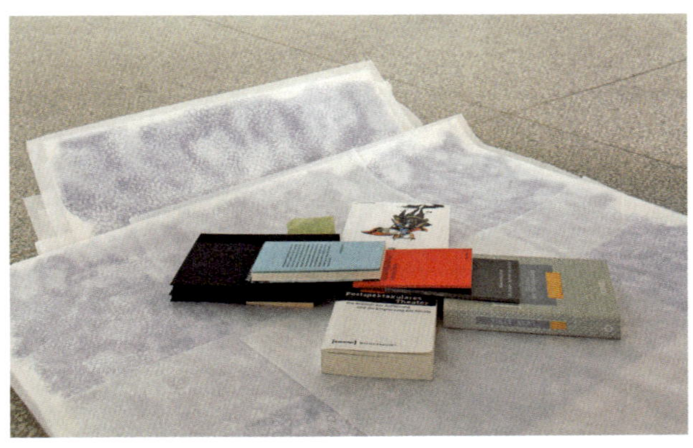

Ulf Aminde, *Prison (excerpt)*, drawings by inmates of the women's prison Schwäbisch-Gmünd, ball-pen on paper, 2011. Photo: Markus Kaesler.

sculptures? We found several solutions for it. Two to mention here: first of all, we did not exhibit single artworks but rather his artistic practice. Further, we screened the video pieces publicly in the presence of the artist, watching them together from the beginning to the end, followed by a discussion with guests.[4]

During our meetings in his studio, I encountered various materials, like photographs and props from different projects, texts in the form of photocopies, and plenty of theory books. I asked him if he could imagine including the books, and certain excerpts from different projects, in the exhibition. Eventually his arrangement under one of the circus stands turned the books into a poetic object on top of a pile of drawings[5] (see image on the left). The excerpts were assembled on a display that matched the width of a central wall as a material collage (see image below). Throughout the five acts, the face of the exhibition changed: makeup was not added, but instead pages, layers, reminiscences of the performative interventions.

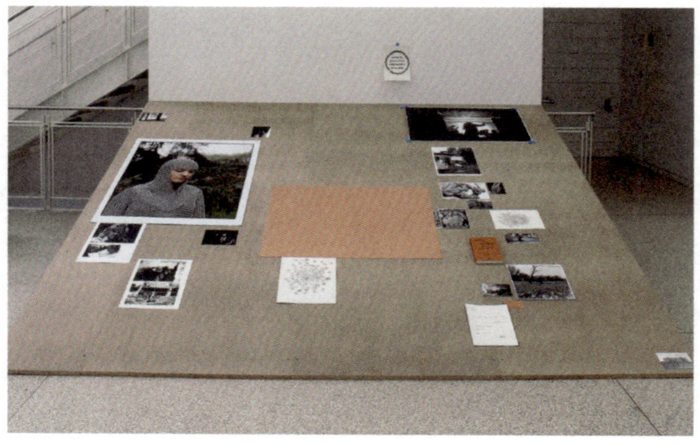

Ulf Aminde, *I.) acted on my fantasies and that's where everything went wrong*, 2012. Photo: Markus Kaesler.

In the next exhibition at Heidelberger Kunstverein I presented *Echoes*, the work of Heide Hinrichs. Heide's approach to sculpture can be read as a translation process. I understand her works as a fragile bodily and a spatial reaction to the literature she is intensely dealing with. Her exhibition brought together works from two main series: first from her long-term body of work dealing with the novel *Austerlitz* by German-born author W. G. Sebald, a recent interaction at the time with the text *Dictee* by Korean American artist and author Theresa Hak Kyung Cha. Both try to bring untold pasts into resonance, to find language for trauma, cultural loss and exile. Heide took the architectural conditions of the Kunstverein into account – the architecture is impossible to ignore – and responded as an echo to the building with woolen blankets to cover the rather cold postmodern-style glass. For Heide's work – which is a response to language and a language itself that reflects on the impact of exile(s) –

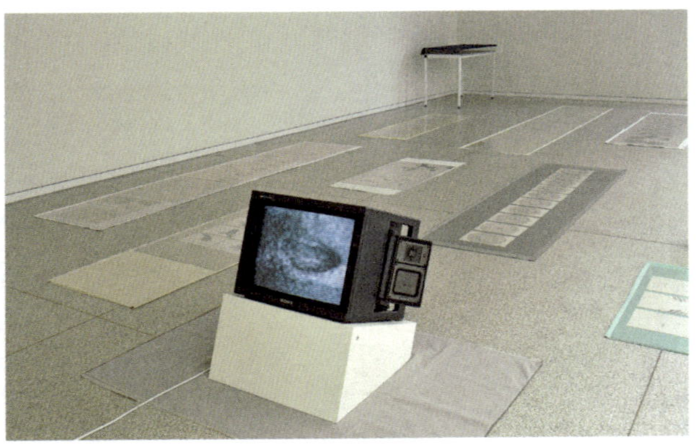

Above: Exhibition view of Heide Hinrichs, *Echoes*, 2012. Video: Theresa Hak Kyung Cha, *Mouth to Mouth*, 1975. Photo: the artist.

Right: Heide Hinrichs, *Blankets*, installation on the outside of the building, 2012. Photo: the artist.

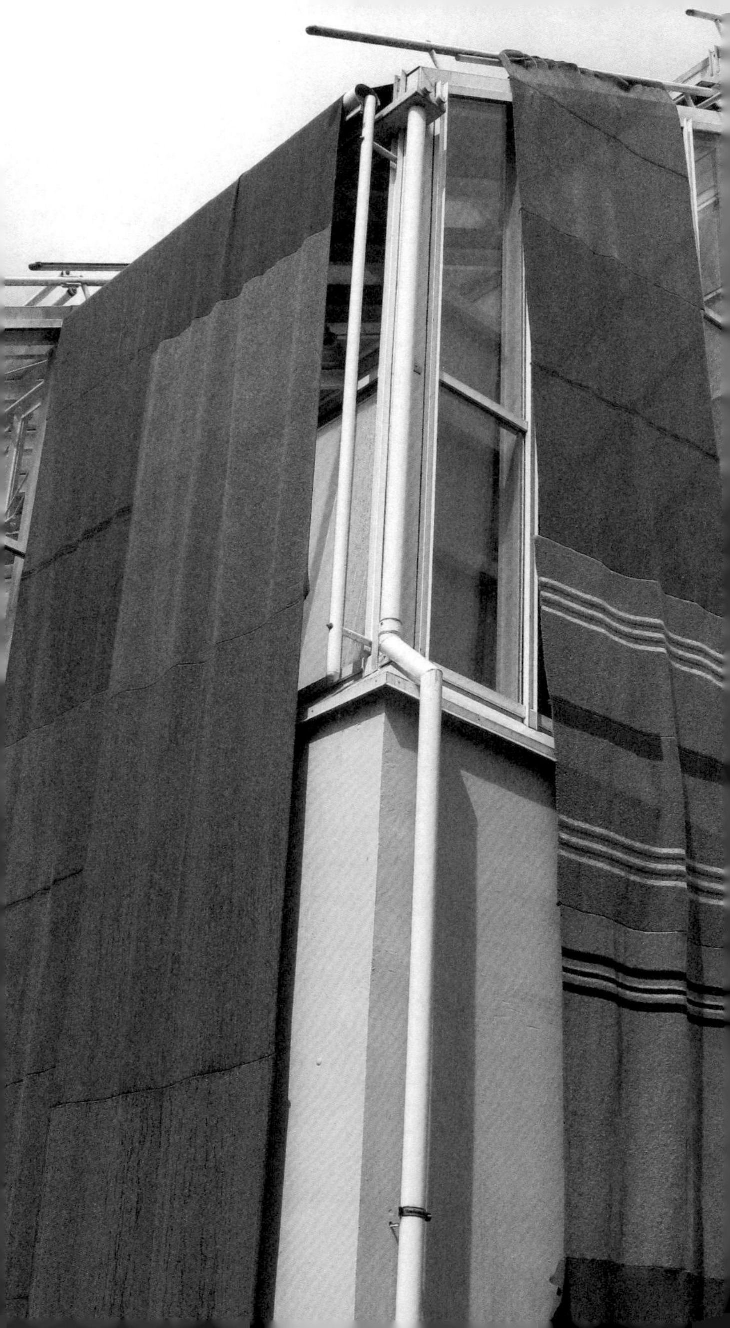

the Kunstverein felt like a massive glasshouse where she decided to place her works on a bed of blankets and other tactile components comparable to seeds. In response to my question of how to give her roots visibility in the exhibition, we decided to show an early video work by Theresa Hak Kyung Cha[6] in which the artist filmed her mouth forming vowels and their representations in the Korean Hangul alphabet (see image on page 120). Seeking representatives for her relationship to Sebald, we went to Marbach, to the German Literature Archive, and looked at his archive boxes which are kept there. I remember my astonishment that Sebald himself documented his process and sources meticulously and chronologically in archive boxes. Everything seemed prepared for the transfer from England to Germany. Further, I remember that I fell asleep next to the boxes while Heide was continuing the research which became a selection of what we planned to include in the exhibition. Finally, it was a showcase filled with key images from *Austerlitz* (see image below). The selection from Sebald's work, in relation to the poetic texture of

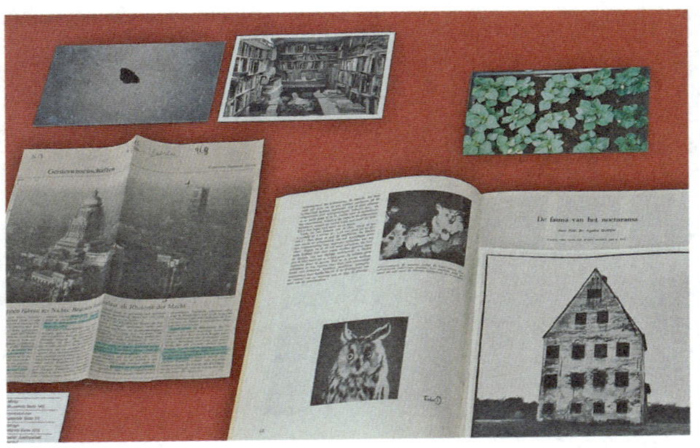

Detail of display case with images from W. G. Sebald's folder related to Austerlitz, German Literature Archive, Marbach. Photo: Markus Kaesler.

Heide's artwork in the exhibition, created the reciprocity of echoes for which the show is named, capturing how intrinsically everyday materials speak through their genealogies.

When I invited artist Annette Weisser into this format, she took my question of influence as a challenge, and quickly responded with a brilliant idea: the complete private library of her aunt Anneliese Weisser. Her good spirit accompanied Annette Weisser during childhood and youth. It was through these books that she began her art education, by looking at reproductions in lavish catalogues of antiquity and Renaissance artworks. And here she internalised the canon of pacifist post-war literature by writers like Heinrich Böll, Bertolt Brecht, and Christa Wolf, among others. We picked up the books, packed up in wooden crates normally used to store apples, at her family home in the Black Forest area. When we arrived, her aunt had already emptied all her bookshelves and I rather felt like an intruder, taking such an important

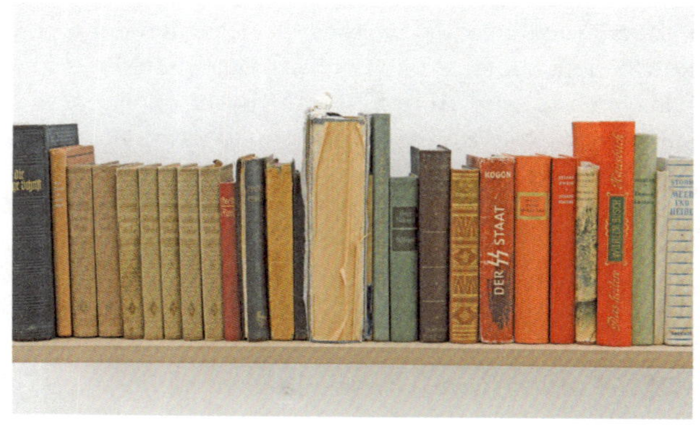

Detail: Annette Weisser, *Anneliese Weisser's library, sorted by date of publication*, 2013. Photo: Markus Kaesler.

part of her everyday life and history out of her private space. But luckily there was also her happiness and pride present in the living room that her niece was going to take her books into an exhibition to Heidelberg, and not only the void of the now emptied shelves.

Back in the Kunstverein, the roughly 500 books were sorted by their publishing date. Arranged on an eleven-metre-long shelf, they turned into a timeline beginning in 1904 (a catechism), with the last bit left empty for new books to come, the acquisition not yet finished. The shelf was installed in the main exhibition hall as part of the exhibition *Make Yourself Available*. For this show, Annette reproduced four architectural fragments of her childhood room (*Jugendzimmer*) located underneath the roof (as those frequently are) complete with slanted ceilings. Some of the fragments were turned upside down or flat on the floor and acted as displays for her woodprints and drawings. They were repainted in the colours Annette had chosen for her room back then, minus one: black, which her parents wouldn't accept.

The best thing about these books were the dialogues they provoked with the audience, as they turned into representatives and echoes. Stories entered the Kunstverein about certain books, about when they had been read and, most interestingly, the experiences surrounding the reading. The personal testimonies about what this and that book meant for the audience enabled a personal connection to Annette's artwork. The link was made and the view opened.

Her motifs are universal yet specific. It is easy to relate to Annette's figures that demonstrate democratic post-war values – from the obedient to the disobedient. Weisser, who dedicated the show to her upbringing

Exhibition view:
Annette Weisser, *Make Yourself Available*, 2013.
Photo: Markus Kaesler.

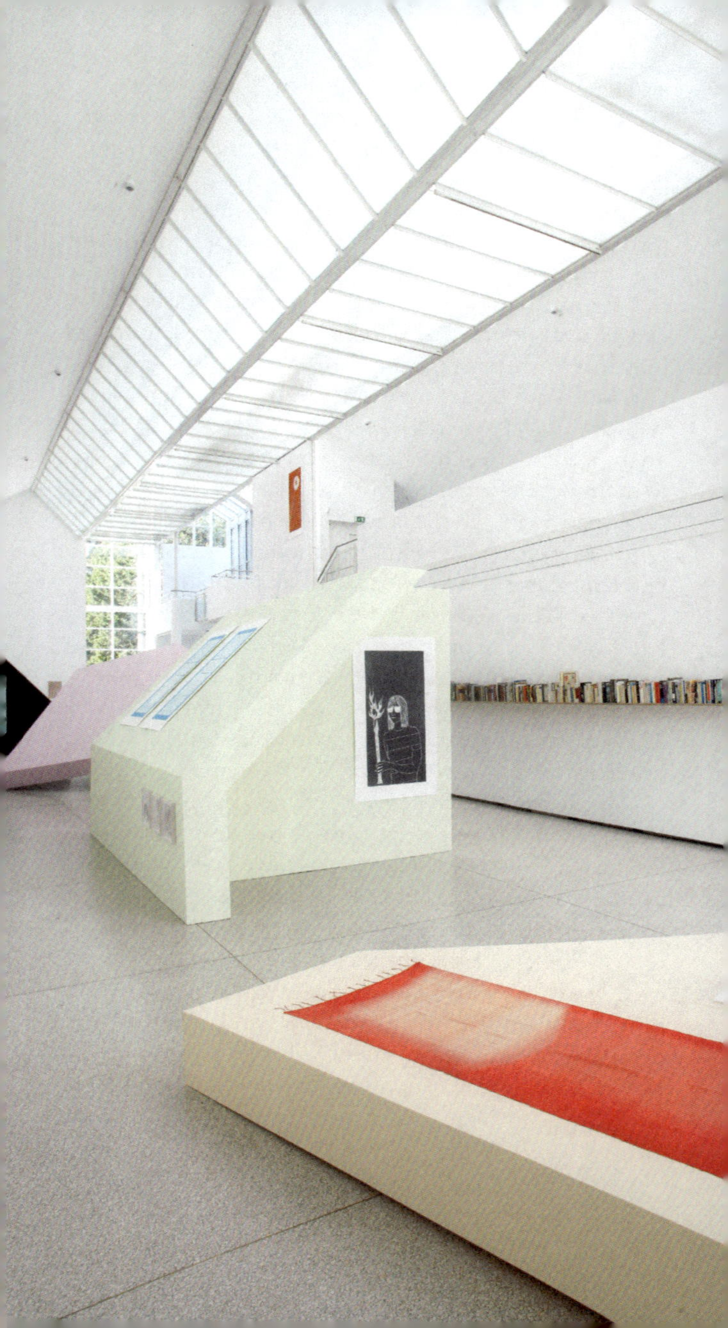

and the related topics of the 1970s and 1980s like the Cold War, acid rain, and the movement against nuclear power, developed the exhibition with a view from her first-floor Los Angeles studio.[7]

Thinking about it now – nearly ten years later – the format probably enabled a more direct engagement with the world inside and outside the studio as there was no mannerism presented but rather personal, social, and artistic testimonies that underlined an understanding of influences in artistic production.

There have been a lot more exhibitions where books, archival material, pamphlets and texts played an important role. One more I would briefly like to mention: the amazing work of Ceija Stojka was published in 2014 in the comprehensive monograph *Even death is afraid of Auschwitz.*[8] Without the work of Lith Bahlmann and Matthias Reichelt I would not have been able to develop the exhibition *Wir leben im Verborgenen (We Live in Seclusion: The Memories of a Romni).*[9] The exhibition title is borrowed from her autobiography which she published in 1988. Ceija Stojka passed away in 2013 but through her testimonies I was able to bring her strong voice into the Kunstverein.

The display, which I developed together with Marei Löllmann, was a response to her hospitality and intimate ink drawings. A generous table built the social centre of her everyday life. On a twelve-metre-long concrete table we presented her deeply disturbing ink drawings. Stojka finds images for the horror and the cacophony she experienced as a child. Her directness of speech alongside her ink drawings and paintings, depicting figures like herself, her siblings, her mother, ravens, barking dogs, shouting NS-soldiers, barracks,

Exhibition view:
Ceija Stojka, *We Live in Seclusion*, 2015.
Photo: Markus Kaesler.

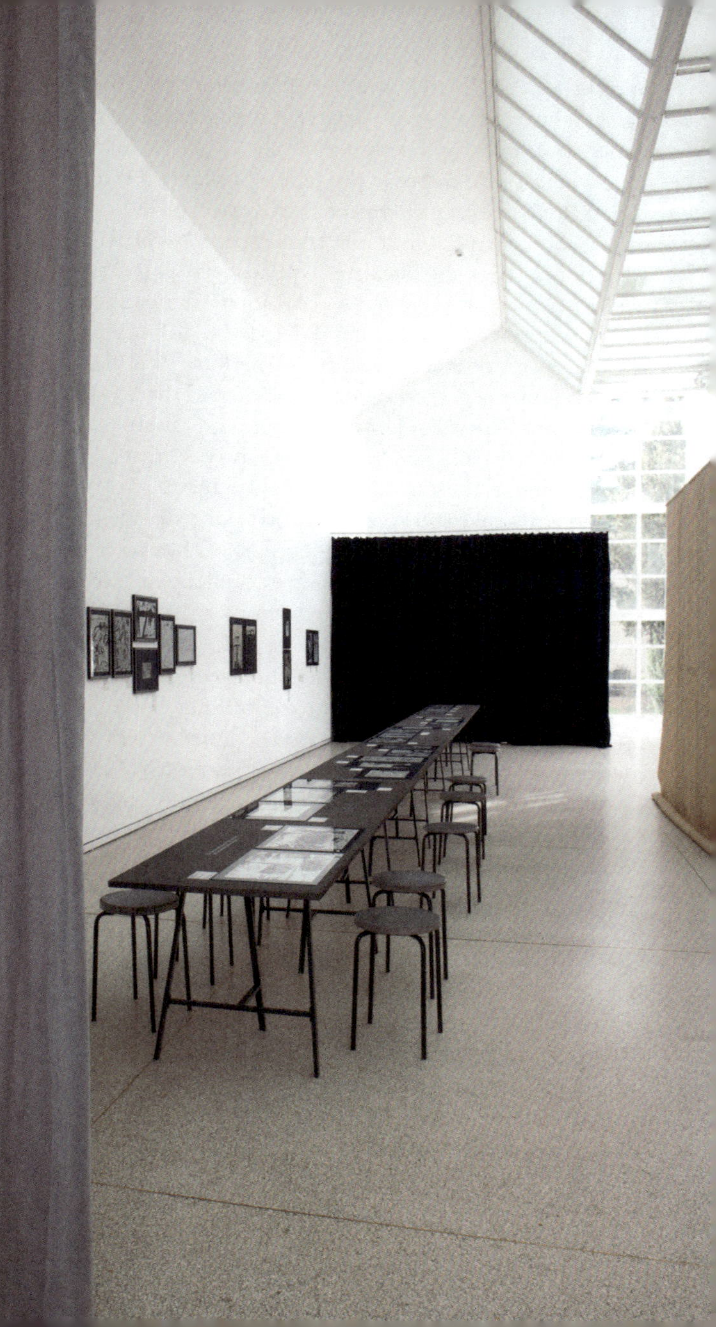

and the woods, form a unique representation of the horror she experienced as a small child in the German concentration camps with her family.

Stojka started to break the taboo of silence in the 1980s. Her artistic work on the brutal past turned into a political intervention in the present. Together with her brother she became a spokesperson and an active political protagonist. As I couldn't ask her about her references and influences, I decided to ask others about important voices within the medium of film. "Kino Romanes" (Cinema Romanes) turned the studio space of the Kunstverein into a temporary cinema. Its programme was curated by many protagonists, each of them expert in the context and medium. The chosen films gave the Porajmos (the Nazi genocide of the European Sinti and Roma people) another voice but also presence to the contemporary conflicts, tragedies and everyday life stories within the broad and diverse Sinti and Roma community.

Personal, biographical and aesthetic conditions underlay all of these curatorial experiments. Earlier on I talked about ties and knots. I find it important to mention that of course ties represent relationships. These relationships can inform the production of an exhibition. The three exhibitions described here were developed with artists I am also friends with. I've known their work over a long period of time, which was very helpful for a mutual understanding that is also based on trust. Ideas could be discussed without being judged. This opened a space for experimentation and reflection. Nevertheless, this space is meant for sharing in the format of an exhibition. To close with Robert Bringhurst: because *we live in it.*

Berlin, October 2020

1 Robert Bringhurst, *The Tree of Meaning: Language, Mind and Ecology* (Berkeley: Counterpoint, 2009), 143.

2 *The Bride of Messina* is a tragedy by Friedrich Schiller. It premiered on March 19, 1803, in Weimar. It is one of the most controversial works by Schiller, due to his use of elements from Greek tragedies (which were considered obsolete at the time it was written).

3 For full text: https://archive.org/details/bridemessinaatrooirvigoog/page/n14/mode/2up.

4 This format was entitled 'Kommentiertes Sehen' (*Commentary Viewing*) and showed selected video works in the presence of a guest (an expert in a related field) who entered into a public dialogue with the artist.

5 The drawings resulted from a workshop Ulf Aminde did with imprisoned women in 2011.

6 Theresa Hak Kyung Cha, *Mouth to Mouth*, 1975. Video, black-and-white, sound, 8 minutes. Distributed by Electronic Arts Intermix, New York.

7 Annette Weisser lived in Los Angeles from 2006 to 2019. During that period, she held a professorship at ArtCenter College of Design, Pasadena. In 2019, she returned to Berlin and in the same year she published her first novel entitled *Mycelium* with Semiotext(e).

8 Ceija Stojka, *Even death is afraid of Auschwitz* (Vienna: Verlag für moderne Kunst, 2015).

9 Ceija Stojka, *We Live in Seclusion: The Memories of a Romni* (Vienna: Picus, 1988).

Pages

Ersi Varveri

Ermoupoli, Syros, November 2020

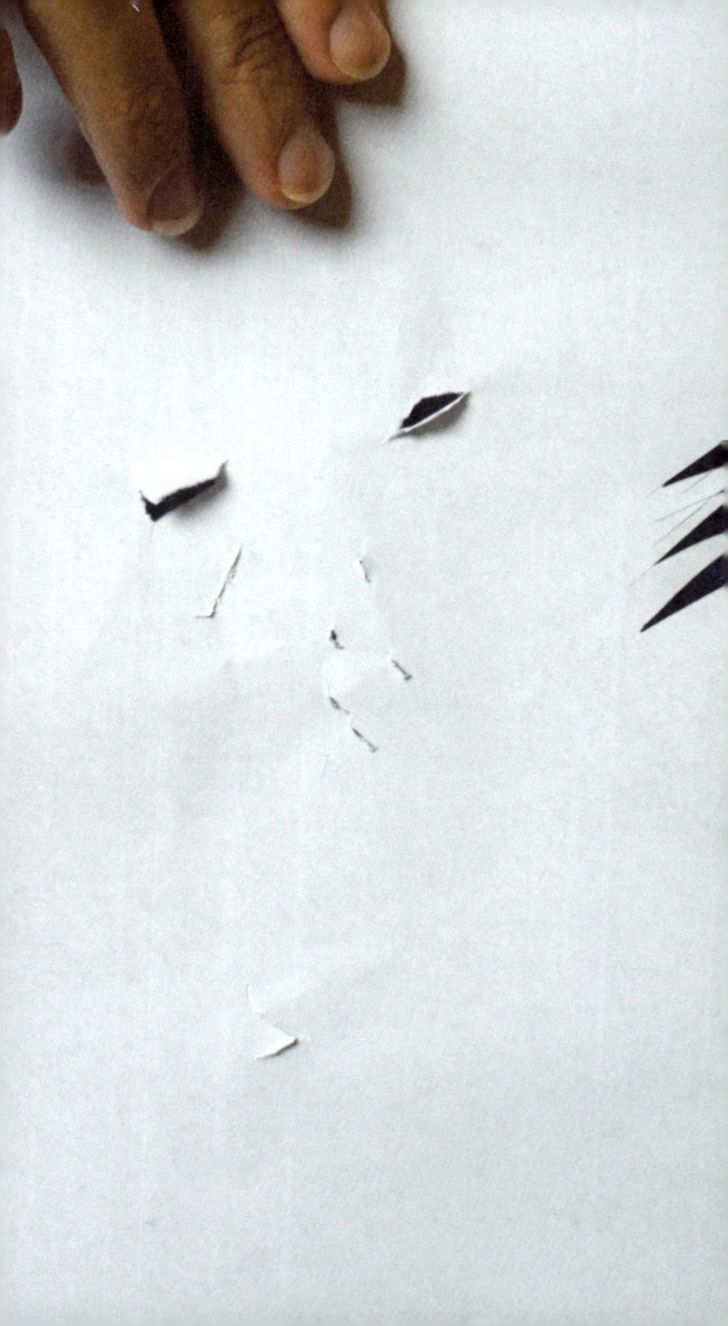

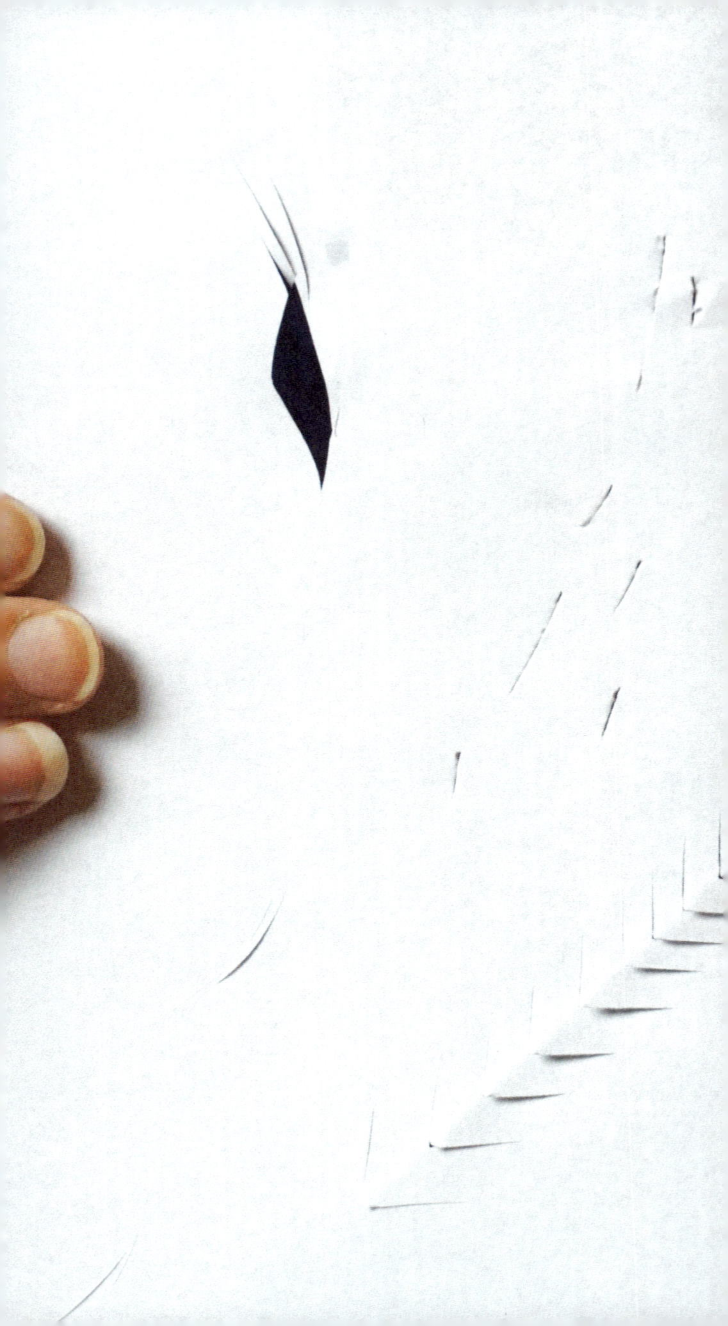

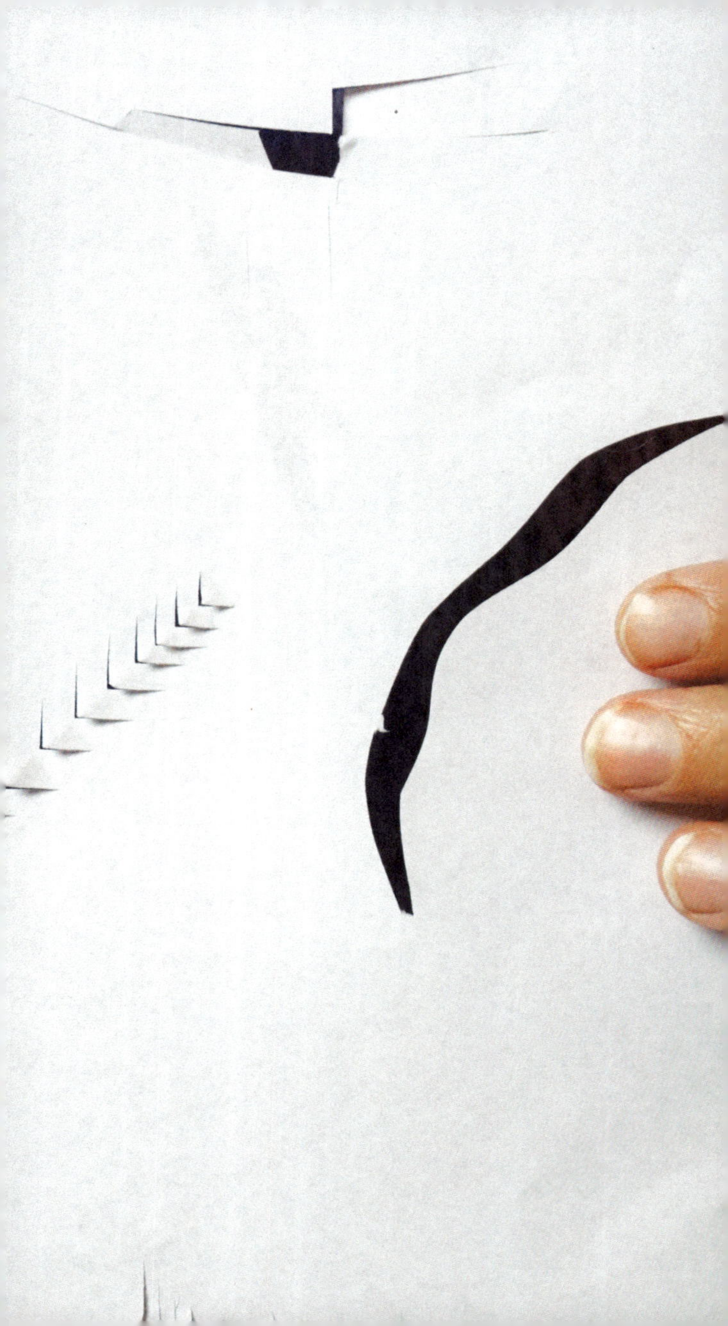

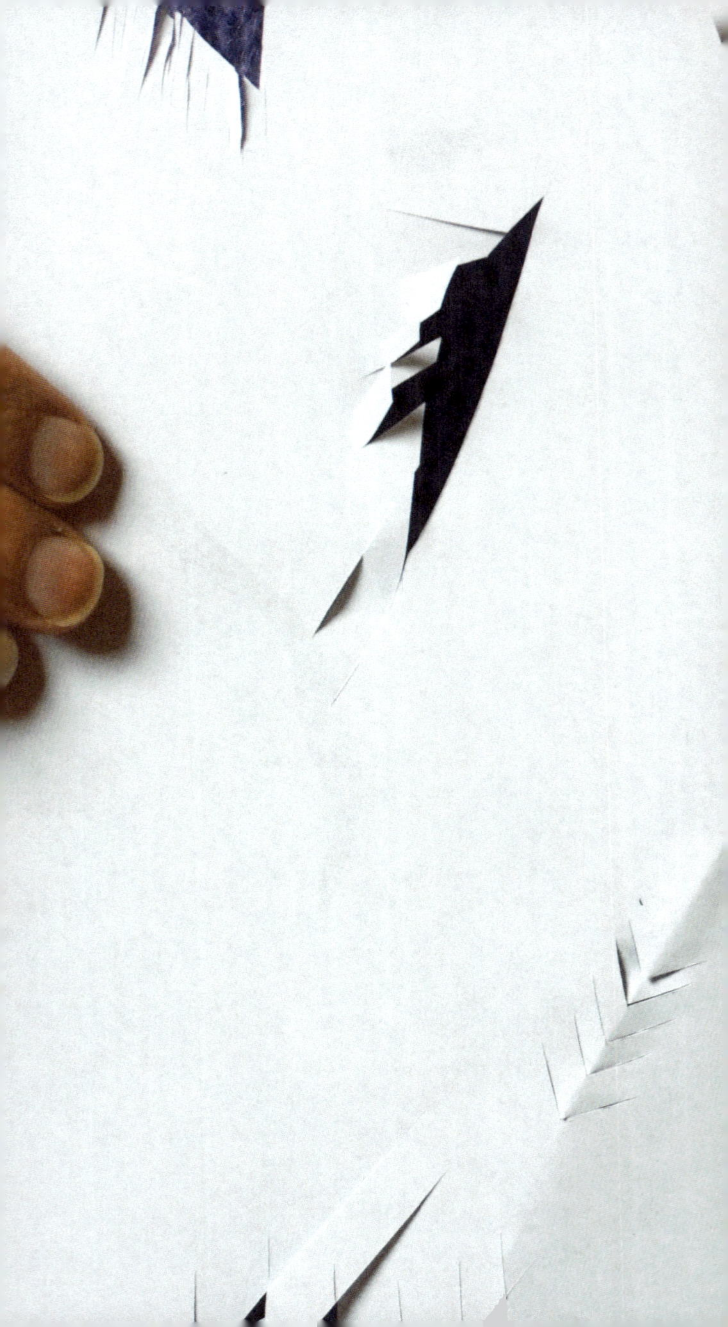

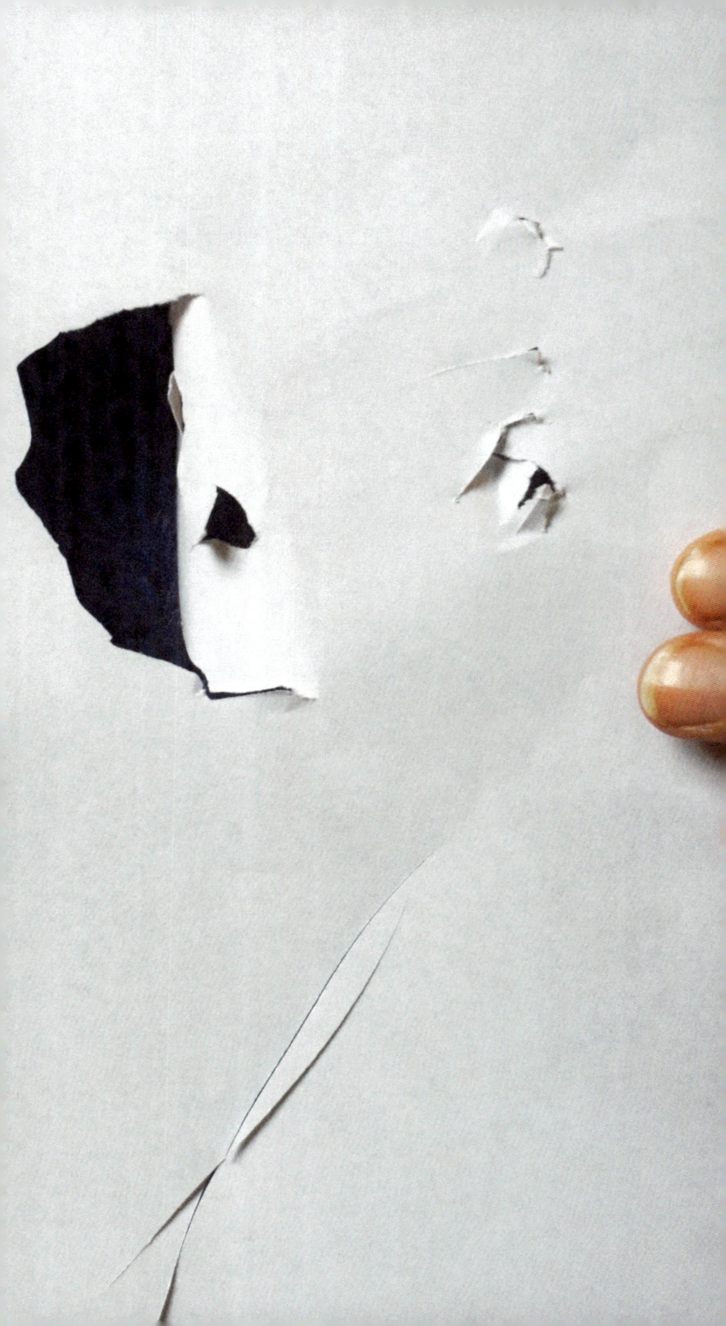

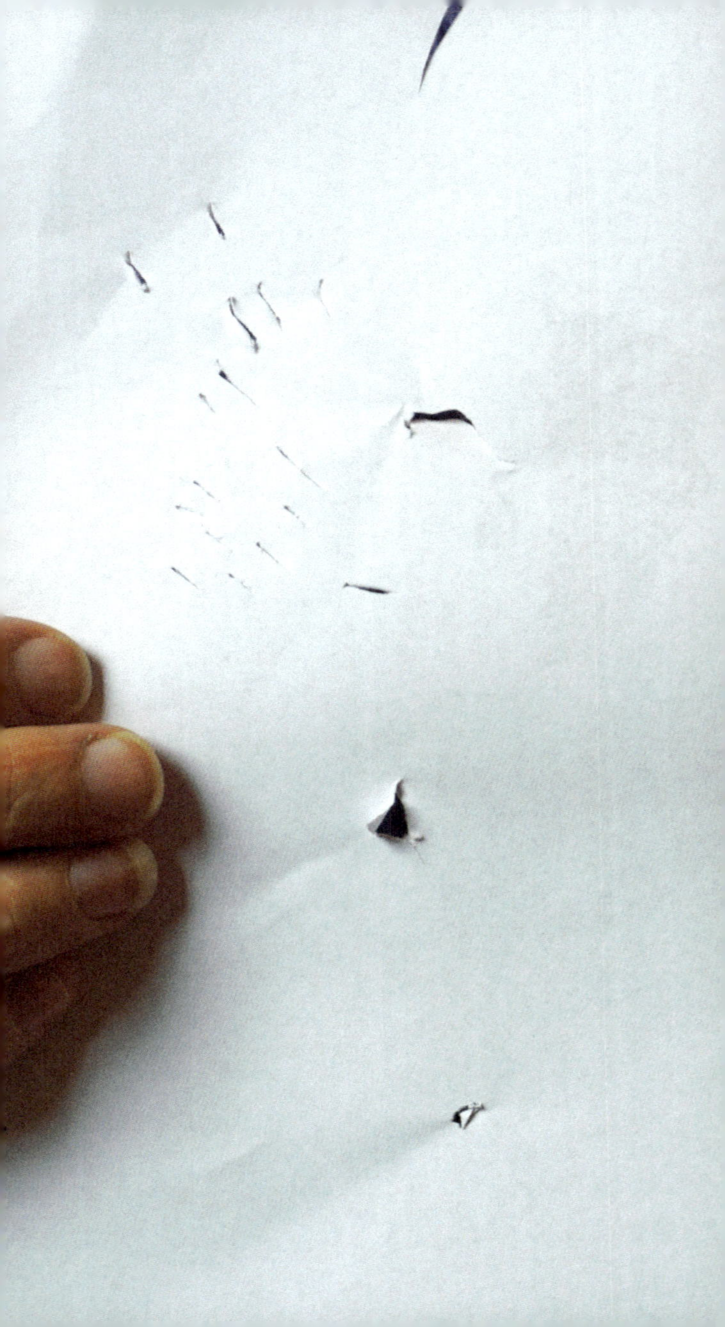

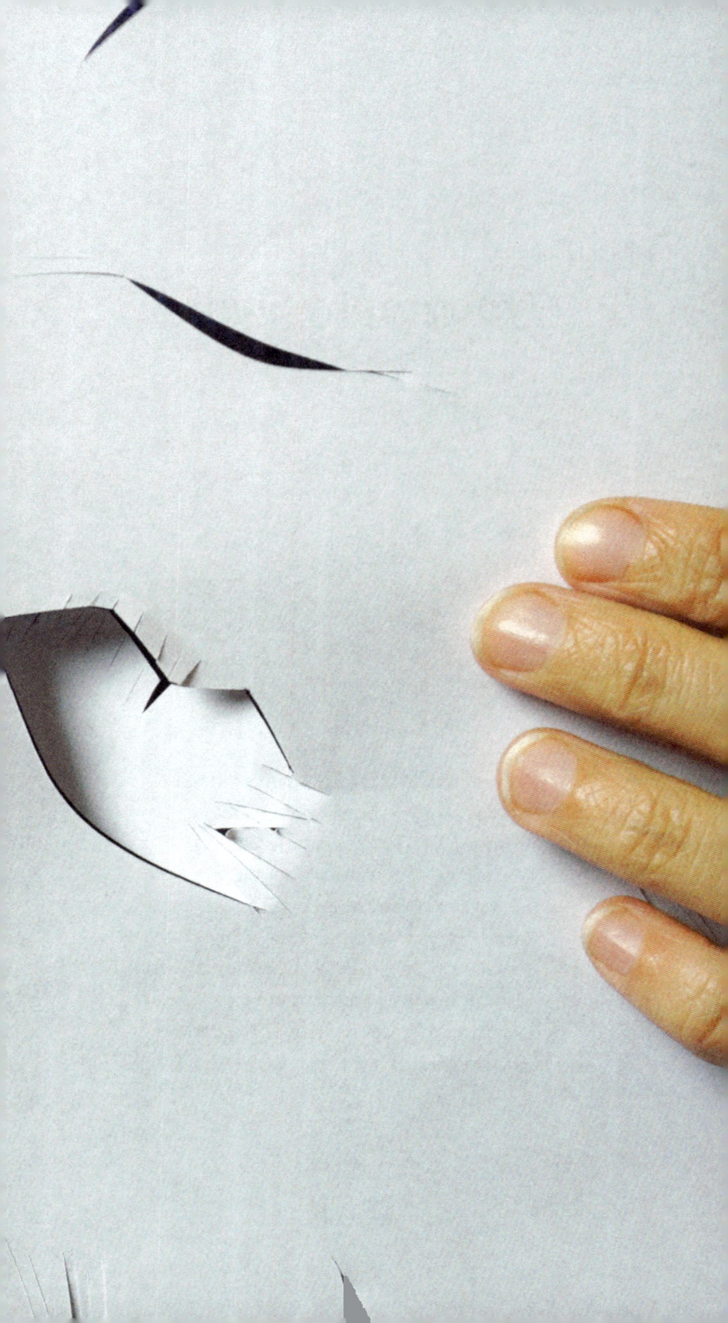

Typography Shelf

Sara De Bondt

The quotes on the following pages are excerpts from typographic manuals in my study library. While flicking through them, I was struck by the inappropriate language they use to describe mistakes and errors in typesetting, referring to women, childrearing, family relations, class, bodily and emotional states. These books remain part of standard syllabi in typography education today, and it is now clear that I need another shelf.

Ghent, November 2020

Orphans have no past, but they do have a future,
and they need not trouble the typographer.

The Elements of Typographic Style
Robert Bringhurst
(Vancouver: Hartley & Marks, 2005), 44.

Widows have a past but not a future,
and they look foreshortened and forlorn.

The Elements of Typographic Style
Robert Bringhurst
(Vancouver: Hartley & Marks, 2005), 44.

Anything loud, vulgar, or discordant was anathema to him. To produce legible books for easy reading by children, for people in a rush, for emotional or other exceptionally differentiated classes – that was not Tschichold's aim. He was not concerned with emotion.

Jan Tschichold: Typographer and Type Designer 1902–1974
Jost Hochuli
(Edinburgh: National Library of Scotland, 1982), 15

A type like Times may thus be described
as large on the body but narrow of set.

Introduction to Typography
Simon Oliver
(London: Faber and Faber, 1969), 18.

Never combine different type families.

The Graphic Artist and his Design Problems
Josef Müller-Brockmann
(Teufen: Niggli Verlag, 1964), 16.

As there is a norm of letter form
– the bare body so to say, of letters –
there is also a norm of letter clothes.

An Essay on Typography
Eric Gill
(London: Sheed and Ward, 1936), 47.

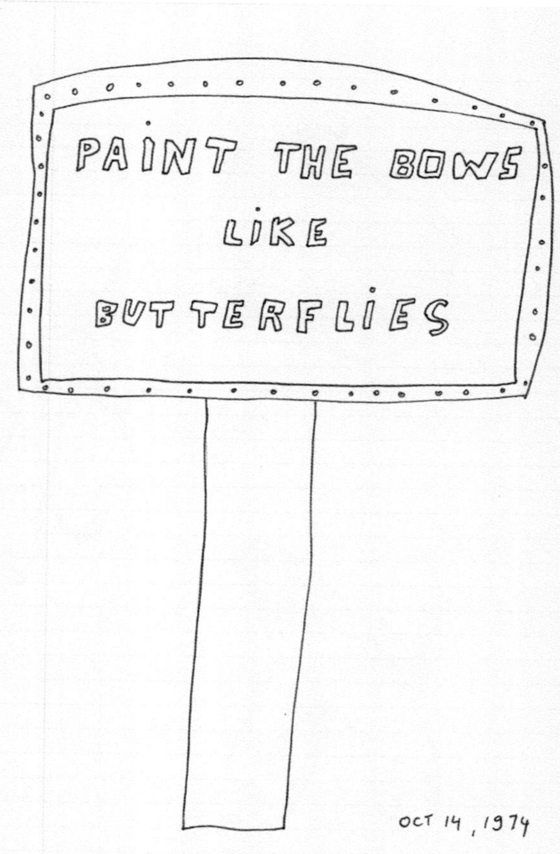
PAINT THE BOWS
LIKE
BUTTERFLIES
OCT 14, 1974

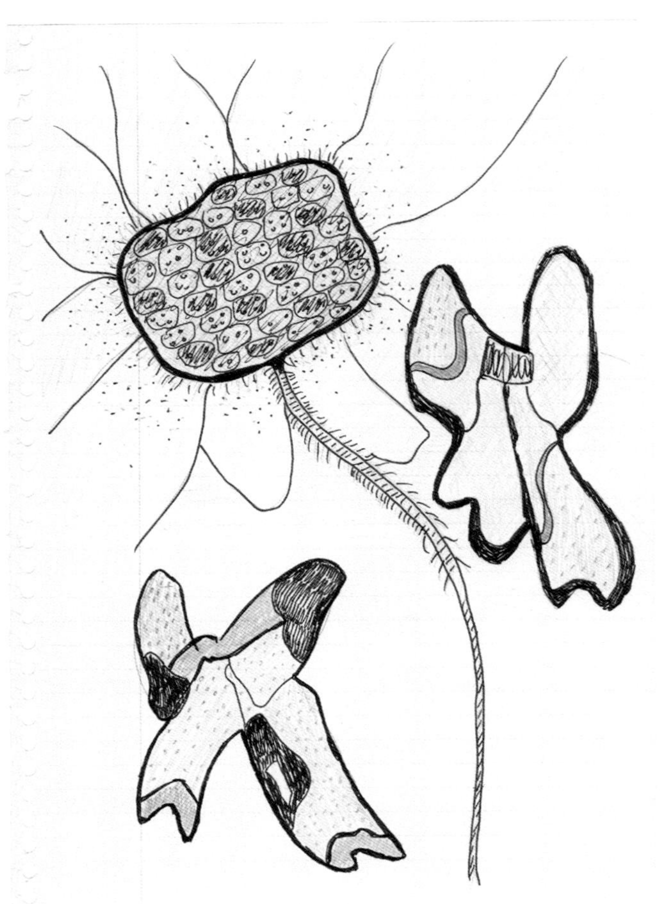

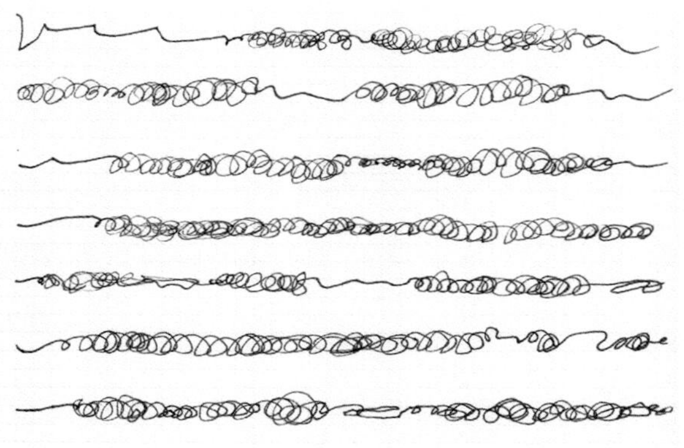

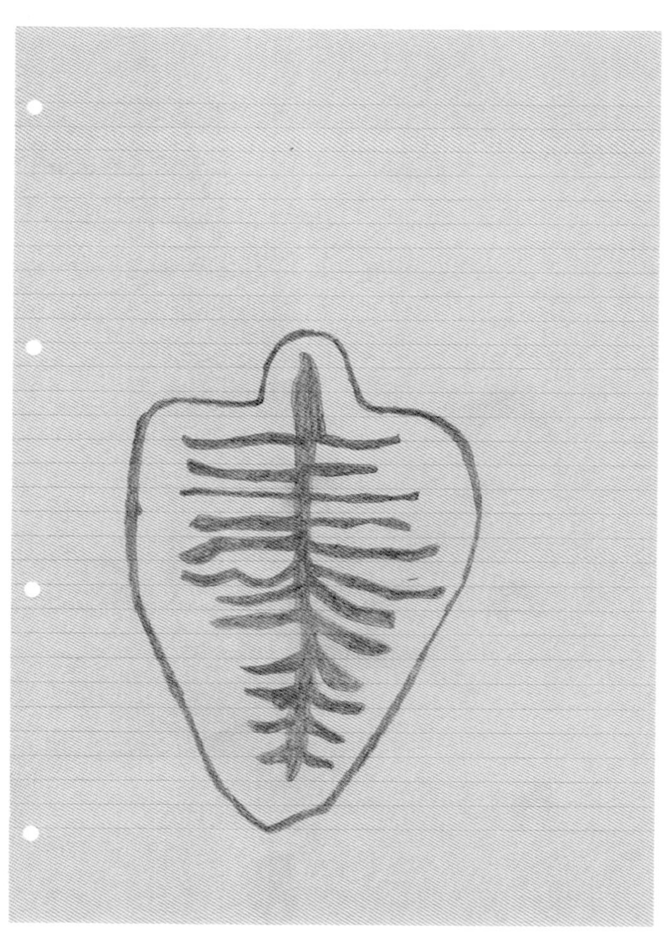

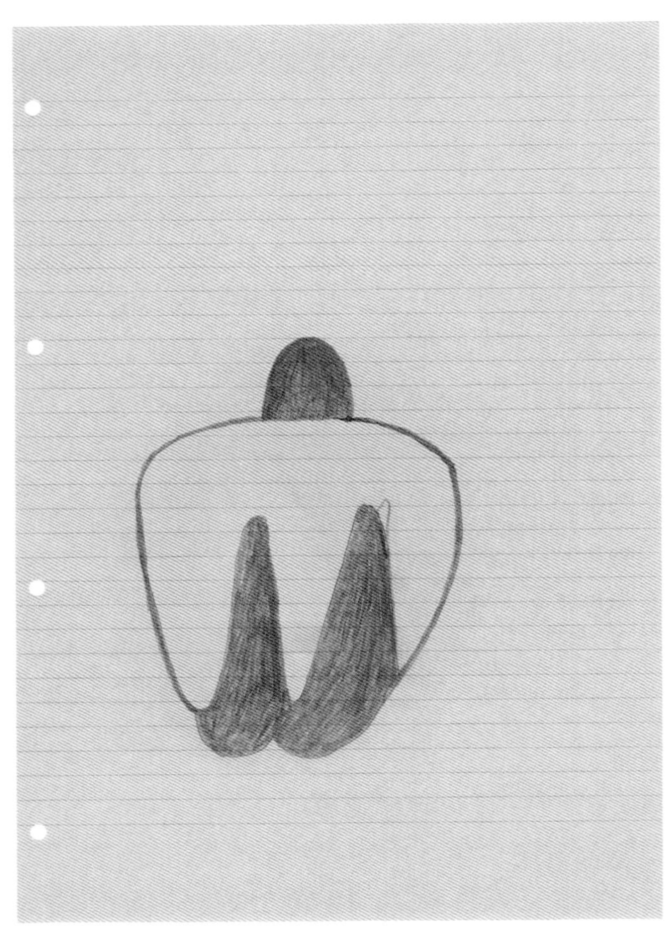

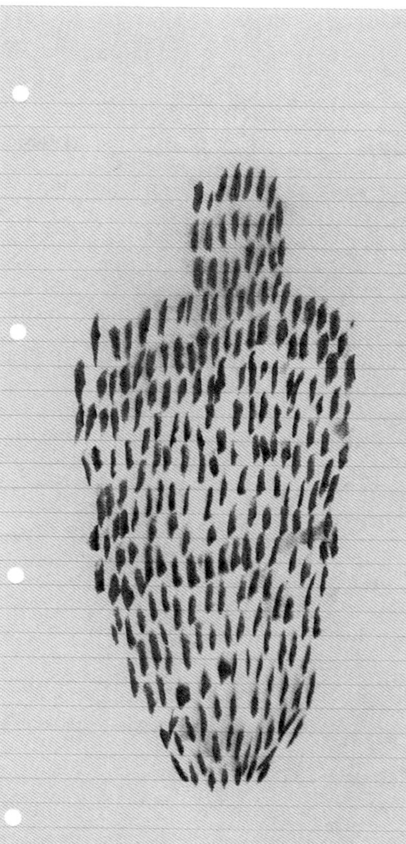

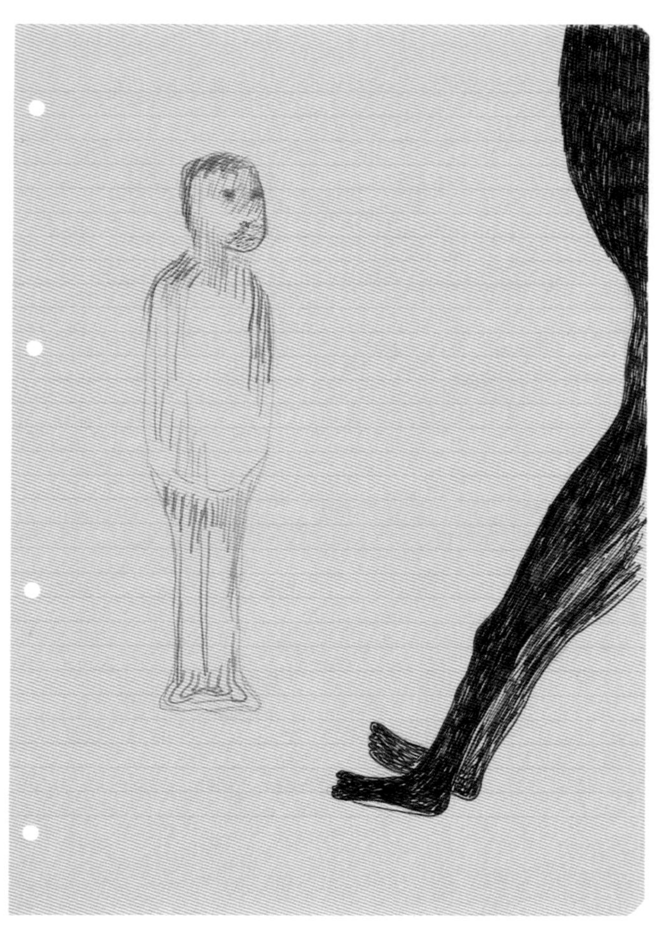

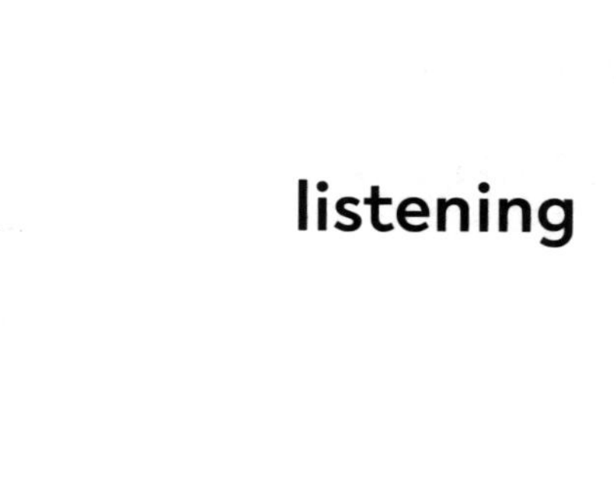

listening

Towards a Feminist Practice: Notes on Listening

Marisa C. Sánchez

> What matter who's speaking, someone said what matter who's speaking.
>
> Samuel Beckett, *Texts for Nothing*

Note #1: In Dialogue

While camping with friends at Logan Lake, British Columbia, this past July, I was alone in my tent on our first evening at the campsite when I heard three animal sounds calling out in the night: the howl of a coyote, the hoot of an owl, and another sound that repeated several times and which I didn't recognize. Its subtle vibration was haunting. Its quality crystalline, expansive, yet hollow. When I tried to classify it in the context of my prior knowledge, in my archive of memories, I couldn't place it—I had no reference for it. This was the first time my body had absorbed this sound, which now entered my memory. The next day, I learned the sound was that of wailing loons.

Describing the loon's call, Greg Budney, audio curator at the Macaulay Library at the Cornell Lab of Ornithology, has noted: "You'll hear one individual of the pair give this long mournful wail, which is essentially saying: I'm here, where are you? Generally, moments later, you'll hear the response from the other member of the pair giving its wail, saying: I'm over here."[1] In this anthropomorphic description of two loons, we hear companions vocally orienting themselves in relation to each other while separated in the darkness.

This dialogue, where each bird produces a sound to reassure the other of its presence, struck me as an apt metaphor for how I had been interacting with loved ones, friends, and colleagues since mid-March, when the province entered lockdown in response to the coronavirus pandemic: reaching out—by voice, by text, by Zoom—with regular check-ins and at times awaiting a response. Prohibited from being in physical proximity, our voices, and these virtual modes of correspondence, were ways that we gave care to one another.

Written amid the unfolding pandemic, this essay was at the same time informed by a number of exchanges and materials that I became immersed in during the summer. As screen fatigue set in, I turned to podcasts, listening intently to voices that began to populate my message thread or were shared on reading lists circulating on social media in collective response to the urgent calls for action against racial injustices and police brutality. These calls arose in the United States, with protests organized in solidarity with #BlackLivesMatter beginning on May 26, 2020, the day after the killing of George Floyd, which reverberated around the world, and precipitated by the killings of Ahmaud Arbery, and Breonna Taylor, and the loss of numerous other Black lives at the hands of police. Calls for collective action to redress racial inequalities and to fight for social justice within educational institutions grew louder, including at Emily Carr University of Art + Design in Vancouver, where I teach as a sessional lecturer in the Faculty of Culture + Community. On July 13, 2020, an anonymous group of students and alumni of the university announced the formation of an Anti-Racist Initiative (ARI), which demands the university be held accountable for not doing enough to support Black, Indigenous, and racialized students and faculty. In a letter to the executive committee, the ARI wrote that the university "actively contributes to marginalized people's dispossession and oppression." They set forth a challenge to the administration, leading to conversations on racial justice, white supremacy, and structural racism. Administrators at Emily Carr have since organized workshops to begin the healing process, including one led by Dr. Tricia Rose, professor of Africana Studies and director of the Center for the Study of Race and Ethnicity in America at Brown University, who spoke on the topic of "Systemic Racism in Post-Secondary Education." With a call to decolonize the university, the ARI aims for a re-education of the academic community so that the lived experiences of BIPOC can be seen and heard. To respond here to the epigraph by Samuel Beckett, whose writings probe questions on existence and survival: it matters who's speaking.

Note #2: Should We All Be Feminists?

At Emily Carr University, I have taught undergraduate modern and contemporary art history surveys from a feminist approach, focusing on the aesthetic provocations of women artists in the twentieth and twenty-first centuries. Through my own experiences, I am sensitive to the fact that the word "feminist" can be an exclusionary term that is often unsettling and difficult for some to embrace. Therefore, to provide a way for students to enter into a discussion on how one might come to identify as a feminist, I typically assign *We Should All Be Feminists* by Nigerian-born writer Chimamanda Ngozi Adichie. Adichie's feminist manifesto describes how she came into an understanding, through her relationships and life experiences, of what it is to be a feminist and to take a feminist position.[2]

Adichie contends that to claim oneself a feminist is to make a choice, to align oneself with a cause that is focused on securing "the social, political and economic equality of the sexes."[3] In the book, she shares a story of a time when she taught a writing workshop in Lagos and a female student told her how she had been cautioned against listening to the author's "feminist talk" for fear that she would be contaminated and "absorb ideas that would destroy her marriage."[4] Underlying this warning is a concern that listening to another voice—one that communicates life experiences that do not mirror our own—can destabilize the self, corrupting the integrity of our own position and system of belief. As such, the voice is seen then to produce an interference within the system, disrupting while seeking to shift and expand an "order of things." We learn how to listen so that we can hear not only what we already know and recognize, but also that which we don't yet know—what we have not yet experienced, and those places where we have not yet arrived.

I was reminded recently of Anishinaabe artist Rebecca Belmore's performance *Vigil* (2002), when I was listening to a story about #SayHerName, a campaign to raise awareness about police violence against Black women that activist and professor of law Kimberlé Crenshaw started in 2014. Crenshaw is known for her theory on intersectionality, which led to intersectional feminists, including myself, to align with her call to consider the intersections of race, gender, and class, rather than having a monolithic approach to feminism. Both Crenshaw and Belmore anchor their calls for justice in the names of women.

Belmore's *Vigil* is a profoundly unsettling and deeply affecting performance staged in Vancouver's Downtown Eastside (DTES), an area known for its poverty, homelessness, and high rates of addiction and mental health issues among the people who live there.[5] In the video of the performance, which students in the feminist survey watch, Belmore moves with intention on the sidewalk in front of an audience. She wears jeans and a white tank top, her arms exposed. Visible on her bare arms are the names of women written in black ink. Suddenly, Belmore emphatically shouts the names, deliberately pausing between each: Sarah, Helen, Andrea, Mona, Theresa, Brenda, Frances, Tanya. Belmore calls out for them yet receives no reply. In naming these missing and presumably murdered

Indigenous women from the DTES, and in her staging this public remembrance for them, she gives them presence by making their names known. The silence that follows the call of the women's names poignantly makes their absent bodies more visible.

Note #3: When Voices Intervene

If intervening means to come in or between with the aim of modifying or preventing a course of events or results, then we can see a number of feminist artists intervening through actions that modify existing discourse to make visible and audible certain absences. What, then, can a feminist approach set into motion? How can a feminist practice intervene into history, an institution, an archive, or a space of thought to create change and at times expose biased systems?

Consider *second shelf*, Heide Hinrichs' artistic research project initiated in 2018, which intervenes into an institutional setting—in this case, the existing, established collection of books maintained and circulated by the library at the Royal Academy of Fine Arts Antwerp.[6] By funding the acquisition of books by artists and scholars who are women, queer, non-binary, and people of color, which are then accessible to faculty, students, and the public, this intervention seeks not only to provide more diverse resources, but also to change and to decenter the process of library acquisition itself.

While this intervention into the library shelves is made at the level of the institution, specifically one dedicated to the teaching and study of visual arts, it allows us to consider, on a micro level, the bookshelves in our domestic spaces. When teaching the surveys, I invite students to look at their personal bookshelves, noting the authors and subjects that populate them. I encourage them to ask: *what authors or topics have I prioritized? What interests and knowledge have*

I privileged? What are the absences? Where are the gaps? In noting the gaps and absences, one can begin to actively do the work of diversifying.

When I consider these questions in relation to my own collection, I see relationships, as some were gifts or passed down, and I also see the priorities of the teachers and liberal arts professors whose teaching and course syllabi, from grade school to doctoral studies, resulted in the purchase of books. For instance, on my shelf is *The Expanding Discourse: Feminism and Art History*, edited by Norma Broude and Mary D. Garrard, which was the textbook for a course on women in art that I took as an undergraduate art history major. From this volume, Carol Duncan's "The MoMA's Hot Mamas," Griselda Pollock's "Modernity and the Spaces of Femininity," and Craig Owens' "The Discourse of Others: Feminists and Postmodernism" are essays I have since included on course syllabi in recent years.[7]

Note #4: Absence—THIS IS NOT HERE

Another important feminist intervention took place in 1971, when artist Yoko Ono curated her unauthorized one-woman show at the Museum of Modern Art in New York. Seeking inclusion, she inserted her work and herself into the context of a leading modern art institution, which since its founding in 1929 had focused on the work of primarily male European and North American modern artists, and was exhibiting and collecting the work of a new generation of contemporary artists at the time of Ono's show. Ono made her work present through a series of performative gestures, which intervened into the art institution and expanded beyond it, into the public realm.

Her self-initiated exhibition was staged over a duration of time and took shape in several parts;

none of which was known about or approved by MoMA. These components included the exhibition, which, "rumor had it," was on view for two weeks in December 1971, and comprised an alleged performance in which the artist stood in MoMA's outdoor sculpture garden and released flies into the environment; a film that documented visitors entering and leaving the museum, which included a man interviewing visitors, asking what they thought about the artist's one-woman show; a man standing outside of the museum wearing a sandwich board with exhibition details; an advertisement announcing Ono's exhibition, which she published in the *Village Voice* and the *New York Times*; and a self-published exhibition catalog, in which the artist printed several photographs that gave evidence to her interventions, including one of her seen standing in the sculpture garden next to a large glass container with a cork in it that was filled with live flies, presumably about to be released. Importantly, when visitors went to see her one-woman show, there was, in fact, no show to be seen.

The circulating advertisement functioned to announce her exhibition on view December 1–15, 1971, and to disseminate her self-published exhibition catalog. Given her Fluxus tendencies, Ono understood well the potential of printed matter to extend the life of the supposed event—her one-woman show. The publication would remain accessible beyond the event, circulating as a record of her actions and as archival evidence, establishing for her career an exhibition history tied to MoMA. The ad included a form that readers could fill out and send away with one dollar to receive in return a catalog in the mail, and it showed a black-and-white photograph of a street view of the exterior of MoMA, which at first glance appears to capture the scene in a straight documentary aesthetic (see page 162). Yet, it becomes apparent that the image has been altered. For instance, the car in the foreground and the view of

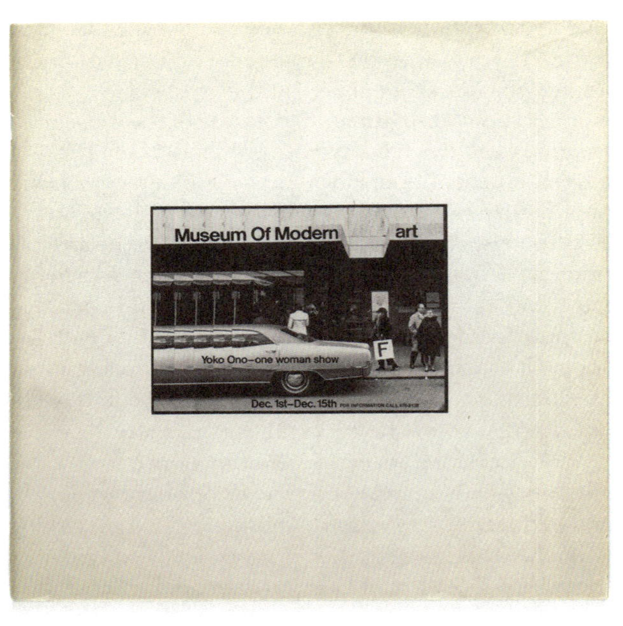

Yoko Ono, *Museum of Modern [F]art*. 1971.
Exhibition catalog, offset, 11 13/16 × 11 13/16 × 3/8"
(30 × 30 × 1 cm). The Museum of Modern Art Library,
New York. © Yoko Ono 2014.

MoMA's entrance are cut and repeated in segments that make visible the image as a construction, further pointing to the fiction of the exhibition itself.

With these modifications, the car, onto which has been printed "Yoko Ono—one woman show," becomes a limousine. The image also shows a handful of people on the sidewalk, including a woman—the artist—dressed in black and standing in profile near the back of the car holding a poster with the letter *F* inscribed on it. With this, the institution's name appears in the photograph and has been modified to read: "Museum of Modern [F]art." Humorous at first pass, the *F* destabilizes one's perception of the institution, encouraging instead a reading that momentarily deflates MoMA's authority, poking fun at how it embodies a certain elitism, cultural refinement, "proper" conduct, and respectable sensibilities when in fact many of the modern artists housed and on view within its walls had radically sought to undo privileged societal and artistic conventions. By "letting the air out," the cultural weight of the institution is called into question, however momentarily, giving way to Ono's proposal that MoMA literally needs an "airing out." With this play on words, the artist's critique addresses an issue that had long been avoided by the institution at that time: the lack of work by women artists—whether collected or exhibited—at MoMA and, even more specifically, in relation to Ono's subject position, the lack of women artists of Asian descent included in MoMA's curatorial and institutional agenda. Further to these absences, at MoMA's admissions desk, the advertisement for her one-woman show appeared and had been marked in pen with the corrective: "THIS IS NOT HERE."

We can read this naming of absence in two ways: first, it functions to let audiences know that they will not find the exhibition on view at the museum; and second, it signals how women artists and artists of color are missing from view. In doing so, Ono, an artist of color, called out the exclusionary agendas of the curators and director (and by extension, the institution at large, including its board) for the omissions that she recognized, and which in fact did exist within the museum at that time. Observing the absences within MoMA and desiring to belong, Ono took it upon herself to add her work to the institution's narrative. Without seeking permission, she used the language of the institution to stage her presence both within and outside it.

Certainly during the 1970s, she was not alone. Many artists, art historians, and critics—most of them women—began calling out the inequalities of the art world, not only launching critiques against art museums, but also calling into question the discipline of art history itself and its methodologies. Linda Nochlin's landmark essay "Why Have There Been No Great Women Artists?" published earlier the same year as Ono's one-woman show is a key example.[8] For Nochlin, however, simply adding names to the existing canon was not adequate. She advocated instead for change within the very structures of the institutions.

Looking back now almost fifty years since Ono's intervention, an action that showed how she was "situated between things," her multi-part performance staked a claim in the space of the art museum. While it went almost unnoticed by the institution and its audiences for some time, it has since become mythologized. In fact, just over four decades later, in 2015, her presence within the institution was made visible in plain sight when the artist was given a solo exhibition at MoMA titled: *Yoko Ono: One Woman Show, 1960–1971*.[9]

Note #5: Decolonizing Voices—Indigenous Feminisms

In March 2018, Tarah Hogue, then senior curatorial fellow, Indigenous art at the Vancouver Art Gallery presented her talk "Radical Signals in (Re)conciliation" to students in my contemporary art survey at Emily Carr University. In this course, students were introduced to a critique of the art-historical canon while taking a historical perspective on the artistic motivations of a diverse range of contemporary women artists working since 1950. Their practices were read through the lens of various feminist methodologies, including the writings of feminist and Marxist art historian Griselda Pollock. Pollock's critique of modernist art history encourages students to see more broadly how the discipline of art history has been, at the time of her writing in the late 1980s, a selective tradition that "normalizes ... a particular and gendered set of practices."[10] She further notes how the privileging of male artists, most often of a particular race and class, which was established by the discipline and upheld by the art-world system, has been perpetuated, in part, through the art-historical canon.

Pollock's call for differencing the canon led to discussions whereby students learned that if, as she claims, "art history is a discourse in so far as it creates its object: art and the artist," then that discourse remains open and, as such, feminist art-historical methodologies, therefore, can acknowledge that the writing into history of a more diverse representation of art and artists is possible, and necessary.[11] While some students embraced these feminist provocations offered by Pollock as well as other art and cultural historians that they read throughout the term, some students were unsettled by them given how a feminist approach seemed to undo or destabilize their foundations of thought, and others were skeptical and called the texts into question. These latter students noted the importance of expanding one's critical view beyond conventional curricula, but they often critiqued the feminist methodologies offered on the syllabus, perceiving them to be situated within a selective academic tradition and therefore, continuing to privilege a certain way of knowing that was embedded within Western pedagogy as it exists within the academy, specifically a colonial university system. Their critiques were situated within a desire to decolonize institutions, an approach that Tarah Hogue, a curator of Métis / French Canadian and Dutch ancestry, offered students in her guest lecture.

Hogue's intersectional practice embraces "Indigenous feminisms, re/conciliation, and cultural resurgence," and is one that "decenters institutional space and history using collaborative methodologies and a careful attentiveness to place."[12] Hogue's talk focused on *#callresponse*, a project she had co-organized in 2016 with Maria Hupfield, an Anishinaabe of Wasauksing First Nation / Canadian artist, and Tania Willard, a Secwepemc Nation / Canadian artist and designer. Through collaboration, *#callresponse* brought together "the work of Indigenous women from across Turtle Island," as they wrote.[13] Five artists were called upon: Christi Belcourt, Hupfield, Ursula Johnson, Willard, and Laakkuluk Williamson Bathory. These five then invited another Indigenous artist or artists to participate. Through this generative process, Belcourt invited Isaac Murdoch; Hupfield invited IV Castellanos and Esther Neff; Johnson invited Cheryl L'Hirondelle; Willard invited Marcia Crosby; and Bathory invited Tanya Tagaq. There is an important distinction to be made between the pursuit of a monographic exhibition, as Yoko Ono desired, and one that is collectively authored, based on collaboration and exchange. An intersectional, Indigenous feminist approach, therefore, may arguably at times distinguish itself from conventional solo shows, which have long privileged the singular voice and artistic vision of one artist. Instead, the form their project took—that of a call and response—was chosen for the reference it made to "call and response [as] a form of rapid, spontaneous interactions of unity building between speaker and listener as demonstrated in the chants of social justice movements."[14] Hogue, Hupfield, and Willard, who refer to themselves as "co-conspirators" on this project, claim that their intersectional Indigenous approach "recognizes and refuses the dehumanization, violence, rape and murder of Indigenous women, girls, trans, two-spirit and gender-variant identities that is systemic to the continuation of the current power dynamics of capitalist and colonial heteropatriarchy."[15]

In advance of her guest lecture to my students, Hogue assigned "Land as Pedagogy: Nishnaabeg Intelligence and Rebellious Transformation," by Michi Saagiig Nishnaabeg scholar Leanne Betasamosake Simpson. In her essay, Simpson proposes that "the academy must make a conscious decision to become a decolonizing force in the intellectual lives of Indigenous peoples by joining us in dismantling settler colonialism and actively protecting the source of our knowledge—Indigenous *land*."[16] And, Simpson further claims:

> We cannot bring about the kind of radical transformation we seek if we are solely reliant upon state sanctioned and state run education systems. We cannot carry out the kind of decolonization our ancestors set in motion if we don't create a generation of land based, community based intellectuals and cultural producers who are accountable to our nations and whose life work is concerned with the regeneration of these systems, rather than meeting the overwhelming needs of the western academic industrial complex ...[17]

In their essay published in the exhibition catalog, Hogue and Hupfield take up Simpson's call "to rebel against the permanence of settler colonial reality and not just 'dream alternative realities' but to create them, on the ground in the physical world, in spite of being occupied."[18]

Importantly, the works within *#callresponse* were commissioned, which further emphasizes an approach committed to creating support structures for Indigenous artists.

Since this introduction by Hogue to Simpson's writing, I have returned to and shared with others her essay many times. It was a watershed moment in my thinking, moving it in new directions by showing me another frame, another worldview, another way of understanding how one comes into knowing, and being in relation to and within this world—with nature, with others.[19] Simpson begins her essay by sharing a story of a young girl, Kwezens (a term used in Nishnaabeg culture to mean "girl"), who learns from the land, from her Elders, and

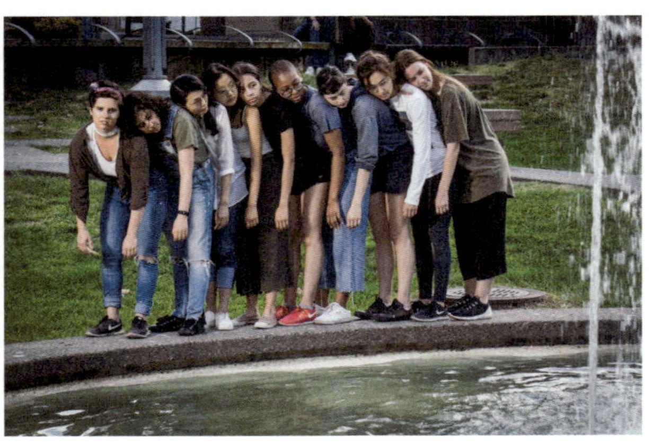

Guadalupe Martinez,
CUERPO, from tree to foundation, performance,
Cathedral Square for the Or Gallery, Vancouver, 2019.
Photo: Luciana Freire D'Anunciação.

from her community. Simpson relays to her readers, in a footnote, that because she identifies as a woman, the central character is portrayed as a girl, but that "the story can be and should be told using all genders."[20] Simpson emphasizes that the story she recounts on Kwezens's life experience is her retelling. As such, her version is but one of several possibilities, thus demonstrating how this knowledge is shared and situated in context, in relation to a body, a voice telling a story again. It therefore remains open for other identifications. We also learn that it is through spoken word, as a story told orally to others, that this narrative is imparted and has been passed on. In her essay, Simpson offers her Indigenous worldview, which while different from my own (given my upbringing, culture, and ethnicity) broadened my experience to embrace and expand my own unlearning.

Note #6: Being In Relation

With a desire to engage feminist voices in my local community, my contribution to *second shelf* has included interviews with Vancouver-based artists Guadalupe Martinez, Carol Sawyer, and Evann Siebens, and with curator Denise Ryner.[21] Our conversations addressed re-enactment, fictional personas, performance, and rethinking curatorial practice by decentering the conventional site of the exhibition while expanding the possibilities of collaboration. While Ryner shows how "to think together and alongside each other" in new ways, Martinez proposes healing "as a form of activism..." She spoke about *CUERPO*, a group of eight women that she formed with some of her former students (see image on the left). Their collaborations—research and performance oriented—offer a new modality for mentorship, pedagogy, and structures of support that encourage collaborative practice outside of academic institutions—lines of collective support that we urgently need.

During the tumultuous events of this year, I have often turned to a quote by Michel Foucault in which he wrote: "There are times in life when the question of knowing if one can think differently than one thinks, and perceive differently than one sees, is absolutely necessary if one is to go on looking and reflecting at all."[22] The feminist practices I have discussed embody this ethos. By situating the approaches of these artists, scholars, and curators alongside my own, I am also speaking from across this threshold, saying: "I'm here, where are you?"

November, 2020

Written in Vancouver, British Columbia, as a guest on the unceded territory of the Coast Salish Peoples, including territories of the xʷməθkʷəy̓əm (Musqueam), Sḵwx̱wú7mesh (Squamish), and Səl̓ílwətaʔ/Selilwitulh (Tsleil-Waututh).

1 The Cornell Lab of Ornithology, "Voices: Common Loon," https://www.youtube.com/watch?v=4ENNzjy8QjU, May 19, 2010, accessed July 30, 2020.
2 Adichie's TED Talk, based on the book, is available online: https://www.ted.com/talks/chimamanda_ngozi_adichie_we_should_all_be_feminists?language=en.
3 Chimamanda Ngozi Adichie, *We Should All Be Feminists* (New York: Anchor, 2014), 47.
4 Adichie, *We Should All Be Feminists*, 25.
5 Belmore's performance, which was documented by Paul Wong, can be viewed on the artist's website: https://www.rebeccabelmore.com/video/Vigil.html.
6 See the project website: https://second-shelf.org/about/.
7 Griselda Pollock's "Modernity and the Spaces of Femininity," originally published in Griselda Pollock, *Vision and Difference: Femininity, Feminism and the Histories of Art* (London: Routledge, 1988), 50–90; Carol Duncan's "The MoMA's Hot Mamas," originally published in *Art Journal* 48 (Summer 1989): 171–78; Craig Owens', "The Discourse of Others: Feminism and Postmodernism," originally published in *The Anti-Aesthetic: Essays on Postmodern Culture*, Hal Foster, ed. (Port Townsend, WA: Bay Press, 1983), 57–82.

8 Linda Nochlin, "Why Have There Been No Great Women Artists?," *ARTnews* 69 (January 1971): 22–39.

9 For further reference, see Klaus Biesenbach and Christophe Cherix, eds., *Yoko Ono: One Woman Show, 1960–1971*, with contributions by Julia Bryan-Wilson, Jon Hendricks, Yoko Ono, Clive Phillpot, David Platzker, Francesca Wilmott, and Midori Yoshimoto (New York: Museum of Modern Art, 2015).

10 Griselda Pollock, "Modernity and the Spaces of Femininity," in *Vision and Difference: Femininity, Feminism, and the Histories of Art* (London: Routledge, 1988), 50.

11 Griselda Pollock, *Differencing the Canon: Feminism and the Writing of Art's Histories* (London: Routledge, 1999), 27.

12 Tarah Hogue and Maria Hupfield, "Radical Signals in (Re) conciliation," in Grunt Gallery, *#callresponse* (Vancouver: Grunt Gallery, 2017), 73. Importantly, this "attentiveness to place" comes through as well in the co-organizers' statement in this exhibition catalog, in which they acknowledge: "*#callresponse* recognizes the numerous Indigenous territories on which this project takes place. We stand in solidarity with Indigenous Nations against the intervention in these territories through conquest, seizure and occupation by settler colonial nation states legitimized by the Indian Act of 1876 in Canada, the formation of the Bureau of Indian Affairs in 1824 and the Indian Removal Act of 1830 in the United States of America" (76). Further, their use of the term "cultural resurgence" brings to mind Leanne Betasamosake Simpson's important essay "Indigenous Resurgence and Co-Resistance," *Critical Ethnic Studies* 2, no. 2 (Fall 2016): 19–34.

13 "Turtle Island" is an Indigenous term that refers to the continent of North America.

14 The *#callresponse* exhibition catalog entered *second shelf* in 2019.

15 Hogue and Hupfield, "Radical Signals in (Re)conciliation," 15.

16 Leanne Betasamosake Simpson, "Land as Pedagogy: Nishnaabeg Intelligence and Rebellious Transformation," in *Decolonization: Indigeneity, Education & Society* 3, no. 3 (2014): 22.

17 Simpson, "Land as Pedagogy": 13.

18 Simpson, "Land as Pedagogy": 8. Also quoted in Hogue and Hupfield, "Radical Signals in (Re)conciliation," 15.

19 Simpson, "Land as Pedagogy": 1–25. This essay has also significantly influenced Guadalupe Martinez's practice. For my interview with Martinez, see: https://second-shelf.org/interviews/feminist-modalities/.

20 Simpson, "Land as Pedagogy": 3.

21 At the time of this writing, four interviews have been completed. Two additional planned interviews will finish the series of six conversations, all of which will be accessible at: https://second-shelf.org/interviews/.

22 Michel Foucault, *The History of Sexuality*, vol. 2., *The Use of Pleasure*, trans. Robert Hurley (New York: Vintage, 1990), 8. Originally published as *Histoire de la sexualité II. L'Usage des plaisirs* (Paris: Gallimard, 1984).

Reading as Activism: the WOCI Reading Group

Interview with Samia Malik

Elizabeth Haines

Samia Malik is an artist and designer, based in London. In 2002, she launched her clothing label *Samia Malik ihtgw*, that was independently sold worldwide. In 2004, she studied MA Womenswear at Central Saint Martins. In 2007, she designed for musician M.I.A. at the release of her second album *Kala*. Between 2012 and 2014, she studied MFA Fine Art at Goldsmiths, University of London. Between 2012 and 2014, Malik worked with artist Indra Moroder who ran an independent gallery in Tower Hamlets, where Malik regularly curated art exhibitions. One of the last exhibitions held in the gallery fundraised to support Palestine.

The central focus of Malik's art practice has been issues of racism, intersectional sexism, Islamophobia and broader social injustices. Malik is the director and co-founder of the WOCI (Women of Colour Index) Reading Group which was created at the Women's Art Library at Goldsmiths University in 2016. Currently, Malik also works with *Shades of Noir* at the University of Arts London, as an Associate Lecturer on the Safe Space Crits, in staff development training and on the Trigger Warning programme. All of these activities utilise Malik's extensive research interest, expertise and commitment to social justice practice as a creative activist academic.

The Women of Colour Index is a collection of material (1983–2002) held at the Women's Art Library, at Goldsmiths University of London. It forms approximately eight linear feet of printed documents that were originally collated for the Women's Art Library by Rita Keegan from 1987, in collaboration with the African and Asian Visual Arts Archive.

The WOCI Reading Group was co-founded in October 2016 by artists Samia Malik, Michelle Williams Gamaker and Rehana Zaman. It is currently organised and facilitated by Samia Malik with Alaa Kassim.

The project aims to improve the visibility of women of colour artists whilst using material in the archive to generate discussions, thoughts around practices of anti-racism, anti-colonisation and political justice. The reading group sessions have been held in galleries, museums, libraries and educational contexts in the UK and beyond.

*

Elizabeth Haines (EH):
Could you start by describing what happens at a typical reading group? I guess they've been different in different places, but how are they set up?

Samia Malik (SM):
We normally do reading groups once a month, maximum twice a month. And when you arrive at the reading group, we'd have around about ten to thirty participants. It can be forty sometimes or it can be less than ten even. We'll do the introduction, first of all, of the Women of Colour Index, and we credit Rita Keegan, who collated the Index. We credit the Women's Art Library at Goldsmiths University and then Althea Greenan, the archivist who's been key in helping me work through the archive as well. And then we also credit 'X Marks the Spot' who did the first publication about the Women of Colour Index in 2015, *Human Endeavour.*[1] So we give all these credits, that's really, really important. And then the facilitators will introduce themselves.

I give a bit of an introduction about how I started working with the Index and then we talk about the aims of the reading group. The aim, right from the start, was to make the archive part of art educational curriculum and to insert the history of Black and Asian female artists into art education. And then after that we do Safe Space rules and we ask all the participants to introduce themselves and give their pronouns. Then we do a collective reading. Normally it's a text written by the artist that we're looking at, or a publication written by the artist. The collective readings work out as a circular activity where we ask each participant to read a line, or they don't have to read if they don't want to. And then we have a discussion.

EH:

One of the things that I really enjoyed about taking part in a reading group session was the way that you run it, and having that kind of circle, and people speaking one after the other, and everyone speaking short sections with this kind of constant flow. Going back to what you were saying I guess maybe it's part of setting up a Safe Space? Your work in signalling about listening to people, with different qualities of voice, with different fluencies of reading, made a difference to how people's voices were received. And often you're reading texts written in the first person. So, the reading group members are directly articulating other people's ideas.

SM:

I guess when we started the question wasn't '*how can we make the reading groups powerful?*' I don't think that was the question. It was more like '*how do we make it workable and engaging for the participants?*' The combination, the team that we ended up being, Michelle, Rehana and myself, it was a good combination, although we didn't really know each other when we met. The format was just a contribution of different ideas from the three of us. Other participants enjoy other elements, such as, some people enjoy the fact that they break into groups to discuss things, so that people manage to network with other people within the reading group space. So, it turned out to be different things for different people, but yeah, you know, I suppose it was definitely an exercise to give voice to the person that's kind of lost their voice, to the voiceless.

EH:
Could you say a bit more about the Safe Space rules?

SM:
Normally we'll say to participants that the Safe Space rules are: to respect everybody in the room, not to talk over each other, and to be mindful of other people's identities and backgrounds. If anyone feels out of place, or if anyone feels kind of offended or uncomfortable about something that's been said, we suggest that person could leave the room if they want to, but if possible, to contact myself or another facilitator of the reading group. The Safe Space rules were inserted after we did the first reading group because there was a transphobic incident where a trans person was experiencing transphobia from a straight white woman. Luckily, that trans person decided to tell me this, which was really useful because then it really set the bar.

We don't discriminate, it isn't a space where we don't allow men, but we've had issues in the past where we do get white straight men who become self-appointed authorities, and we have to tell them, 'Look, you are taking up the space'. We don't want to kind of turn it into some sort of war zone, but Black and Brown artists have already been discriminated against by institutions. And also, myself, being an Asian woman, I know how, you know, anything we can say and do, we'll be totally ostracized anyway. So, it's a bit kind of naive to walk into a space and expect everybody to automatically be respectful, because people do walk in with their own personal agendas or their own privileges that they're not totally aware of. So, the Safe Space rules are pretty important.

EH:
You say that at the beginning of each reading group, you give some of the background of the history of the archive and how the reading sessions kind of came out of it. I wonder if you could run through that?

SM:
The archive was collated by Rita Keegan in the early 1990s. And she collated one hundred and twenty Black and Asian female artists. And at the time, they were using the term 'political black'. So that term 'political black' meant, Black and Asian people, so Afro-Caribbean people and Asians. The 'political black' isn't really valid anymore, especially with the younger generation, and the term 'black', they often prefer for it to be associated with people of African descent. I suppose that's another conversation on its own. But I have to sort of highlight that when you look at the Index you will see the term 'black' being used by Black and Asian women. They say, 'we black people,' and when they say that they mean, Asians and Black people.

'Political black' has a huge history. Back in the day, when you arrived in the UK as a migrant, you had two boxes to tick: 'black' or 'white'. So, if you weren't white, you would be the 'black' box. And the term was also used because of street-level racism. For people in my dad's generation, here in the 1960s and 1970s, the street-level racism was so rampant that, you know, it was standard to see a Black or Brown person being beaten up, actually. Yeah. So, the idea was that 'political black' meant a street-level sort of solidarity where you looked out for another Black or Brown person in the road. That's a brief kind of explanation of 'political black', which is really important.

So, Rita Keegan collated the Index in the 1990s. Myself, I've studied in art institutions since the age of 18. I was at Saint Martins [Central Saint Martins,

University of London] doing a Foundation in Art and Design, then I went and studied Fashion at Winchester [School of Art], went back to Saint Martins where I did an MA in Womenswear, then I did an MA Fine Art at Goldsmiths University [of London] in 2012. And I've just been like living in and out of art institutions, all my life. In a way I've grown up in them. My friend, he was working in a secondary school in Bethnal Green, this was around 2015, he said, 'Look, a lot of my students are Asian young women, aged 15–16. I'm a white man. Can you come in to teach the students about some Black and Asian artists?' And I couldn't really think of many, actually, at the time.

Then I remembered that somebody had mentioned an index at the Women's Art Library. So, I thought, okay, I would go in and look at the Index to research what to present to the students. But when I found the Women of Colour Index (that's what I was told to look at), I was really perplexed that I'd never seen it before. I really thought that the only Asian or Black female artists were the people that I knew. I just didn't realize there was this whole generation of them, who had such solid practices and made really great achievements. And that was thirty years back. And there were so many things, you know. I was making artwork that was similar to their artwork, and things they were thinking about thirty years ago I'm talking about now.

Then of course, the other biggest question, was, well, I've studied in all these institutions, but I can safely tell you that I've never, ever, been given any insight into this Index or most of these artists. Okay, I knew about Sonia Boyce, I knew about Mona Hatoum. But there's one hundred and twenty of them! And they've done like, lots and lots of work. Some of them, I kind of knew about, but also understood they were underrated. They didn't achieve what they could have really achieved for the kind of work they were doing at such young ages. Out of all the artists in the Index, only Mona Hatoum has had a solo show at the Tate. Even Sonia Boyce has not been given that kind of platform. Sonia Boyce is now meant to be showing at the Venice Biennale next year [now in 2022], she's going to be the first Black female artist to show at the Venice Biennale in the British Pavilion.

It was five years back, and things have changed quite a bit since then. Lubaina Himid hadn't won the Turner Prize and I was actually discovering her through the Index. And then her partner, Maud Sulter, she passed away in 2008, but she was very active and did amazing work. These were names that I was just discovering in 2015, when they had been there for years and making really important artwork that was absolutely relevant to me, and that I could identify with.

So, it became a really restless exercise for me because I had all these other plans I suppose that I wanted to do as a designer. I was thinking about designing a collection, but I kept on getting back to the Index. So, I was like, 'This is really strange, am I imagining this? Has anyone seen this?' Ego Ahaiwe (Sowinski) was there, who is part of 'X Marks the Spot', and she was just launching the publication *Human Endeavour* by 'X Marks the Spot'. So that was a really interesting time because I was kind of just getting to know the Index, and the first publication about the Index came out. They talk about censorship, in that publication, kind of describe it to you.

But then I also started asking my friends to come over and have a look. I curated a couple of art shows at the Women's Art Library with my friends' artwork in response to the Index. And what I wanted was my friends to tell me how they'd also *not* seen the Index. I was asking 'Am I just imagining that I've not seen this?' Because it turns into something psychological like a paranoia. 'Am I just imagining this?' Working with two female artists who were also Black and Brown, they were both like, 'No, we've never seen this before. And we wish we could have seen it when we were younger. It could have really helped us'. The Women's Art Library gave us some funding to curate two small shows. They were very small shows, but it was really interesting, and this was all between 2015 and 2016.

So, then I thought, 'Okay, we've got to try to find a way to make this Index more accessible to the students. We are inside a university (Goldsmiths), the Index is inside a university'. I was not teaching at Goldsmiths at the time, and neither was I studying either. I'd left the Fine Art course by then. And a few months down the line I met Michelle and Rehana and it was quite important for me to work with them because they were teaching on Goldsmiths Fine Art courses. And they both just happened to be Asian women as well. So that's when the reading group work really started, around 2016 in October.

There was also a reading group that my friend, Nadia Chan organised, about Malcolm X and Fanon, and we were going through a lot of anti-racist theory at the time, in this reading group. And that was just the summer before the WOCI Reading Group started off in 2016. I mean, it wasn't like I had some master plan, it wasn't ever like that. It was more like, 'Okay, I love going to my Malcolm X reading group, maybe we should do a reading group, for the Index? But how do we get the students engaging?'

Really the Index sessions are not 'reading' groups. I mean, when I was going to the Malcolm X reading group we would go through chapter by chapter. So, I was going to reading groups in the summertime, which were proper reading groups, but, although I was fascinated by the theoretical material of the Index, the art was obviously really, really important as well. So, I mean, in the reading groups really ... we read a bit of material, but then we have to look at the *visuals* as well, which is really important, the artwork. So, they're not like, you know, kind of classic reading groups, if you understand what I mean. I suppose you could call them study groups, but also, they're more like workshops, I suppose, aren't they?

EH:
That's really interesting. One question about the name of the Index, because you mentioned that lots of the artists in the archives are using the term 'political black' rather than describing themselves as 'Asian', 'African', 'Afro-Caribbean' or 'of colour'. So, do you know when the transition was? Was the archive already called 'Women of Colour' when you started using it?

SM:
Rita Keegan named it the Women of Colour Index. Rita Keegan is from the US, and there they've never ever used the term 'political black', even to this day. I think I've never actually spoken to Rita in a lot of detail about why it was called the 'Women of Colour Index'. But I think Althea mentioned that, because Rita's from the US, for her the term 'color' was more viable, I think.

I've got to mention that Eddie Chambers initiated that project, and yeah, I have contacted Eddie Chambers to have a conversation about the Index, but he never responded at the time. I've got a good friend who's one of the artists in the Index. And she talks to Eddie Chambers directly. He does know about our work with the reading group. But he's a busy guy. I suppose hopefully one day we'll get to talk to him. But Eddie Chambers, from what I understand, he initiated to the Women's Art Library, to have an archive for Black and Asian artists. So that was when they put a job vacancy out for someone to collate the archive, and Rita got the job.

I can't, off the top of my head, remember the exact details, but what I do remember, Rita was from the US, and the term 'colour' was more viable. I don't want to kind of make it concrete that this is what it was, I'd rather be very honest that either I've forgotten or it stands quite vaguely, I need to go back and, you know, investigate why the term 'women of colour' was used at the time, you know.

EH:
Could you describe a bit about what the contents of the archives are?

SM:
As I mentioned there's one hundred and twenty artists represented in the archive, Black and Brown female artists. Some of them were not born in the UK, but they've been educated here. So, a lot of them could be referred to as the diaspora. I don't necessarily like the term 'diaspora', there's a lot of terms I don't like, I don't like the term 'colour' either, but those terms are located around these histories now somehow.

The content mainly is art publications and artwork by the artists. There's a slide gallery that is also part of the archive. On a very practical level, it is just files and folders for the one hundred and twenty artists. Some folders are empty, by the way, or have one photocopy or publication on the artist. But you know, Sonia Boyce's folder, or Lubaina Himid's folder, or Mona Hatoum's folder, they're very chunky folders. They've got publications, press releases of art shows, artwork they did, letters they've written. So, a lot of it is photocopies.

From what I know, Rita sent a call out in the early 1990s and said to artists, 'Please bring your work to the Women's Art Library and whatever you would like to put in the archives'. I know that Eddie Chambers collated some of the material and gave it to Rita. And

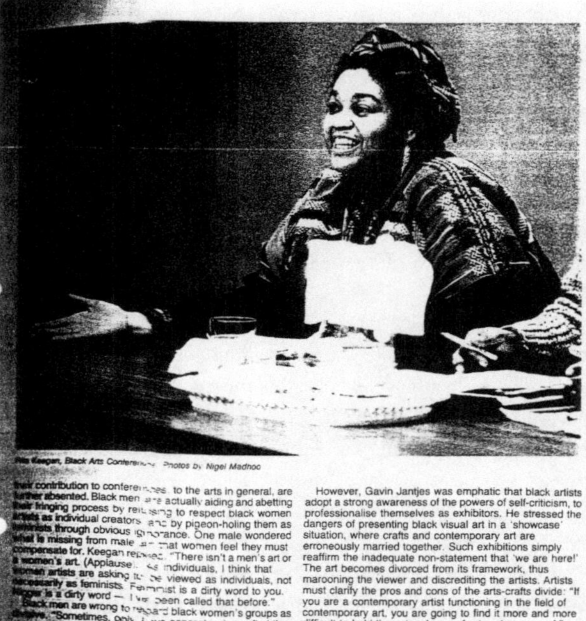

Rita Keegan, Black Arts Conference. Photos by Nigel Madhoo

their contribution to conferences, to the arts in general, are further absented. Black men are actually aiding and abetting their fringing process by refusing to respect black women artists as individual creators, and by pigeon-holing them as feminists through obvious ignorance. One male wondered what is missing from male art that women feel they must compensate for. Keegan replied, "There isn't a men's art or a women's art. (Applause). As individuals, I think that women artists are asking to be viewed as individuals, not necessarily as feminists. Feminist is a dirty word to you. Nigger is a dirty word — I've been called that before."

Black men are wrong to regard black women's groups as divisive. "Sometimes, only if we separate, do we find the strength to do what we have to do for ourselves." If black women are viewed as competitors in the race for equality, they have no choice but to record and define their work for themselves.

Is Craftwork Art?

One aspect of the defining process is the question of the acceptability of craftwork as Art. This very issue reflects the extent to which black artists have internalized western definitions of art in general over the years. Many women are [illegible], hence by erecting a wall between art and [illegible] black women are being further alienated in the visual arts field where work on walls is held as the apex of art [illegible]. Functional, utilitarian artwork is relegated to the ubiquitous non-art category through sexist prejudices.

However, Gavin Jantjes was emphatic that black artists adopt a strong awareness of the powers of self-criticism, to professionalise themselves as exhibitors. He stressed the dangers of presenting black visual art in a 'showcase' situation, where crafts and contemporary art are erroneously married together. Such exhibitions simply reaffirm the inadequate non-statement that 'we are here!' The art becomes divorced from its framework, thus marooning the viewer and discrediting the artists. Artists must clarify the pros and cons of the arts-crafts divide: "If you are a contemporary artist functioning in the field of contemporary art, you are going to find it more and more difficult to hold those two forms of art under one roof."

The importance of the catalogue

Another pitfall facing artists is an underestimation of the significance of exhibition catalogues. "The catalogue is the stepping stone into history, we must use it." said Jantjes. The catalogue is extremely important in the necessary correction of the art history which the Europeans claim as theirs. It also provides us with the historical framework within which to authentically criticize Black art. When an exhibition ends, the only evidence that remains is the catalogue. If 'The Establishments's' assistants mis-present it, the artists' reputations are marred, not theirs. The artists' resources and strengths lie not in being in exhibition space but in the historical documentation and dialogue which is ours.

The Conference was divided on the issues surrounding

21

Image of Rita Keegan, original curator of the Women of Colour Index. The photocopy is an extract from the article 'Talking About Black Art' by Ade Solanki, Patricia Hilaire, and Karin Woodley that was originally published in *Artrage*, Winter 1985. This was read by the WOCI Reading Group at a session at the Museum of Impossible Forms, Helsinki, Monday, 19 November 2018. Material held at: The Women of Colour Index, Women's Art Library collection, Special Collections and Archives, Goldsmiths, University of London.

I know that some artists gave in their own material. I don't know all the details such as, did Rita go and do her own research? Now? I'm sure she did, you know, but I don't know if she sort of dug into *Feminist Review* at the time and said, 'Okay, get a copy of Chila Kumari Burman's essay', you know, or did Chila give it in? I don't know these sorts of details, but I know you can find essays by Chila Kumari Burman, or a letter Sutapa Biswas wrote to a racist gallery owner.

EH:
So, then the next question. Is there anything that you do that you think about or do differently because of the reading groups in your own practice? Whether that's as a practitioner or as an educator or an activist. Are there things that the reading groups have changed for you?

SM:
Before I started working in the Index in 2015, in that year I was doing frontline activism, so lots of occupations, and it was getting very dangerous, to the point where I'd already been given one injunction and we were accosted by the police all the time. So, it was just getting far too dangerous, like physically. All the causes I was fighting for were really important, but I needed to do something else with my activism. And I went to some lectures about archives at the time, and they were talking about archives as a form of activism, so it gave me another way to resist, you know, to fight all the causes that I was fighting for.

But the other thing was, that I was invited to do PG Cert course by *Shades of Noir*, by Aisha Richards at the University of the Arts, in 2016.[2] So I had already been working in the archive for about a year and then Aisha invited me to do a teacher training course. There was a group that started at the University of the Arts called *UAL So White*, and Bolanle Tajudeen was one of the main organisers of this group, and there were various other people that were helping with this group, but I was kind of helping with this movement as well at that time. *UAL So White* led onto a panel discussion, confronting the University of the Arts, the Deans and the university management about institutional racism and the lack of Black and Brown teachers. And this was all like, I think, around March–April 2016, and I was invited to chair the panel which was one of the first of its kind. And it initially was kind of galvanised because of this campaign *UAL So White* and there was another campaign that stood alongside it called *Diversity Matters* as well, that was led by a woman called Kai Lutterodt. And then I was invited to, you know, come in to do a teacher training course.

I had always avoided teaching. As much as I love education, and I've spent a lot of time in education, I didn't want to be a teacher actually. I was always put off by the fact that I didn't want to be teaching about Picasso and Van Gogh. I thought that once you become a teacher in an institution of these sorts, you're going to be expected to teach certain things. Things that I know about, but that I don't want to be teaching. So, when I was invited to do the teacher training course, it was like, okay, I've been given this platform. Aisha Richards was given funding to train twenty Black and Brown teachers, so I thought, this is not going to limit me and there won't be this expectation to be fulfilling some curriculum. I'll teach what I want to teach.

So, this is when I think the reading group work became extra important because I was doing my teacher training course, and I was starting to teach. And then I was like, okay, I know about Picasso. I know about Matisse, and Van Gogh, and the only women that I really knew about were Frida Kahlo, or Tracey Emin, maybe. And I felt that as a teacher, I'm not actually educated enough about these histories that I'd like to be teaching. So, although the reading group started off quite casually, it was like, okay, but I need to get this in place for my own practice as an educator. I'm not really qualified, I'm not informed enough to teach this history, and the only way I can become informed is if I learn more about it, and that's when the reading group work became essential. If I want to be the kind of educator I aspire to be, then I need to learn about these issues.

EH:
And what about in terms of your own practice? Because you mentioned the experience of finding artworks and issues that you identified with in the Index. Did having this artistic and intellectual resource affect your own personal practice?

SM:
Completely. We organised an art show to fundraise for Palestine in 2014 during 'Operation Protective Edge' which was a Palestinian genocide by Israel. The artists that were submitting their work to the show, some of them were talking about Palestine, but a lot of the artists' work was very apolitical. And you're like, 'Well hang on, we need to be a bit more blunt to get the message out there, if we're going to do this properly'. The person I was working with at the time, Lydia Cohen, she had been to Israel and she had seen what happened in Palestine. And we needed to find a way to make political artwork, and as artists to be more confident to make this kind of artwork, because we get trained in a very apolitical way in art school. So, I started making text-based work, just being very blunt about anti-racism and imperialism, and Zionism.

And, of course, I pissed off a lot of people at the time, and I got kicked out of art shows. A lot of people didn't want to know me, and it became quite an isolating experience. So, when I started working in the Index, it felt like a saviour to me. I felt like, 'Oh my god, these women that have spoken about this before, I'm not the only person'. So, it became a bit of a guiding tool to me as an artist. For me, individually, beyond what we've done in the reading group it was so nurturing to find this. Being in Art School as an artist or a designer, all my references were white and apolitical. Even at Goldsmiths in 2012 there were times when I was in the studio and my teachers were like, 'I see what you're trying to do, but what are you going to do when you put it in a commercial gallery?' And I thought, 'Well, but if you're *not* making work to put it in a gallery in Mayfair?...'

So, I think the Index is really fascinating to look at. Some of these artists make different kinds of artwork now, they're doing different things with their art practices. But a lot of them were making political work before Margaret Thatcher was in place. And after the Thatcher rule was in place in the early 90s, a lot of things changed. My generation were trained, deliberately, very apolitically, we couldn't make that kind of artwork. And if you wanted to make political work, you had to step away from an art space. But the artists in the Index were able to talk about politics. When I talk to some of the artists in the Index (I'm not quoting here, just giving you some vague examples), they will tell me, 'We were at art school in Liverpool, my teacher said this to me, and I could do this, they encouraged me'. But it was a different time, you know, and the politics were different, and laws were different. And then you know, when you're trained so apolitically it's almost like you're trying to escape from the cage all the time. And, that's an explanation of how the Index has affected my current practice.

EH:

I mean, I guess one of the things that occurred to me as you've been talking is the contrast. The 1990s were a time when London was supposed to be celebrating multiculturalism, and diversity, a melting pot cosmopolitan centre. The idea that you could go through art schools and years of creative practice and never encounter these artists and their voices is ironic. No, it's tragic. That you were working in this supposedly super-multicultural environment while, in fact, all of those women's artistic voices were totally repressed.

SM:
Yes, we talk about this at the University of the Arts a lot, because the school is based in London, right? It is based all over London, one site in Camberwell, one in Kings Cross, one in Oxford Street. And when you are a child of migrants like I was, you grew up in a really multicultural area of London, a suburban area, like I did in Hounslow. So, you are growing up with a lot of migrants and children of migrants. In the secondary school that I went to there were actually not that many white girls there. It was mostly the kids of migrants that were Black and Brown. I grew up around a lot of Asian girls, you see. Then when you end up at the University of the Arts, like I did, at Saint Martins at the age of 18, you're away from that community, your own community, and immersed in a different culture of London. You're surrounded by internationalism, a lot of international students who don't speak your language, and a really middle-class environment, with a lot of kids that have a lot of money. And you come on the tube from a very working-class part of London and then you end up in art school, with all these culture shocks that come along.

So, by the time you get into the studio, and you're being taught art, you're coping with all these other things. And your teachers are all white as well. My teachers at secondary school were white too, but they had become very familiar with the conduct of such a large Asian community, so the kind of oppression and institutional racism that happened at university level couldn't take place in my school, not at that level and that scale.

When I started at Saint Martins in 1998, you're seeing racism... I saw my white teachers make fun out of Muslims quite openly in the middle of the Fine Art studio. This was before 9/11 even. My teachers at secondary school wouldn't do that because there were so many Muslim girls there. But, you know, then at art school you're in a very white environment, there's no Muslims there. At age 18 I was not even half as confident as I am now, and was really nervous. I tried to be like, 'No, you can't take the piss out of Muslims', but the whole class looked at me like, 'What the fuck is she saying?' because it was a very normalised thing to do.

What I'm trying to tell you is that you don't even expect to be given these references [of women artists of colour] because you're already in this environment, the walls are white, the place is white, and the money is white, everything is white. You're not even expecting anyone to tell you about anything Black or Brown anymore. What you want and what you try to do is actually survive in the environment, that's it. I meet some former students or people that did say to their teachers, 'I want to see more Black and Brown references', but I never even asked for that because I think the scale of racism you witness, you don't know how to calculate it.

You know, I've been in situations, at Saint Martins. In 2004 the head of the course in an interview asked me, 'So what kind of Muslim are you?' So, this was my interaction. I didn't know how to vocalise it. I didn't know how to talk about it at the time, but I think maybe you're the first person who has asked this question. I've never actually thought about this. When I found the Index, yes, it *became* important, but I never actually thought, 'Where were these references?' at the age of 18. No, I wasn't even wondering. I just thought, 'I've got to get my degree and just get through it and play the game'. You know what to say, and you know what not to say.

EH:
My experience at art school, in fact at the University of the Arts, at around the same time, was that there was quite a kind of cult of personality around the teachers. So, it was actually very difficult to contradict them or to ask them to be different than they were, because we had very few teachers and they were individually so powerful in the development of your artistic practice. My teachers were all white, and I'm trying to think, I guess they were like eighty or eight-five percent men, and it was quite authoritarian. So, I can see how you felt there wasn't a space for challenging your teachers to think differently or to question them.

SM:
There definitely was no room for that. But, I mean, it was quite intimidating for me, if you could understand, I went to a girls' school, where students were mainly Black and Asian actually. And then I hadn't really interacted with men, apart from my brother and his friends. I'd only seen guys in sixth form. And then most of these guys were Asian. So, my interaction with white guys was almost non-existent and then you end up just with male white teachers, who are a lot older than you. They're very intimidating, and they're racist. But on top of that the space itself is so exclusive, with invisible symbols of discrimination that say, 'This is not a space where we entertain that conversation'.

Things have changed now in education. The students challenge these things. They still have to be challenged. But at the time, white males, they owned the space, and you were only lucky enough to be there basically.

EH:
My last question is about the reception of the reading groups. You've done the reading group sessions in different kinds of places, with different kinds of participants. Could you talk a bit about the sort of reaction that you've had, and the reception of this from

the people who've taken part, or from the Index artists who were involved in the sessions?

SM:
All of the reading groups have been really important to me. And, I think sometimes, it was a bit of war zone, in a way because there's a lot of conflict that arises when you bring up these histories and, you know, you're working with an archive that has so much violation around it. You've got to bear in mind that as many compliments as we've had about the reading groups, we've been individually scrutinised and policed to pieces, by other Black and Asian women, by institutions, by men, and there's been a lot of things that have happened. I'm not saying that it has wrecked our lives, it definitely complemented our practices. We gained a lot from meetings as facilitators, as individuals as well, and it's been really important for other Black and Asian women. But I'll be very honest with you, right now I'm in a reconciliation process with Michelle and Rehana. There's a lot of turbulence that arised between the three of us, because of the reading group. The kind of the heaviness of the politics that we work with and what it does, and where it can go, and what it can mean to us individually. You're dealing with your whole entity, right, when you talk about these topics, and how they affect us.

So, I have to be very honest with you, and say that I can't really single out a reading group that I can say, look, that was my best reading group. I think there were lots of powerful moments, you know, that moved me a lot, right from the start. But what I think I have to live with is the conflict, and then the conflict which stands out, unfortunately, because you don't expect that to happen. Actually, you don't want it to happen. You do organise these things for the good parts you see, you organise it for the powerful parts, to make changes, that was the intention. But the level of conflict that occurs when you do these sorts of activities, and you work with these types of histories, you don't prepare for it, and there's not a guideline of how to deal with it when it happens. So, that is something that I have to deal with, at the present time, to sort that out. Like, what video was played, what I said when that video was played, what I thought of Stuart Hall when he said this. What I'm trying to tell you is although it's been four years almost since the reading group started, the work isn't really completed. We're still in a really critical phase of it, where it has made some achievements, but of course, it hasn't sorted everything out. Being in this critical phase means that I don't really get the time to kind of like celebrate it. It means that I need to reflect and work out what the problems were, what I did wrong, and what I said wrong, what I don't agree with about what that person did. And how do we move forward with these problems?

EH:
I think that's really helpful. I guess, when people come to these projects, and I guess that's what I was drawn to, they have a sort of utopian kind of vision of reconciliation, talking, sharing … but it's so much more complicated than that in so many ways.

SM:
When we entered into conflict, me, Michelle and Rehana, it was very triggering. You've got this really great partnership going on, a great project, that suddenly becomes a no-go zone. When it arrived, I started talking to the artists from the Index to try to get their feedback. They were like, 'Yes, it's happened before, we've done it before, we've experienced it all before'. And I said, 'Well, why don't you talk about it

then? You should write a manual, it could have helped me out here'. Because they had a lot to say about it! 'Oh yeah, it always happens, you should do this, you should do that'. And I say, 'You guys have written about other parts of your experience, but you should have written about these parts, too'.

One part of me thought, 'Should I tell you right now about this in the interview or not?' But then I thought, 'I should tell you it as it is'. I need to be honest about it. Because I don't want to create some sort of history where the reading groups are this utopia. It's not, because you're dealing with this big battle, basically, and I think it's unfair actually, to pass on a message, or inform another generation, that it can all work out perfect. I think it's only fair for people to know the truth.

I do also think that institutions have a big hand in dividing people. Because there's a lot of tokenisation of Black and Brown people. We had an incident within the reading group where a white male curator was very selective in the way he dealt with me, Michelle and Rehana, which caused a lot of conflict between the three of us. I told this curator (I won't mention his name, but he is pretty well known), 'Look, you're doing something that is blatantly dividing three Brown women'. The whole divide and rule, you're ticking all the boxes of what the empire does, divide and rule. That, despite the fact he's written a book, organised art shows, about Black and Brown people.

I won't go into that, but, you know, it's a catastrophe. If you can enter the space with the fact in mind that you are entering a battleground, I think it only helps you to deal with it. Because it will cause a lot of mental health issues, it'll cause a lot of anxieties, personal turbulence, turbulence amongst your peers as well, your friends. If you aren't going to be honest and pretend it's okay, or to try to force it to be okay when it's not, then that's even more of a problem. Once you open up, it is so personal, and it has affected my personal and professional life in so many ways.

In all though, four years on after starting the reading group, it's been a fruitful journey and I feel a lot more educated about the histories of Black and Brown female artists. The reading group has made some excellent achievements.

London and Didcot, 3 September 2020

1 X Marks the Spot (Artists' collective), Joan Anim-Addo and Althea Greenan, eds., *Human Endeavour: A Creative Finding Aid for the Women of Colour Index* (London: Women's Art Library, Goldsmiths, University of London, 2015), https://research.gold.ac.uk/19685/1/XMTS_HumanEndeavour_e.pdf.

2 A Postgraduate Certificate in Education (PGCE) is a UK qualification for teaching. *Shades of Noir* is an independent programme initiated by Aisha Richards that creates opportunities for marginalised groups and their need for safe spaces to articulate self-determination and liberate the struggles from oppressive structures both in education and society. *Shades of Noir* has set up a number of initiatives working with staff and students at the University of the Arts London. https://shadesofnoir.org.uk.

Inscriptions

Interview with Heide Hinrichs

Susanne Weiß

Susanne Weiß (SW):
Heide, I wanted to talk to you about the beginning of your drawing series entitled Inscriptions. *Where did it start?*

Heide Hinrichs (HH):
Yes, so the drawings started in Seattle. I had just moved there and I didn't really know the place. It was my first time in the US and so I had to make myself comfortable. I had also no place to work and, at that time, The Seattle Public Library, a Rem Koolhaas building, had just opened, and so I went there and used the art section to take notes, to redraw drawings that were reproduced in catalogues, but without really any intention, just because I didn't know what to do. And it happened that these would be artists that had also a connection to Europe and that they were female artists like Eva Hesse, Meret Oppenheim and Louise Bourgeois ...

SW:
... who were influential for you anyway.

HH:
Exactly, artists I felt an affinity with.

SW:
Do you think it was more like a subconscious act?

HH:
I did not really know what I was doing. I did this without purpose. I just had to do something and that was how it started.

SW:
But then you continued and it became a project.

HH:
Yes, but much, much later.

SW:
And when was that?

HH:
So these drawings happened in 2006. And then I really started to think about copying, about the act of reproduction, and what kind of position the artist takes related to gender. But that was after my return from Seattle to Europe, to Belgium, at the end of 2010. There I started to conceptualize these ideas.

SW:
But when did you start copying the drawings again?

HH:
I think that I picked it up again when I was in Florence. I went to Villa Romana in 2013 and there I started copying again. It was also out of a given situation where I was new to a place which was the total opposite of Seattle. Florence is overloaded with textures and inscriptions of art and history. So, I think I fell back on something that was basically not connected to the place, but that gave me a guiding line.

SW:
How do you choose the drawings you copy, and how does it feel copying or appropriating when you come close to the original?

HH:
I think that my drawing process helps me in the interpretation of the original works, like a reading. So that the interpretation happens in thinking through how to redraw, deciding on what to emphasize. There are some artists, like with Agnes Martin, where I feel

like what I am doing is the opposite of what she did. My drawing is so quickly done and her drawings are so minimal that it feels a little bit ridiculous: how can one make it more minimal than she did? This form of concentration, I don't get it. I always felt with these drawings that I failed. It seemed impossible and absurd. That's a feeling I had at the beginning. I chose these artists that were at one point important to me. They show a chronology of what has informed my own artistic practice.

SW:
You can quickly recognize certain styles like those of Miriam Cahn, Silvia Bächli, Agnes Martin. They are rooted in our understanding of an artistic visual language system. But a drawing has these manifold meanings in each artistic practice as well, right? It's either a sketch or daily practice, like a meditation. Silvia Bächli, for instance, draws what she has in front of her eyes and in front of her mind, and then afterwards she starts the sorting of what comes into her collection and what not.

HH:
The drawing is the most direct articulation from the body towards the outside – there is only the hand. In between the hand and the paper is only the pencil, or whatever you're using, but it is the body that speaks through that stick, and through the trace that you leave on the paper. So there's not much mediation in there. It's very direct.

SW:
How many drawings are there and how many artists are now in your ongoing project?

HH:
I think there are about 240 drawings. I don't know if that is a lot or not. If you look at the series of *Inscriptions*

I think you see that it has never been a daily practice. If it was, there would be thousands of drawings. And that's not the case. It's really a selection. I think there are 25 artists.

SW:
The title Inscriptions *really relates to your form of appropriation.*

HH:
Yeah, this idea of inscribing something into your personal references. The inscription is an act of redoing, a form of circulation – from the eyes, through the body, out of the hand, again to the paper.

SW:
Your drawings are in general very specific in the sense that they are drawn in a simple and direct way. There's no mannerism. Your way of drawing is always related to space, or questions spatial conditions like the floor…

HH:
…taking an imprint of what has been imprinted on the floor, traces that have been left over time.

SW:
So it's always like a much more conceptual way of drawing. I wondered where your idea came from, of hanging the drawings into chains, like it was presented in the exhibition at Beeler Gallery?

HH:
They were not chains, but you saw them as chains, and you saw them as chains of art history. They were hung up into the chains of art history (*laughing*). No, but they were ropes.

SW:
Oh, yes, yeah.

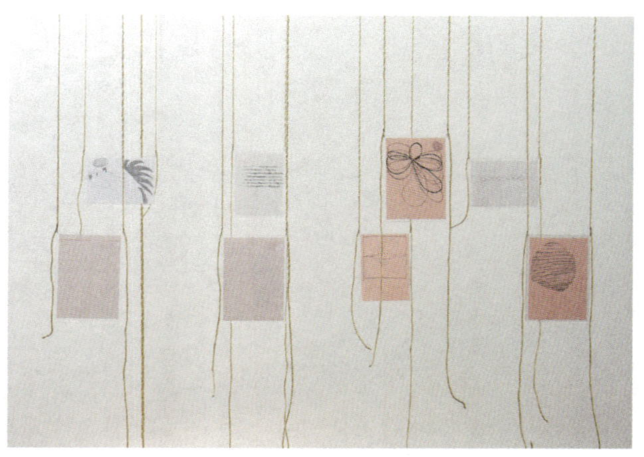

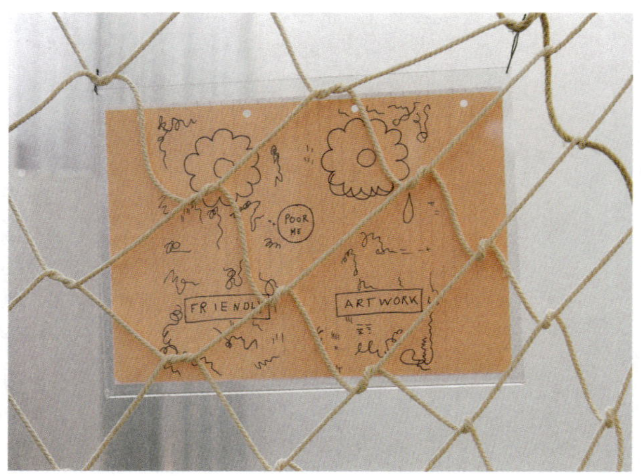

Above and next spread:
Heide Hinrichs, *Inscriptions*, 2006–2020,
as part of *Follow the Mud*, conceived by Jo-ey Tang and co-curated with Ian Ruffino and Marla Roddy, Beeler Gallery at Columbus College of Art & Design. Photo: Stephen Takacs.

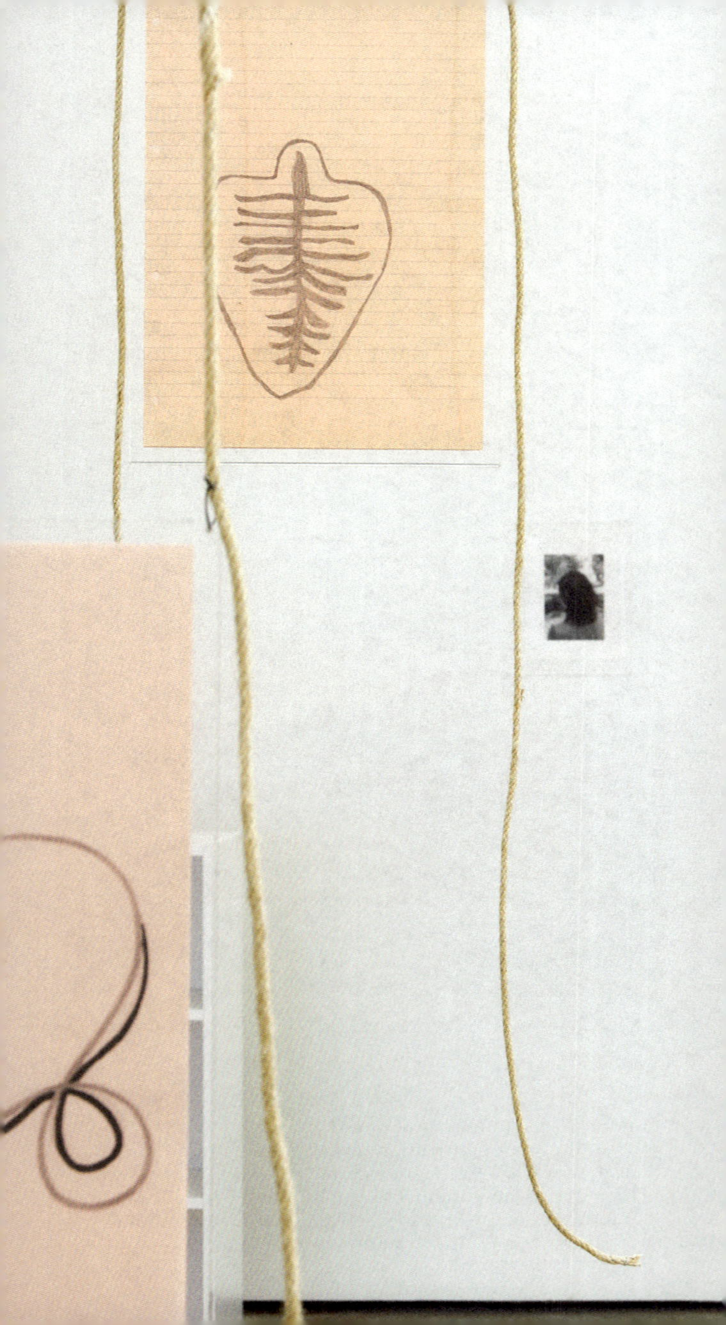

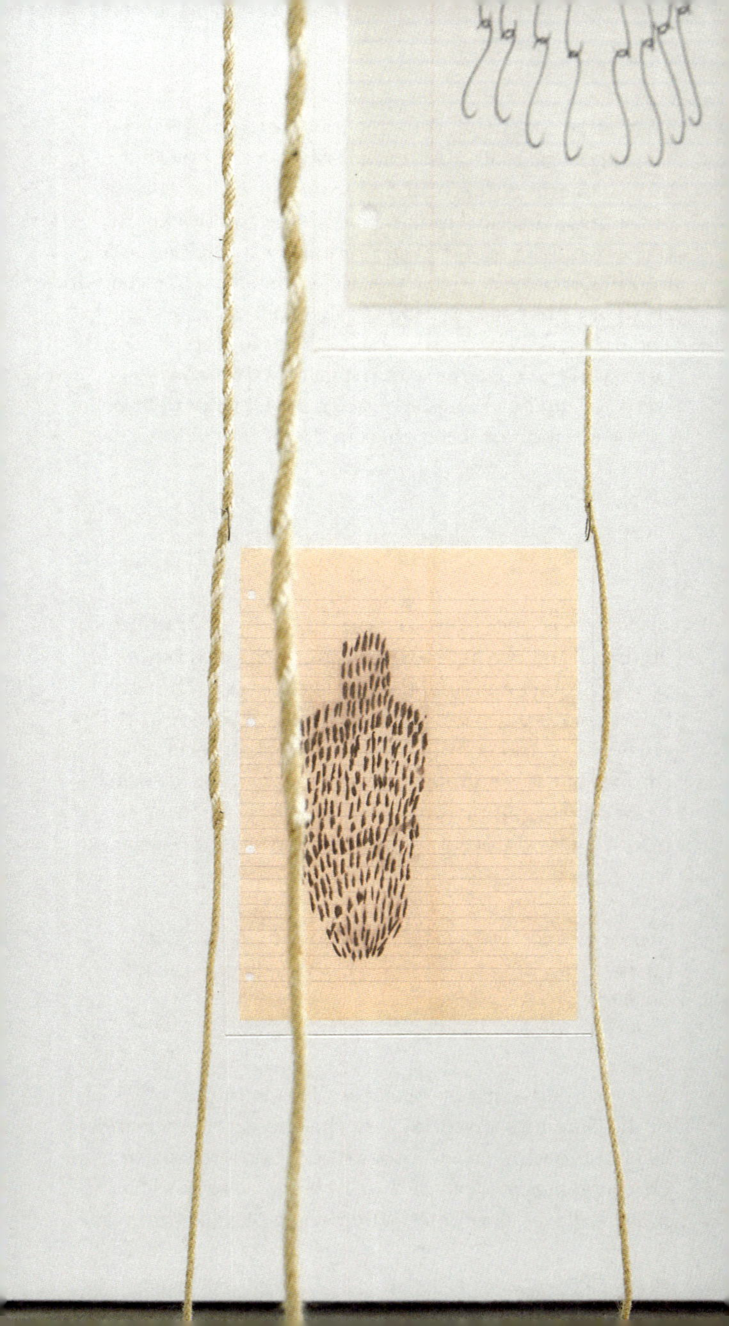

HH:
They were ropes that the drawings were connected to. The ropes are really just about bringing the line that is on paper into the third dimension; like a gesture of enforcing a line and making it thinner and thicker in the space. They're a transgression into space, but also into materiality. And in this case, the space was situated above another at Columbus College of Art & Design: The Beeler Gallery on the ground floor and the Packard Library in the basement. In the gallery the drawings were hanging on ropes whose locations were defined by the position of the shelves in the library below.

SW:
Wow!

HH:
And there is one rope that goes from the floor of the library all the way up to the ceiling of the exhibition space through a hole in the exhibition floor. Though this is one straight line, pointing toward the idea of chronology and continuity, it was made thicker and thinner at different places to emphasize that we don't work out of an innocent space, but that our work is informed by different assumptions and ideologies.

SW:
And the way you're planning to present the drawings for the exhibition at WIELS? Do you plan to present them one next to the other chronologically?

HH:
Yes, I needed to get an overview. I hung photocopies of the drawings in a grid, very close to each other and, as I had no idea how to order them, I ordered them chronologically. Most of the drawings were made after *second shelf* was developed. Their conceptualization was,

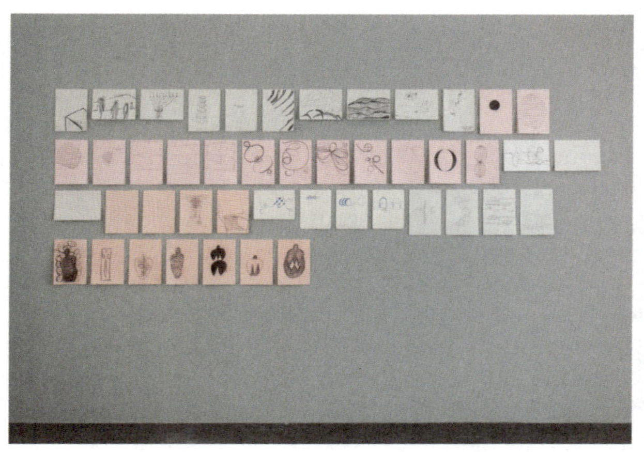

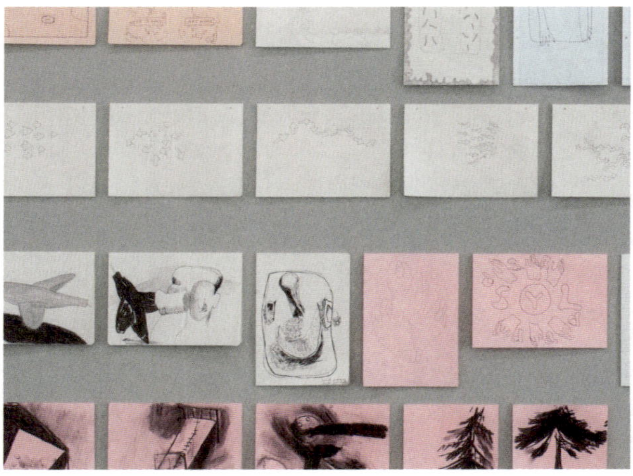

Heide Hinrichs, *Inscriptions*, 2006–2020,
as part of *Risquons-Tout*, curated by Dirk Snauwaert
with co-curators Zoë Gray, Devrim Bayar, Helena Kritis,
and Sofia Dati as curatorial assistant, WIELS, Brussels, 2020.
Photo: Philippe De Gobert.

in part, a response to the one-dimensionality of the library of the Royal Academy of Fine Arts Antwerp where I had started teaching, and started to connect the idea of the drawings to what a library at a school means, like the library is the reference space for what is taught at the school. For many reasons the library holdings were a mirror of the interests present. There were only very few female artists represented, and there were other gaps, so I started from there to develop *second shelf* as a collaborative project. I invited Marisa, Jo-ey, Elizabeth and you to expand the collection from your expertise, and to also activate the space of the library within the academy with lectures and workshops. The gesture of redrawing happened alongside this institutional intervention.

SW:
Do you decipher the drawings – so we know which artists you are copying? Do the drawings have numbers? Or when visitors look at them, at this body of work, or body of drawings, can they figure this out? Do they each have individual titles?

HH:
They carry the initials of the artists.

SW:
But if there is 'SB' for Sylvia Bächli, for example, how am I supposed to know it's for her?

HH:
In each exhibition there's a way – exhibition guide, poster – to connect the drawings to the artist being copied. There is a possibility of identification if you want but I'm not interested in a comparison between the original and what I did. It is much more that they stand also on their own as a language by themselves. Though of course it has also to do with paying a tribute. I don't

know, but it certainly has also to do with admiration or respect that I feel for them. These are all figures that matter to me. In that sense I think it is really like a memory for myself. A record of ideas or a record of references, but not as a photocopy or as a JPEG but as …

SW:
… inscribed. And I mean it's also about the dimensions. I mean, you copy from the book, which is not the original.

HH:
Yes, and that also says something about the place where I encounter a lot of drawings, how things are circulated. Of course nowadays a lot of things are circulated in the digital space, but I think here, this is really to emphasize the materiality of printed matter. And the space of the library is also a space that I believe in.

SW:
So true. Libraries really have therapeutic qualities for me. I think this body of work is truly connected to the healing moments of printed matter and the spaces where it is worshipped and contained.

HH:
It is another form of transportation, a sort of redirecting or rechanneling or repositioning of something, and in that sense it is more than me keeping my private notes.

SW:
Heide, thank you very much for this talk.

Outside of Kunstbibliothek, Berlin, 18 August 2020

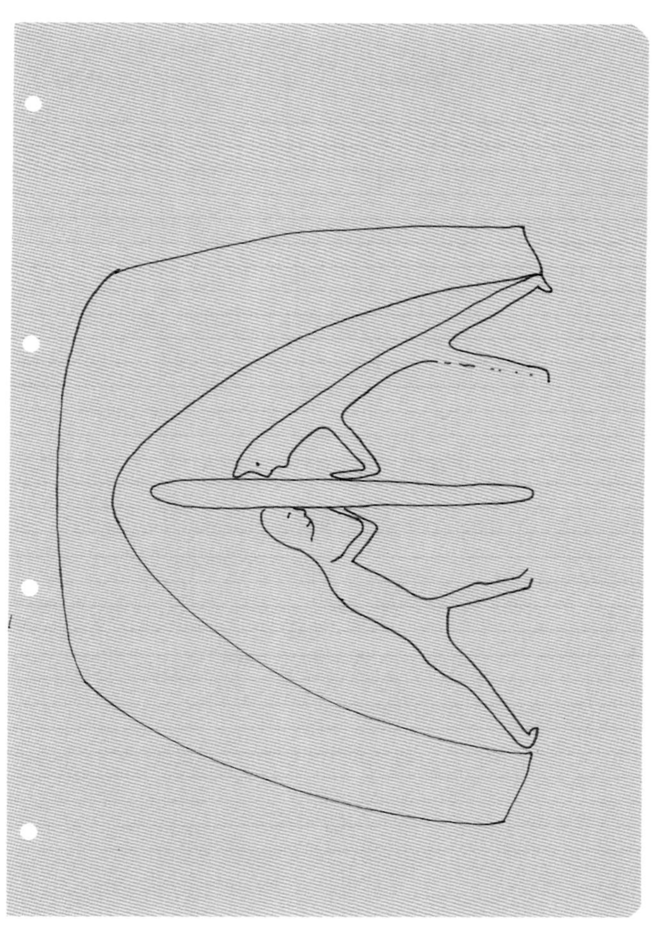

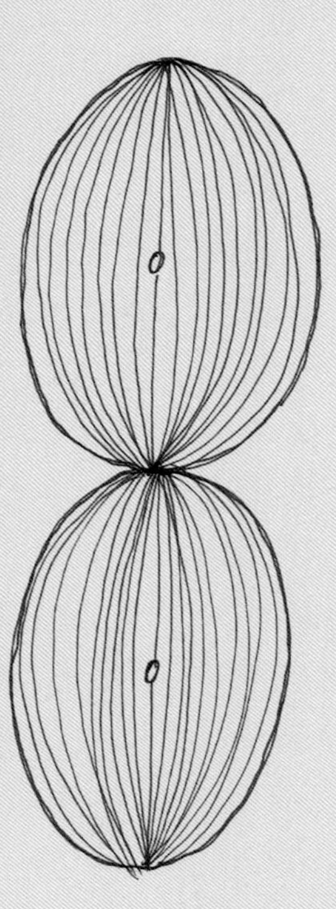

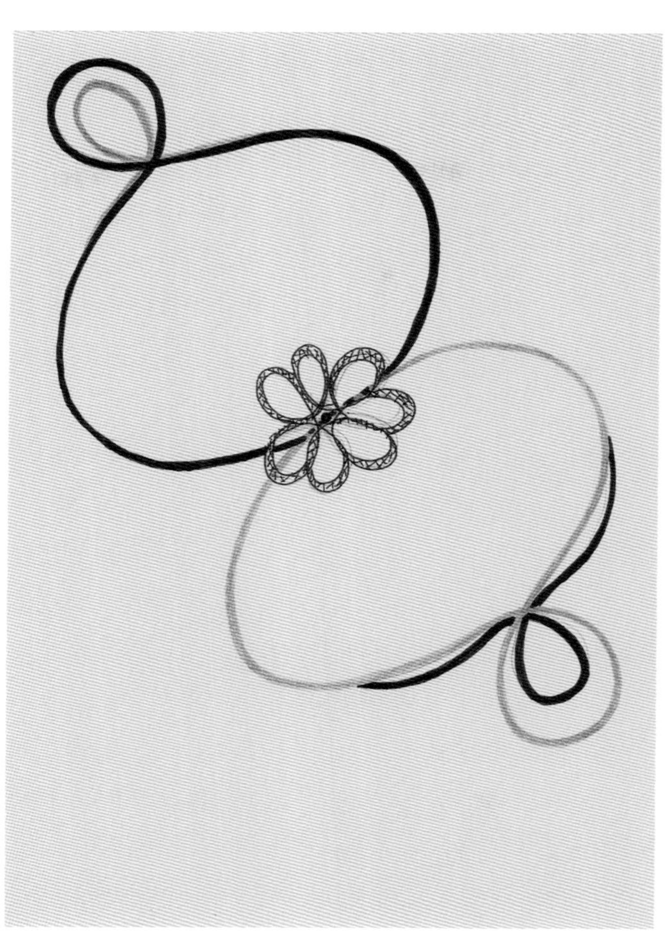

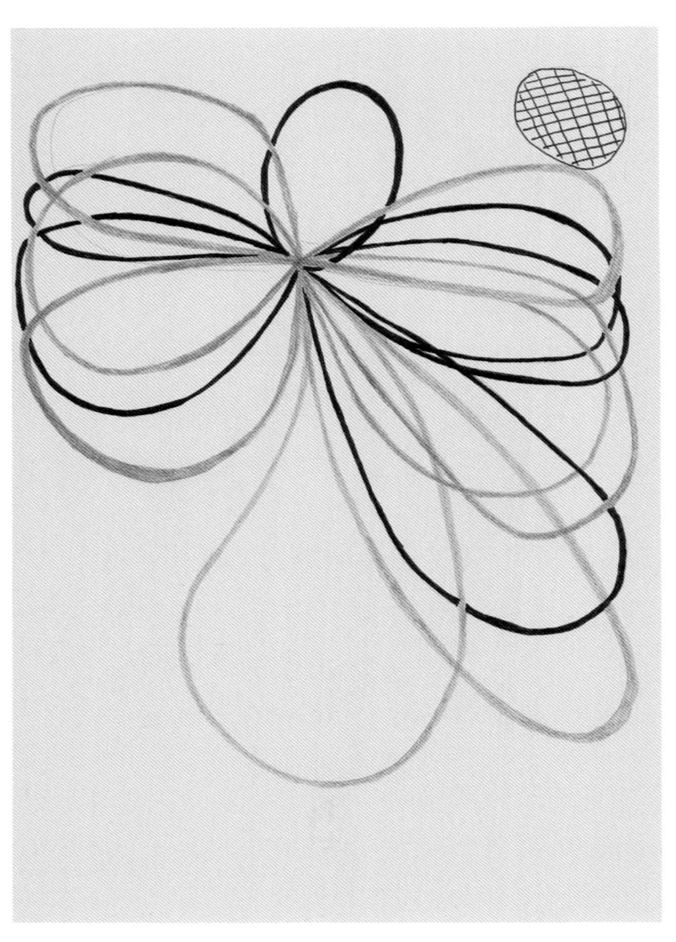

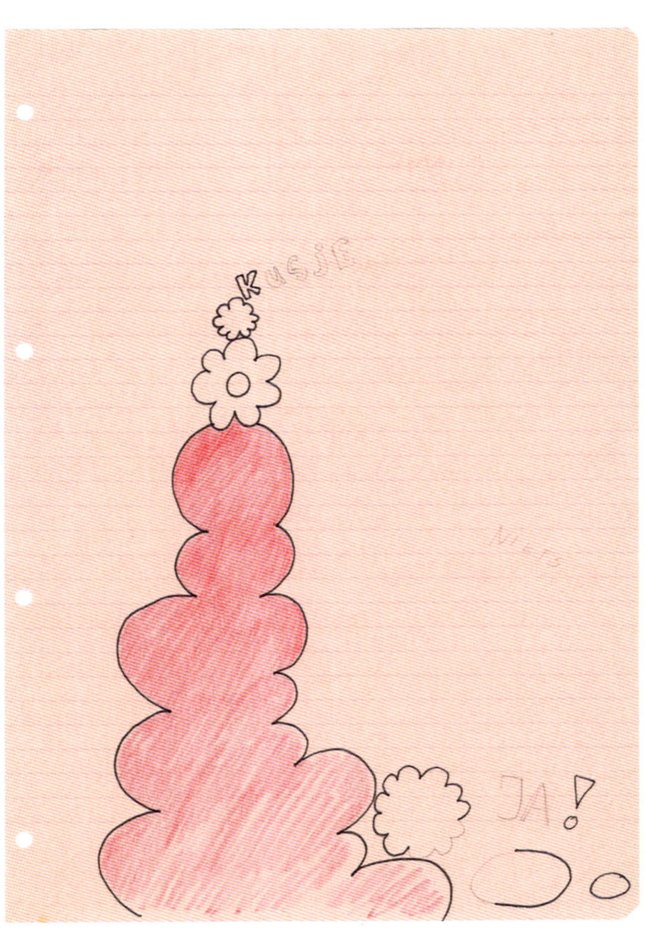
Kusje
JA!

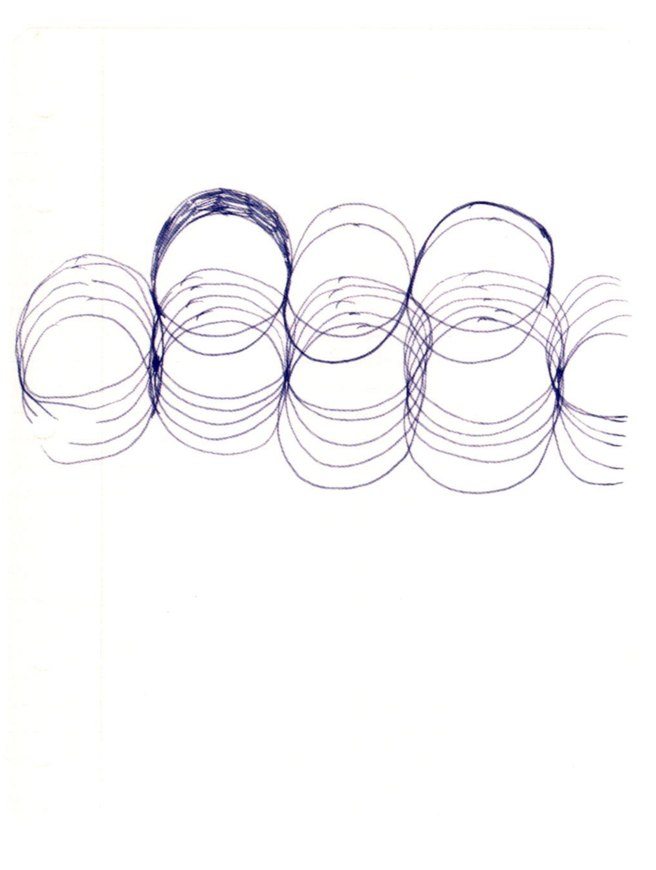

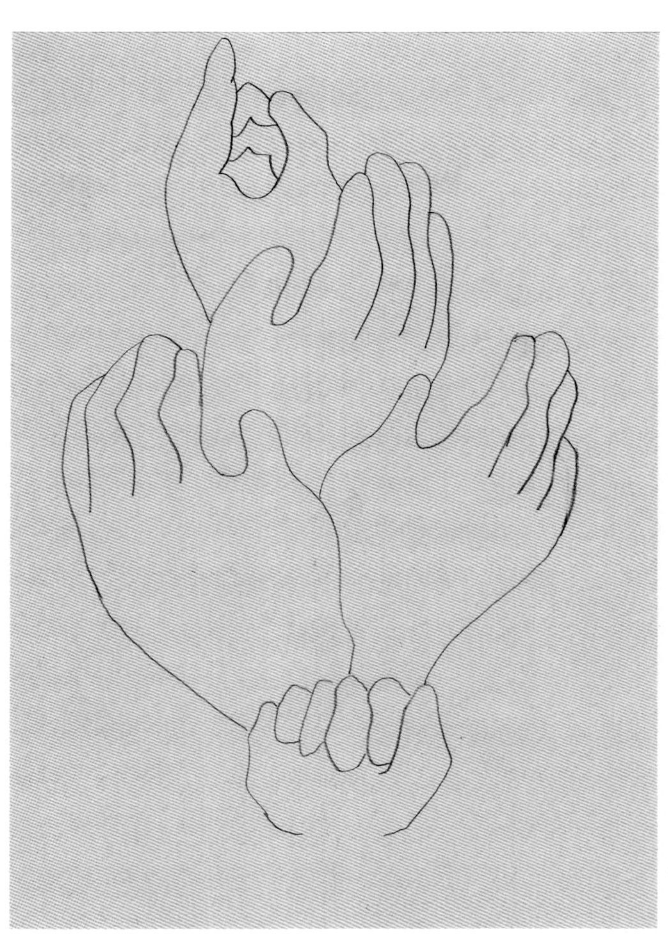

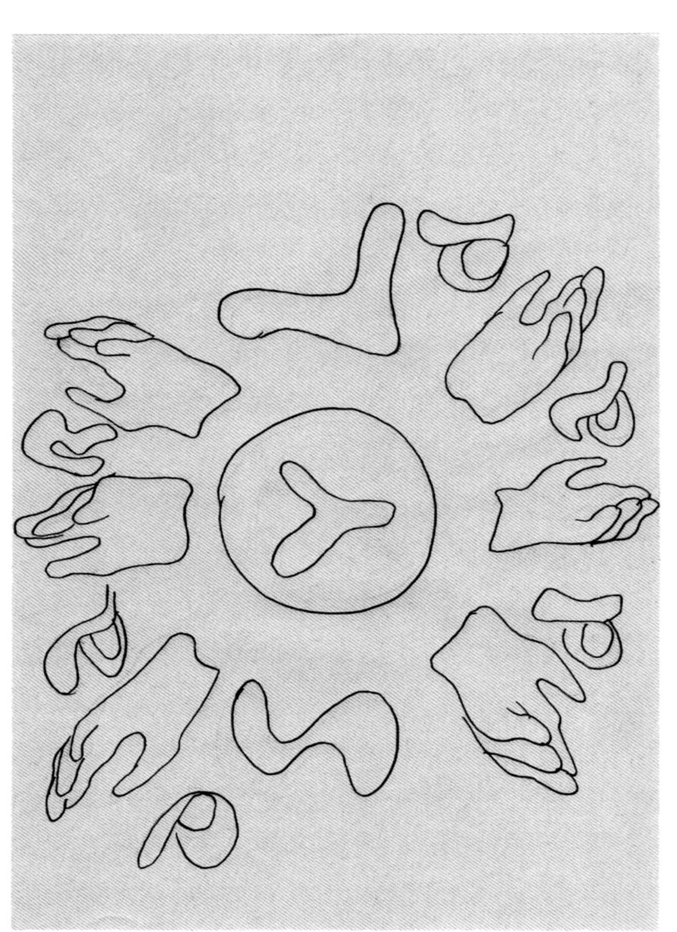

the body

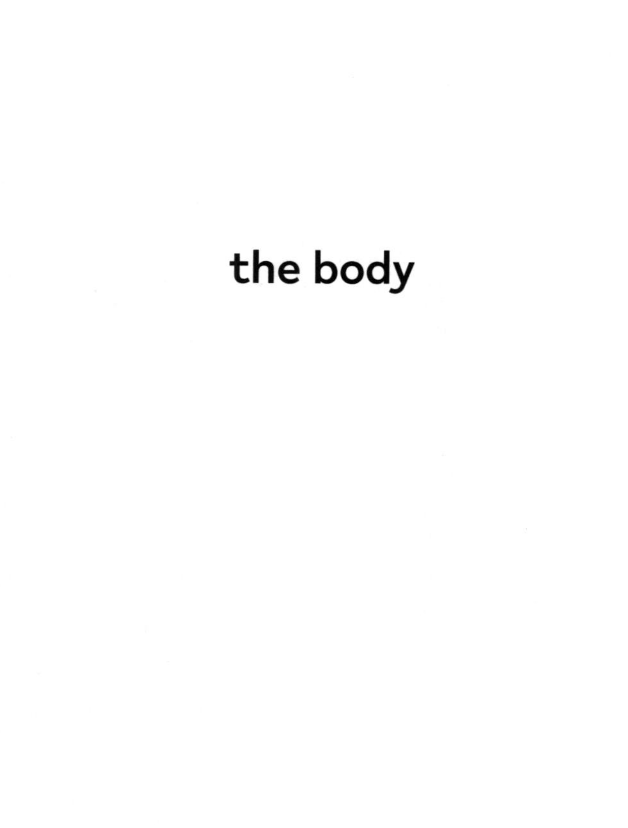

Camouflaged for Fire

Melanie Noel

Present and absent

you I crawl (crawl) inside the body of (of) in your my eyes

Dandelion
in the goldfish

prone in the

eye body : eel blanket

the little glass of water saying *I am the sun* ::

Seam furies to pleat   in rain clings

with a shadow's diplomacy   Rippling in the drape   a glint divides the eye.

Something unfolds from the water.

*

In Anaheim dawn you check out the Space Place costume for Tomorrowland. Yellow dickey. Orange polyester pillbox hat. Red-orange culotte. Cap-sleeved synthetic scoop-neck with a wide elastic waistband. You check it out at the start of your shift; at the end, you check it in.

*

Destruction *hides inside* the woman –

animates the wall where she is ____ frames per a life.

Eel shimmers.

Walls withdraw.

        Something unfolds.

*

On the remains of the pedestrian overpass

locks locking nothing beside other locks,

        & a strand of orcas

open the path's root   the they-you

you-blur

x echo

stride writing back to stride.

*

The boy jumped and fell, landing on the wrong foot from the top of the stairs. He was crying on the ground when a column revealed his father. The father gestured for him. Though the boy was four or five, his father cradled him like an infant. When he was done crying, the boy explained what happened. His voice was very clear. The father's kisses landed on his injured hand the opposite of eating   landing as   parachutes   The boy   tried the jump again   *Try from a lower step,* the father said.

*

Rippling with arhythmia, hands   anonymous in fin mittens tread the flood.

From its afterlife   the sheep sings down.

Matthew rides an invisible horse. Wax melts inside its form.

Elby practices to be a statue. He kisses the statue within. It climbs to the surface awkwardly and there is met by skin.   Together they mount the pedestal. Paint flickers in the space between his fingers.   And then he falls.

The floor   as cloth   as water   captures him.

He blinks from the water

Eyelash   antennae

*

*

*

From the sea of grandmothers

Cabanillas's eyes

Bruises rip through them in clouds of silence

Iron ropes turn ether in dark rooms

Mama Sane as Ada's eyes

The eyes repeat on buildings

Fanta in Amina Kane's eyes

We remove Bataille's violent eye from the shelf.   *creaaaka creeeck*

From the cavity of violence   we stir a corrective dark fell

the weak scaffold   The ladder rattles

Vicuña's eyes

We must be blood to reach   for them to bear our weight –

New cones form in our sight   we sip

on the nectar of negative space

volcanic with eyes.

*

Behind my eyes

is the chrysalis at the end of Brooks's *Riot.*[1]

I hear its *physical light*

"… Alive in Ice and Fire"

the intimacy found (in)in(out)side the collective wake.

Two longings are portrayed as one.

We share the street unfolding.

We (I) leave the eyes that are not (ours) mine   form releases form

*

No one knew he played piano. He played for twenty years and no one knew except a stranger who'd left a note saying *you play beautifully.* After that, he didn't play for a year. When he resumed practicing, it was at the public library, in one of two small soundproof rooms. It wasn't possible to book more than an hour at a time. He practiced during his lunch hour. His most private hour in confidence with shared commons
Pedestal antithesis

The piano was a place.

*

To the pharmacy in feral silence we go

erupting with yellow roses.

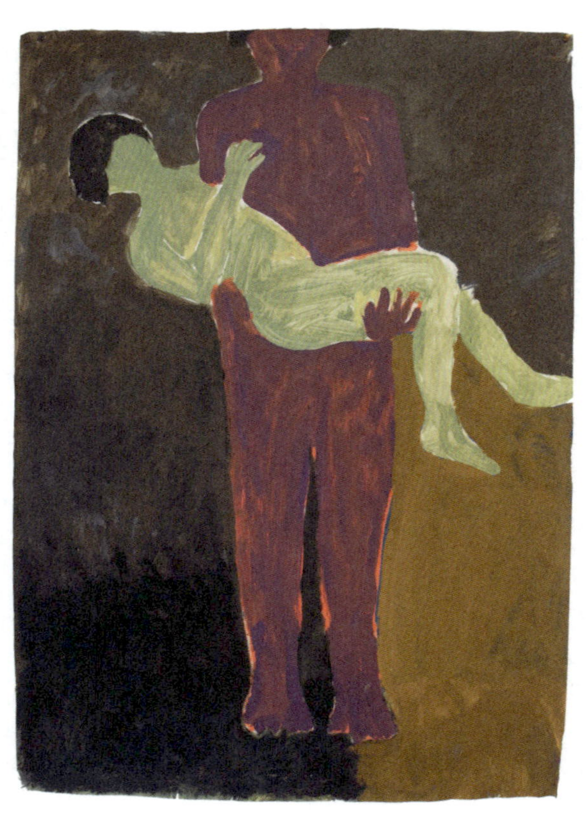

Matthew Offenbacher
untitled, 2018
acrylic on paper, 6' 1" × 4' (175 × 122 cm).
Photo: the artist.

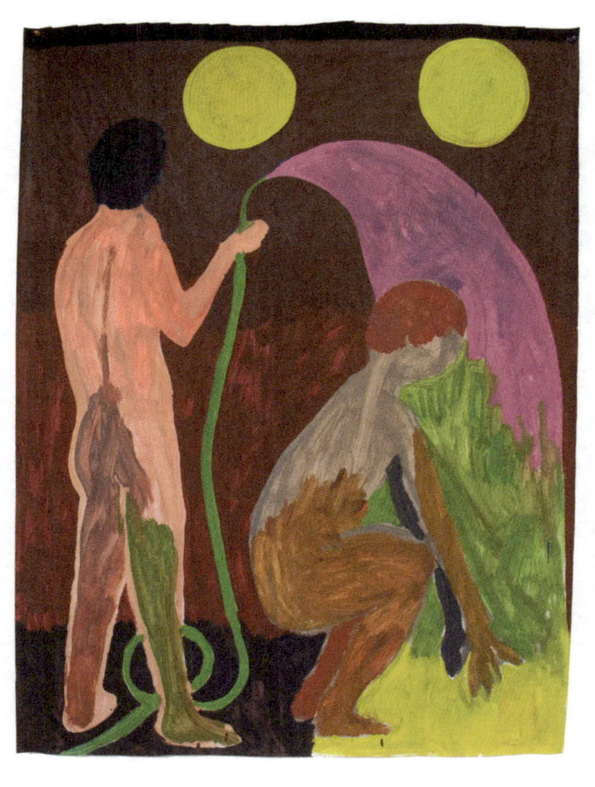

Matthew Offenbacher
untitled, 2018
acrylic on paper, 5' 8" × 4' (164 × 122 cm).
Photo: the artist.

Postscript

"Camouflaged for Fire" began as a response to Matthew Offenbacher's *Feelings*, an installation and dance performance at the Oxbow Gallery in Seattle, Washington, in June 2019.

Feelings is ninety-six chalky tempera paintings in brilliant colors of around 6 × 4' (183 × 122 cm) that were pinned on three adjacent walls, five across, four down. Paintings were pinned beneath paintings as well, so they sometimes fluttered open like recently read books. Matthew based the figures in the paintings on the ancient Greek romance novel *Daphnis and Chloe*.

One afternoon the paintings served as a set and score for a dance performance in three parts. First, the five performers—Matthew, Elby Brosch, Alex Leydon, South and Jeremy Steward—struck the poses of the painted figures. They imitated them by stopping still in their poses for a minute or so and then slowly moving on to create a new one. Next the performers worked in pairs, imitating the poses of two things in a painting together. Comical entanglements ensued. The stiffness of the living stood out against the vitality of the still paintings. In the final act, a performer would strike a pose on a pedestal, this time imitating monuments and statues that exist in the world. The other performers surrounded the frozen one and as the statue began almost imperceptibly to lose its balance the group would form a swift energetic negotiation to catch and remove the person-statue from the pedestal and set them prone on the ground until they dissolved and became human and mobile again.

I found the performance inexplicably moving. The objectified beings, static and silent on the wall, seemed released through the dancers. The dancers' eyes took and then embodied what they saw, and then, it seemed, gave something back, or up. The mimesis seemed a chimera of mockery and eros; as if rocks were skipped in Narcissus's pond, and then became some new species of boomerang, part rose. Matthew wrote that he was "thinking about the links between things we call 'classic' and supremacism," about what it means to be in a body, and what it means to be in a body moving through space, particularly in relation to identity. My writing was an attempt to explore what I thought I saw taken and given by the bodies in *Feelings*—paper and flesh, past and present, and also not present, but possible—and how.

Present here, with my deepest gratitude and admiration for the artists, is the ending of Gwendolyn Brooks's poem *Riot*, murals and paintings by artists Isabel Cabanillas and Cecilia Vicuña, Georges Bataille's *Story of the Eye*, and Mati Diop's film *Atlantics*.

Reykjavik, October 2020

1 Gwendolyn Brooks, *Riot* (Chicago: Broadside Press, 1969).

All the Women I Know

Laura Larson

Ongoing since 2018

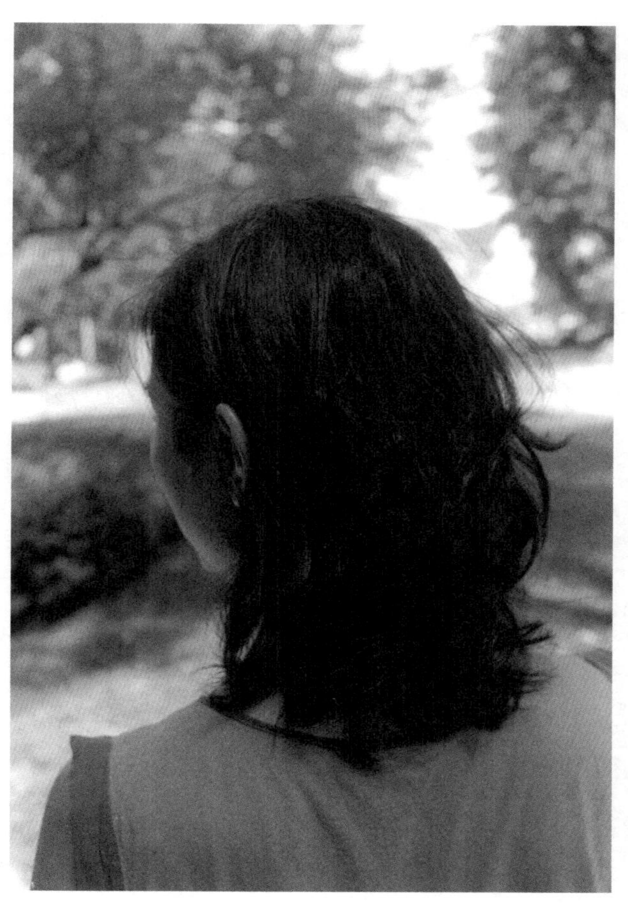

Gina
2019

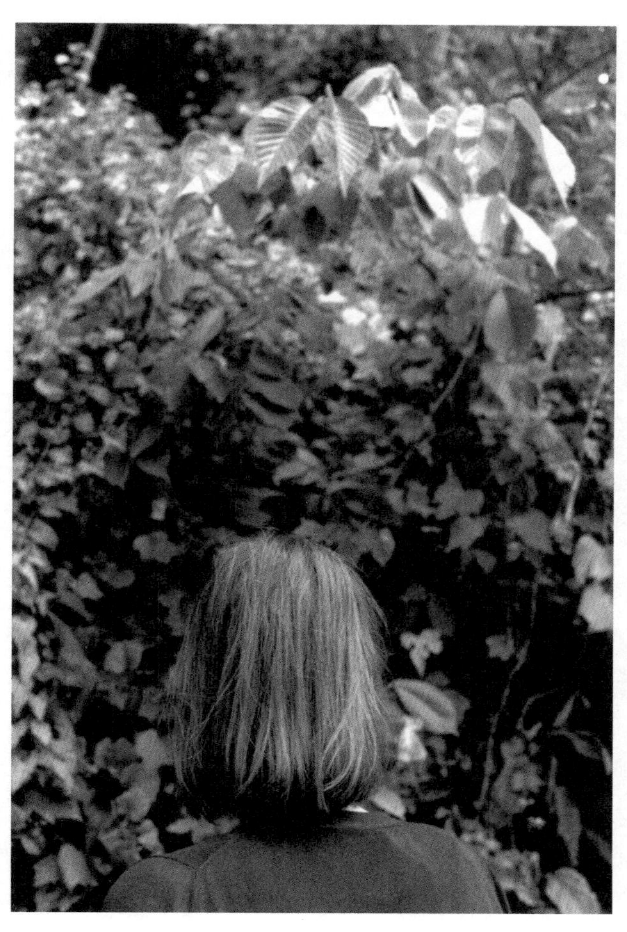

Christine
2019

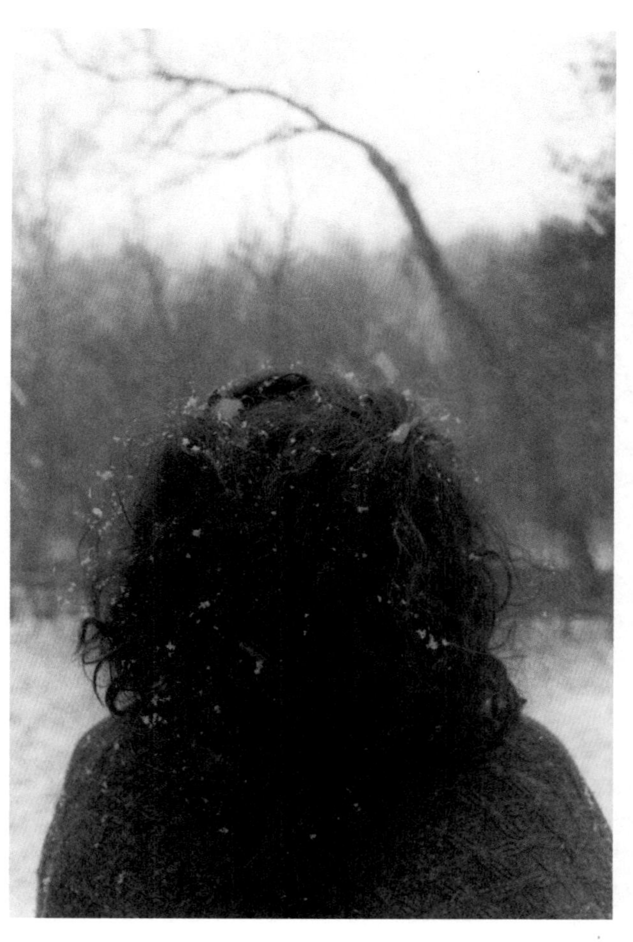

Alex
2019

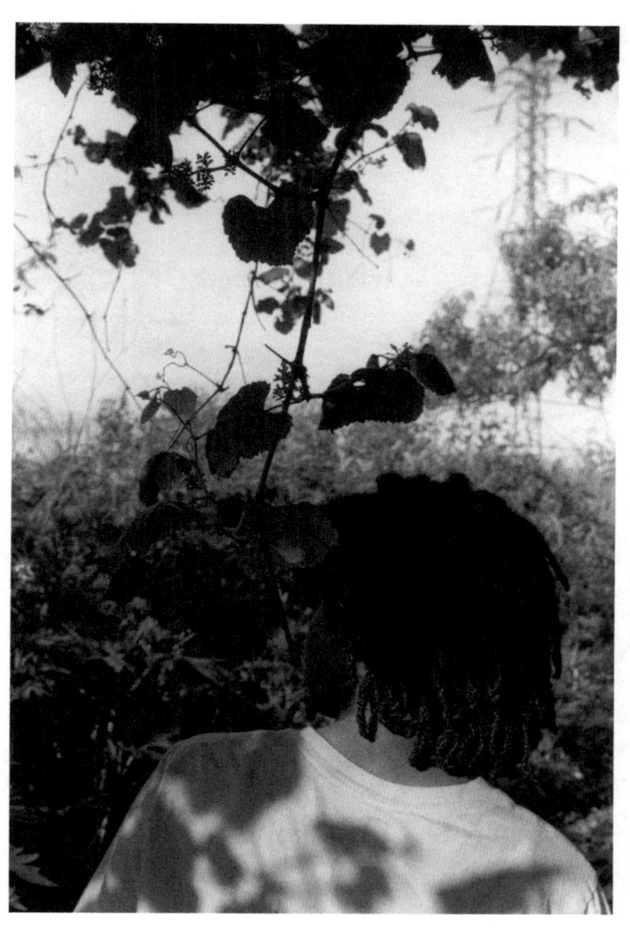

Gadisse
2019

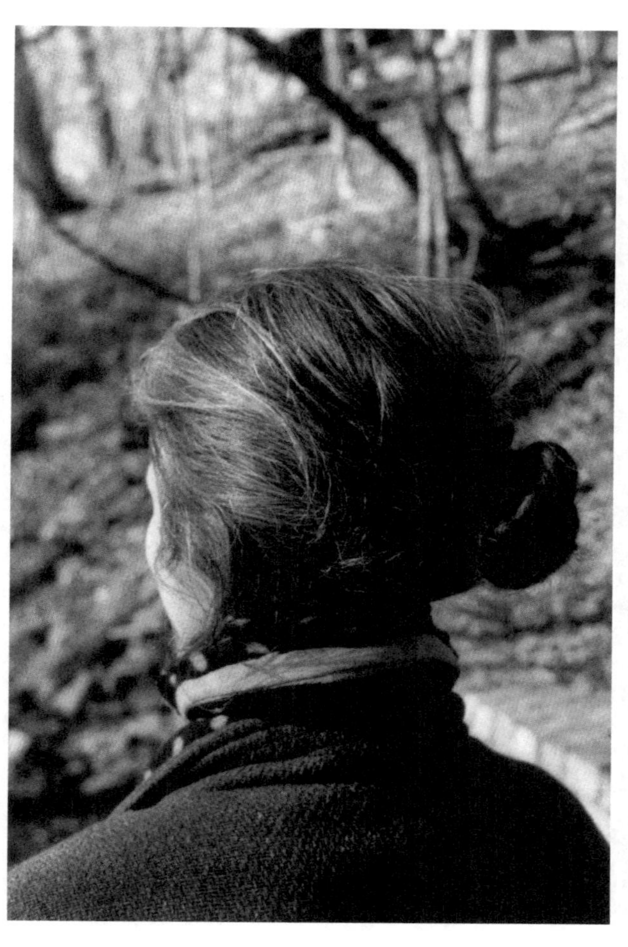

Heide
2020

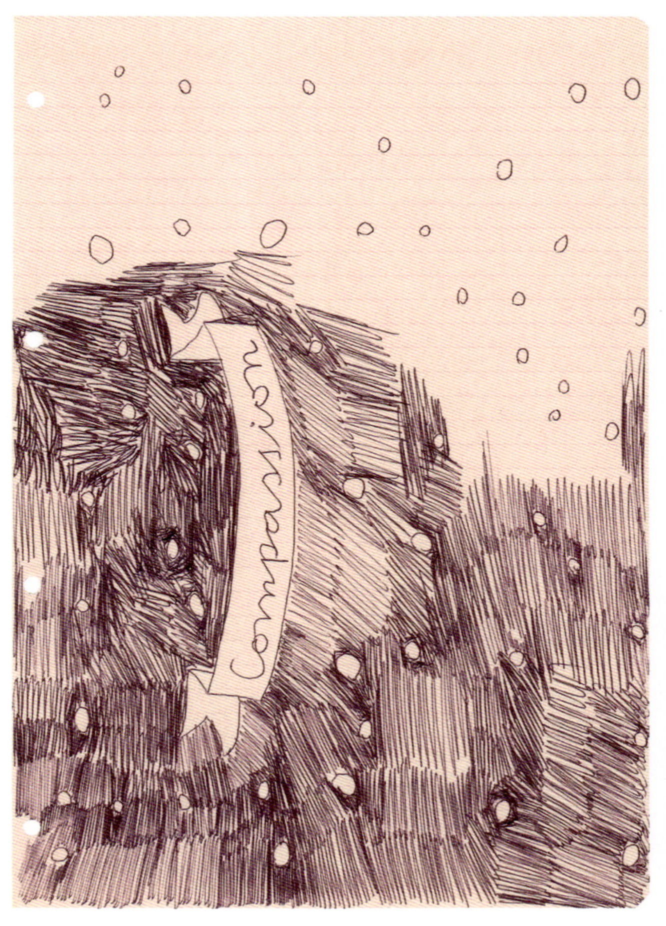
Comparison

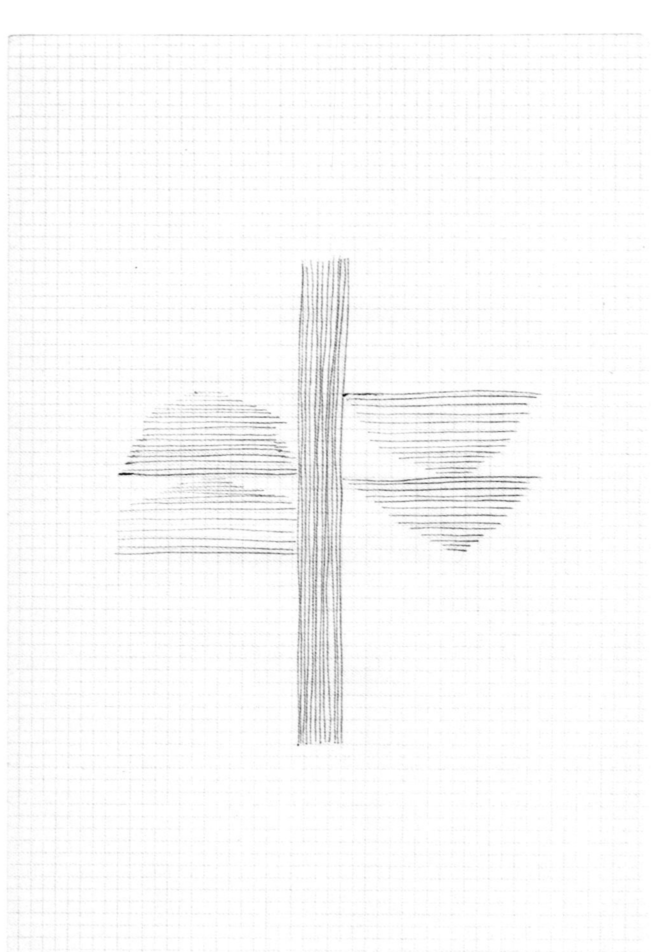

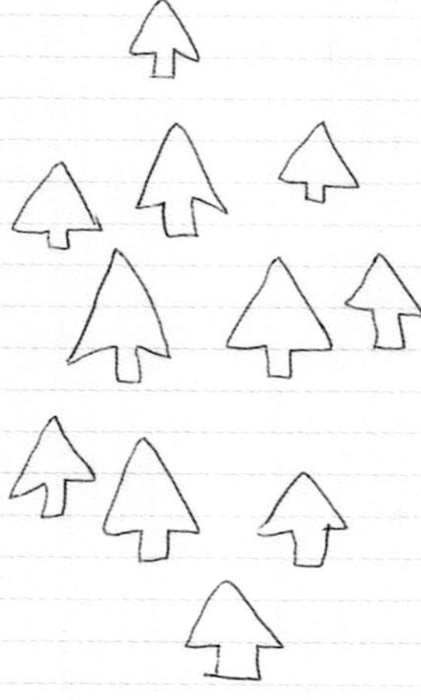

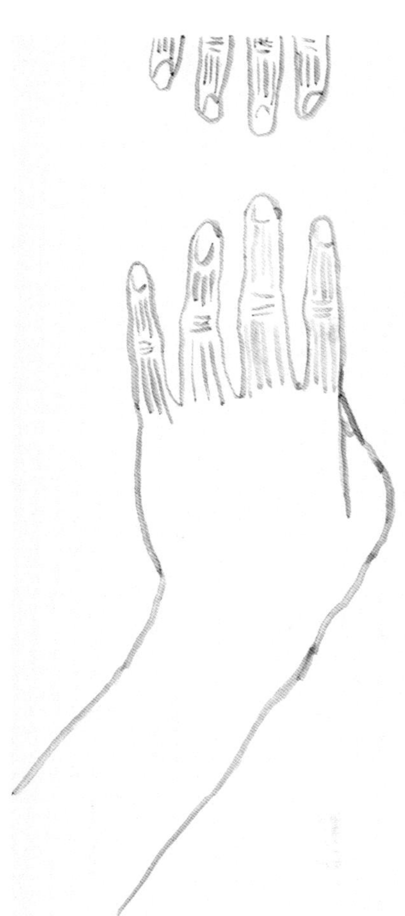

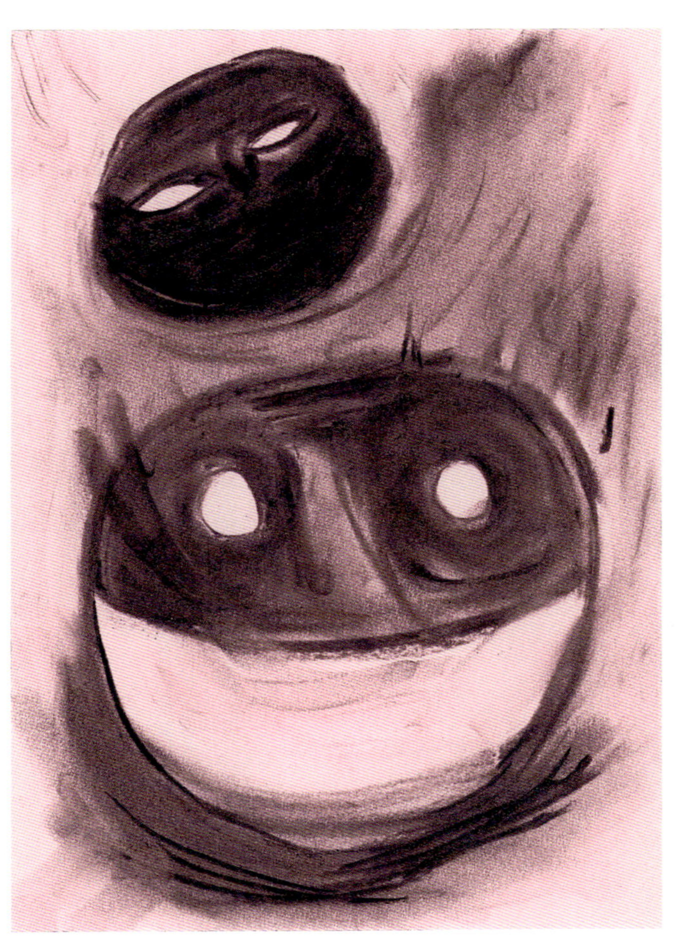

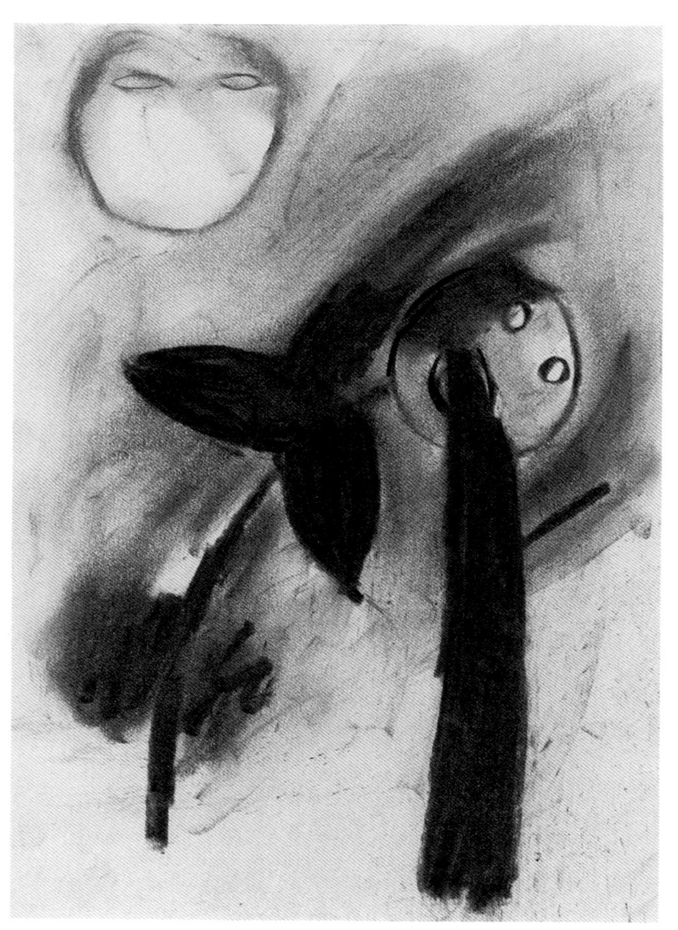

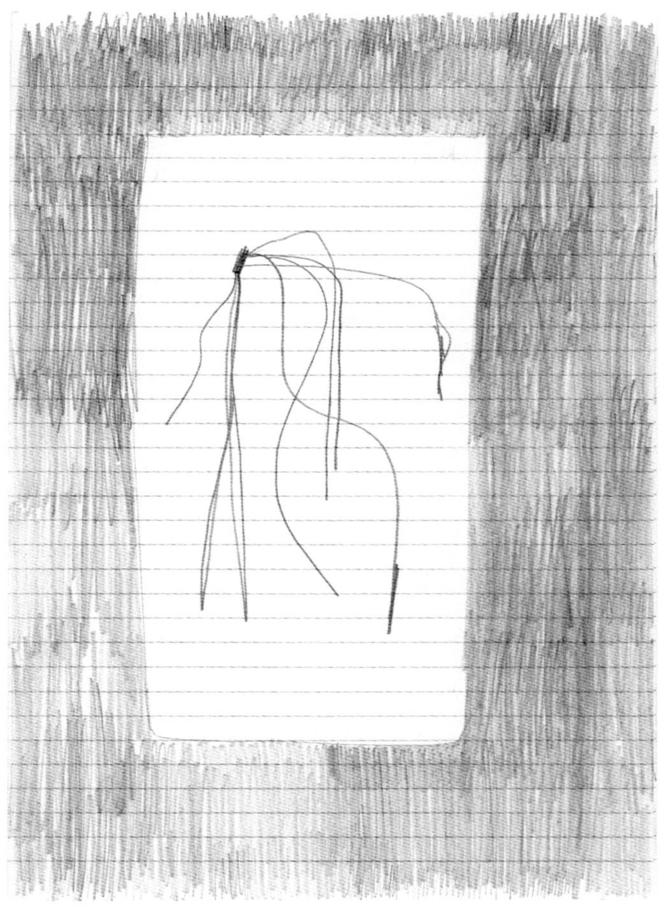

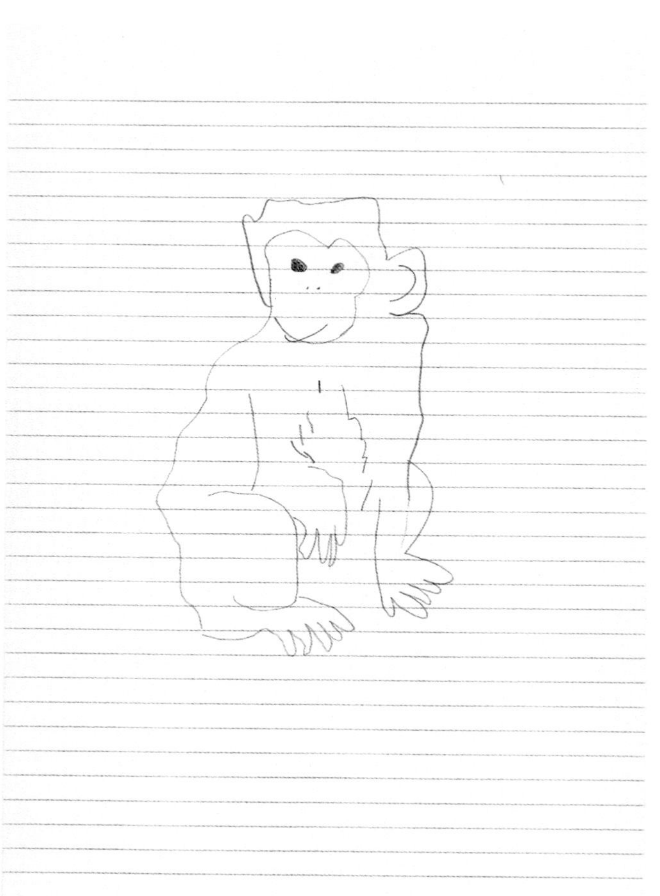

Biographies

Sara De Bondt is a Belgian graphic designer working mainly for cultural clients. In 2008, she founded the non-profit imprint Occasional Papers with Antony Hudek. She is a PhD candidate at KASK School of Arts Ghent, where she teaches. See also occasionalpapers.org and saradebondt.com.

Rachel Dedman is Curator of Contemporary Art from the Middle East at the V&A, London. From 2013 to 2019 she was an independent curator based in Beirut, Lebanon, where she curated for institutions large and small across the Middle East and Europe. Current and recent work includes projects for Kettle's Yard (Cambridge), the Whitworth Gallery (Manchester), Ashkal Alwan (Beirut), Sursock Museum (Beirut), Serpentine Galleries (London), and the Palestinian Museum (Ramallah). Rachel is published extensively, and is one third of Radio Earth Hold, a research collective creating and commissioning broadcasts from artists and writers. See also racheldedman.com.

Elizabeth Haines works at the National Archives of the United Kingdom, and was previously Vice-Chancellor's Fellow in History at the University of Bristol. Her interdisciplinary interest in the materiality of knowledge production draws strongly on her education in Fine Arts. One strand of her research focuses on mapping and the lived experience of land rights in twentieth-century Africa. In another strand of research she has been exploring what scholars can learn about the recent past when they begin their research with objects. Elizabeth is currently working on projects with the Science Museum Group, Bristol Museums, Galleries and Archives, and National Museums of Kenya.

Heide Hinrichs is an artist based in Brussels, who works with found and existing materials. For the first Kathmandu Triennale (2017) she developed the project *On Some of the Birds of Nepal (Parting the Animal Kingdom of the East)*. In 2018 Hinrichs published *Silent Sisters / Stille Schwestern*, an unauthorized German translation of Theresa Hak Kyung Cha's text *Dictee* (Tanam Press, New York, 1982). Her drawing series *Inscriptions* was shown in 2020 as part of *Season Two: Follow the Mud*, Beeler Gallery at Columbus College of Art & Design, Ohio; *Risquons-Tout*, WIELS, Brussels; and *ringing critical forests*, KIOSK, Ghent. Currently she is also researching and teaching at the Royal Academy of Fine Arts Antwerp. See also 4h-club.org.

Laura Larson is an artist and writer based in Columbus, Ohio. Mining the intersection between politics and poetics, her work looks to photography's history as a documentary practice to tell personal and sociocultural narratives. She has exhibited her work extensively including the Bronx Museum of the Arts, Centre Pompidou, Columbus Museum of Art, Metropolitan Museum of Art, Museum of Fine Arts, Houston, and Wexner Center for the Arts. Her image-text book, *Hidden Mother* (Saint Lucy Books, 2017), presents a lyrical account of becoming a mother through adoption mapped through nineteenth-century hidden mother photographs. The book was shortlisted for the Paris Photo–Aperture First PhotoBook Prize. Her second book, *City of Incurable Women*, will be published by Saint Lucy Books in 2022. See also lauralarson.net.

Samia Malik is an artist and designer. In 2002, she launched her clothing label *Samia Malik ihtgw*, independently sold worldwide. In 2004, she studied MA Womenswear at Central Saint Martins, London. In 2007, she designed for musician M.I.A. From 2012 to 2014, she studied MFA Fine Art at Goldsmiths, University of London. The central focus of Samia's art practice has been on issues of racism, sexism, Islamophobia and social injustice. Samia is the director and co-founder of WOCI (Women of Colour Index) Reading Group. Currently Samia also works for *Shades of Noir* at University of Arts, London as an Associate Lecturer.

Melanie Noel is the author of *THE MONARCHS* (Stockport Flats) and *A Ringing* (Goodmorning Menagerie). Her poems have also appeared in *Spiral Orb, La Norda Especialo, GUEST*, and *The Arcadia Project*. She's written for short films and installations, and curated *IMPALA*, a reading series that took place in her grandmother's car. She's an independent teacher and editor whose experiential workshops invoking synesthesia are becoming more performative.

Marisa C. Sánchez is an art historian and curator of modern and contemporary art, with teaching and research interests in feminist art histories, methodologies of art history, exhibition histories, and the intersection of visual art and Samuel Beckett's writings. Prior to receiving her PhD from the University of British Columbia, Vancouver, she was Associate Curator, Modern and Contemporary Art at the Seattle Art Museum. She's currently preparing a book proposal on her dissertation, *The Beckett Effect: The Work of Stan Douglas, Paul Chan, and Tania Bruguera*. Marisa lives and works in Vancouver as a guest on the unceded territory of the Coast Salish Peoples, including territories of the xʷməθkʷəy̓əm (Musqueam), Sḵwx̱wú7mesh (Squamish), and Səl̓ílwətaʔ/Selilwitulh (Tsleil-Waututh).

David Senior is the Head of Library and Archives at the San Francisco Museum of Modern Art. Formerly he was the Senior Bibliographer at MoMA Library in New York. For the last twelve years, he has organized a program of events, The Classroom, for Printed Matter's New York Art Book Fair and more recently, at the Los Angeles Art Book Fair. Senior edited *Steven Leiber Catalogs* (2019) on the work of book dealer Steven Leiber, published by Inventory Press and RITE Editions. He serves on the Boards of Directors of Primary Information and Yale Union.

Jo-ey Tang (Hong Kong, based in the US and France) can be an artist, a curator, and a writer. Art: Musée d'art contemporain de la Haute-Vienne; IAC Villeurbanne / Rhône-Alpes; Komplot, Brussels; Lyles & King, New York; Galerie Joseph Tang, Paris. Roles: Arts Editor, *n+1*; Curator, Palais de Tokyo, Paris; Director of Exhibitions, Beeler Gallery at Columbus College of Art & Design. Curatorial projects: Centre Pompidou, Paris; Institute of Contemporary Art, Philadelphia; chi K11 art museum, Shanghai; Rupert, Vilnius; FUTURA, Prague. Writing: Artforum.com; *The Brooklyn Rail*; *Flash Art*; Wexner Center for the Arts; S.M.A.K., Ghent; Shimmer, Rotterdam. He is director of KADIST San Francisco since August 2021. See also jo-eytang.com.

Ersi Varveri is a visual artist living and working between Antwerp, Athens and Syros. She is currently conducting a research project connected to the Royal Academy of Fine Arts Antwerp with Gijs Waterschoot, visual artist, entitled *one space becoming another*. They are using their experience in the Pink House (an artist-run space in Antwerp) as the basis for research into new possibilities and necessities for artist-run spaces. Ersi is developing a newspaper edition *How to become* ______ that is published every month, sharing material from her ongoing research and exploring the idea of a portable space in a printed format. See also ersivarveri.com.

Susanne Weiß is a curator, art mediator and writer living in Berlin. Since March 2021 she has co-directed the ifa-gallery with Inka Gressel, a partnership that began in 2015 developing the ifa touring exhibition *The Event of a Thread – Global Narratives in Textiles*. Between 2012–2016 Susanne was the director of the Heidelberger Kunstverein. Her curatorial practice gives attention to the overlooked, the social-political realm within an artistic practice, and also to mediating its contexts. This enables a multitude of voices, counter narratives and a critical re-reading of history. See also mukimaki.de.

Index

Colophon

shelf documents: art library as practice
Editors: Heide Hinrichs, Jo-ey Tang, Elizabeth Haines
Authors: Sara De Bondt, Rachel Dedman, Elizabeth Haines, Heide Hinrichs, Laura Larson, Melanie Noel, Marisa C. Sánchez, David Senior, Jo-ey Tang, Ersi Varveri, Susanne Weiß
Copy editor: Melanie Noel
Copy editor for Marisa C. Sánchez: Greg Gibson
Proofreaders: Devrim Bayar, Sofia Dati, Zoë Gray, Helena Kritis, Brian Raiter

Graphic designer: Sara De Bondt
Graphic design assistance: Sarah Horn
Typefaces: Diotima by Gudrun Zapf von Hesse and Lelo by Katharina Köhler
Printer: Graphius / Stevens Print, Ghent

Cover image: Detail of Heide Hinrichs' *Inscriptions SB 1*, 2019.

Both American and British spelling and grammar are used within *shelf documents* reflecting the different geographies in which the contributors live and work.

Thank you to Liene Aerts, Leontien Allemeersch, Laëtitia Badaut Haussmann, Anne-Christin Bielig, Ine Boogmans, Sonel Breslav, Wei Ling Chang, Florence Cheval, Marina Coelho, Anna Dasović, Cara Davies, Simon Delobel, Loraine Furter, Stephan Geene, Arthur Haegeman, Leslie Jankowski, Zane A. Miller, Clare Noonan, Matthew Offenbacher, Min Park, Vijai Patchineelam, Thomas Peeters, JiaHao Peng, Marla Roddy, Ian Ruffino, Gintaute Skvernyte, Dirk Snauwaert, Cédrik Toselli, Wim Waelput.

Track Report
Royal Academy of Fine Arts Antwerp

b_books

This publication is part of Heide Hinrichs' research project *second shelf* at the Royal Academy of Fine Arts Antwerp.
second-shelf.org

Publisher: Pascale De Groote
Lange Nieuwstraat 101, 2000 Antwerp

Editor-in-chief: Johan Pas
Coordination: Stefan Vanthuyne

Track Report documents research in the arts at the Royal Academy of Fine Arts Antwerp AP University College, Mutsaardstraat 31 B-2000 Antwerp.

TR 20/02
Legal Deposit: D/2020/411/2

Co-published by b_books, Berlin
bbooks.de

ISBN: 978-3942214384

First printing: January 2021
Supported by Beeler Gallery, KIOSK and WIELS
Print run: 600 copies

Second printing: November 2021
Supported by KIOSK
Print run: 800 copies

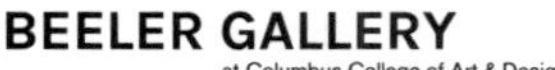

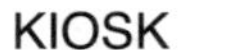

WIELS

List of Drawings

Inscriptions is based on drawings by artists present in the *second shelf* collection: Anni Albers, Lutz Bacher, Silvia Bächli, Louise Bourgeois, Andrea Büttner, Miriam Cahn, Ulises Carrión, Hanne Darboven, Mirtha Dermisache, Ulrike Grossarth, Eva Hesse, Hilma af Klint, Emma Kunz, Lee Lozano, Agnes Martin, Ana Mendieta, Ree Morton, Meret Oppenheim, Lygia Pape, Lily van der Stokker, Sturtevant, Paul Thek, Cecilia Vicuña, Annette Weisser, and Rachel Whiteread. The series consists of 240 drawings in total of which sixty-four are included in this book. They are drawn on A4 and letter-size paper and are dated between 2006 and 2020.

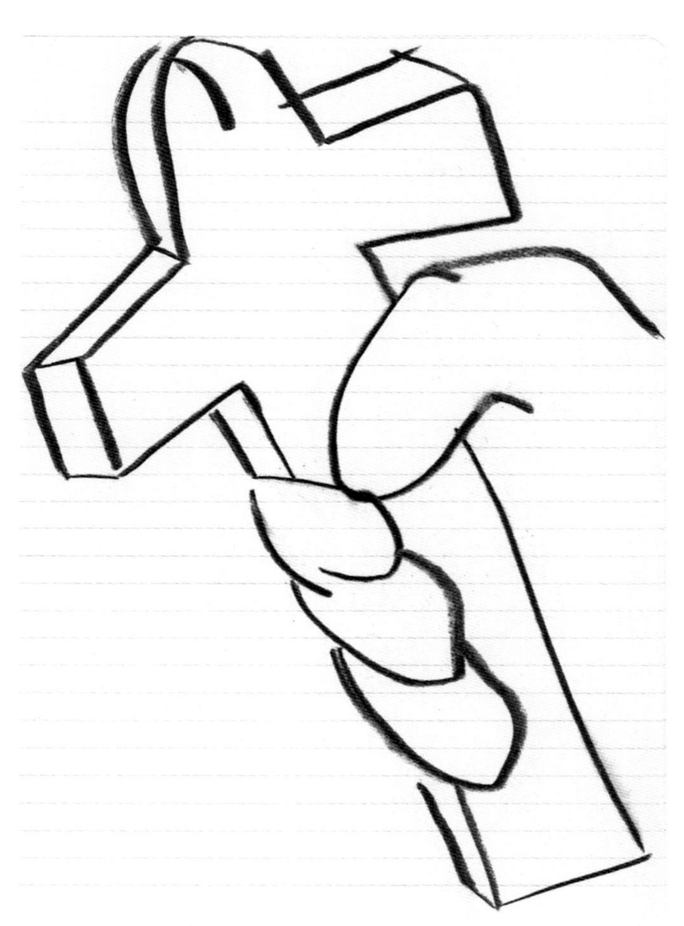

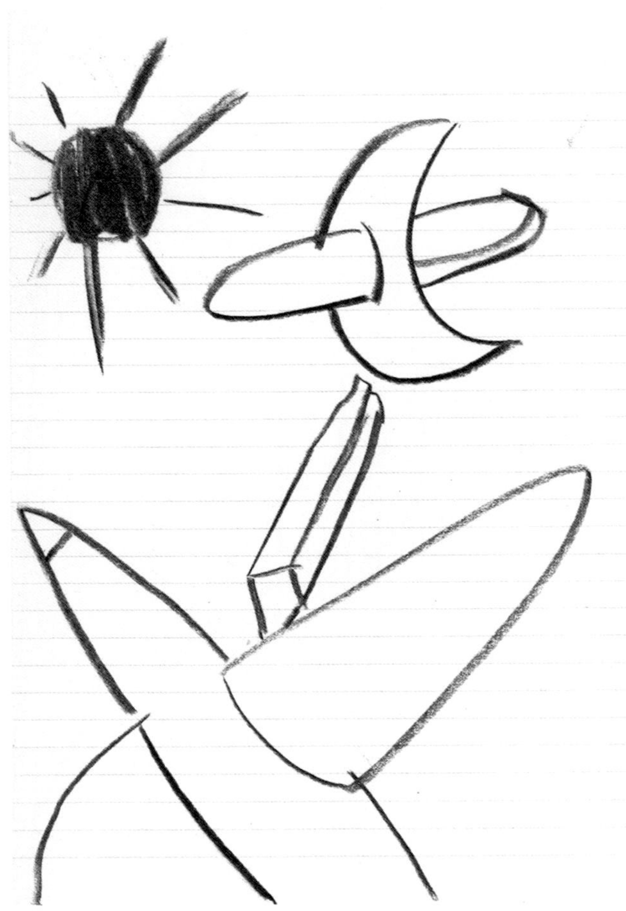

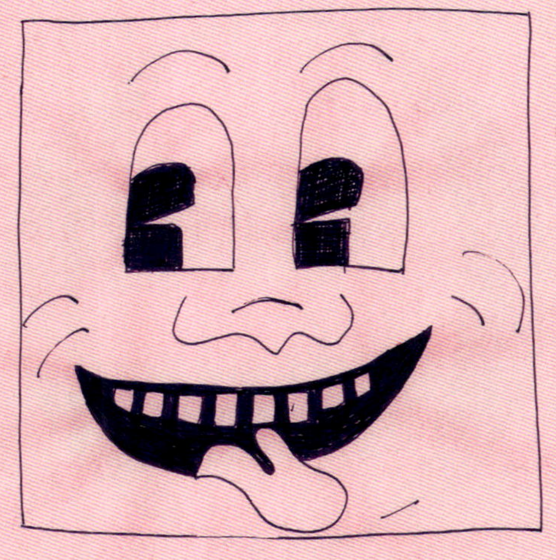

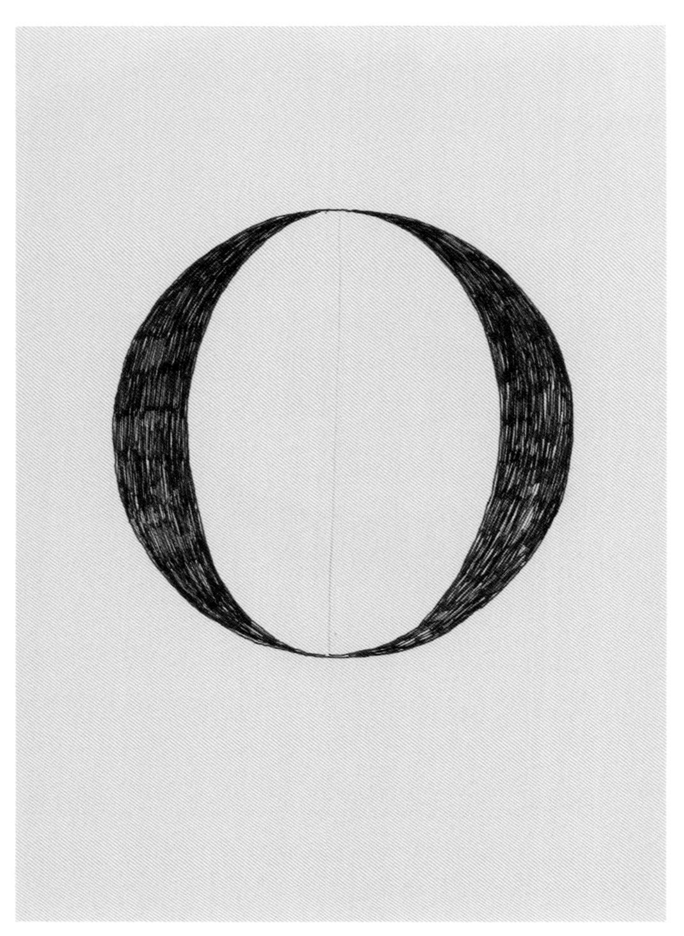

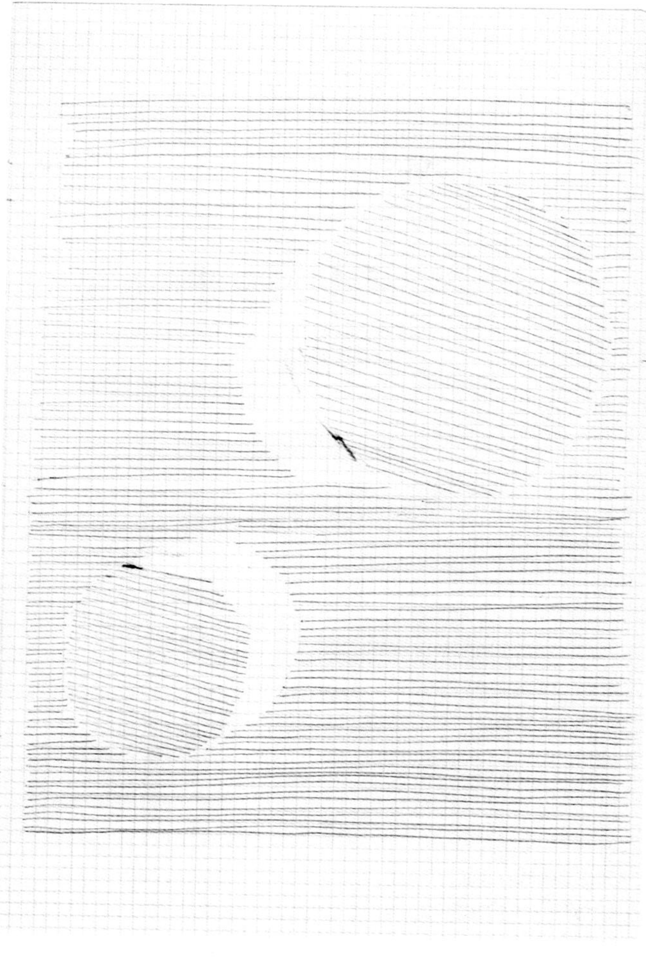

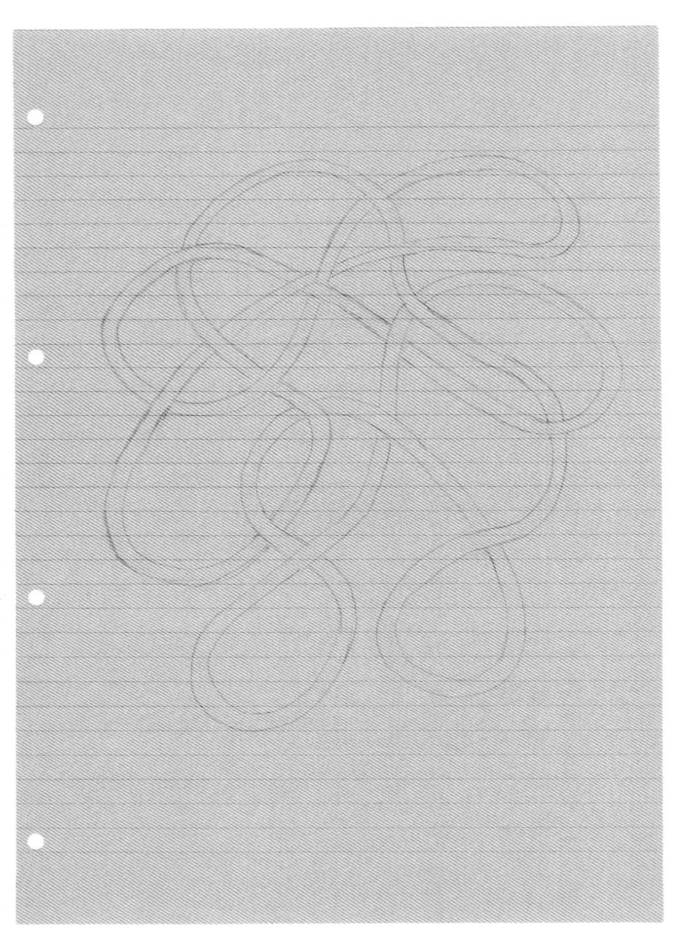

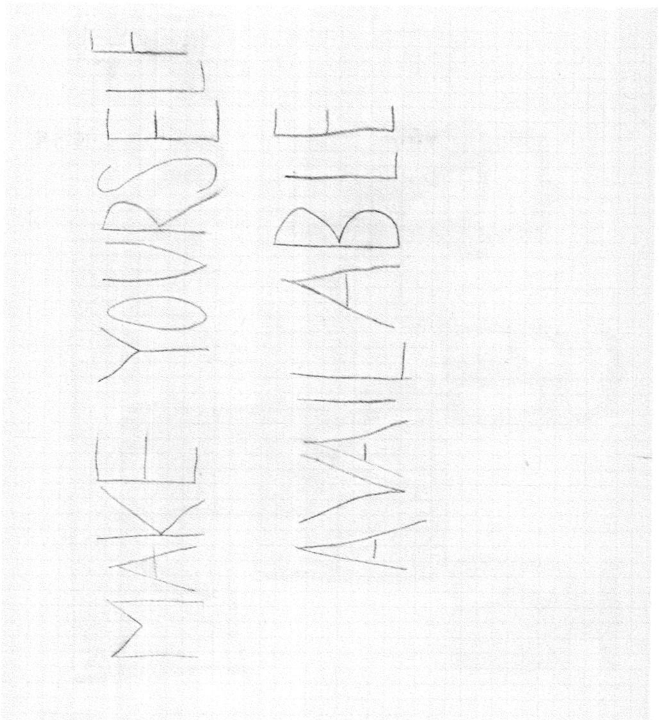

MAKE YOURSELF
AVAILABLE

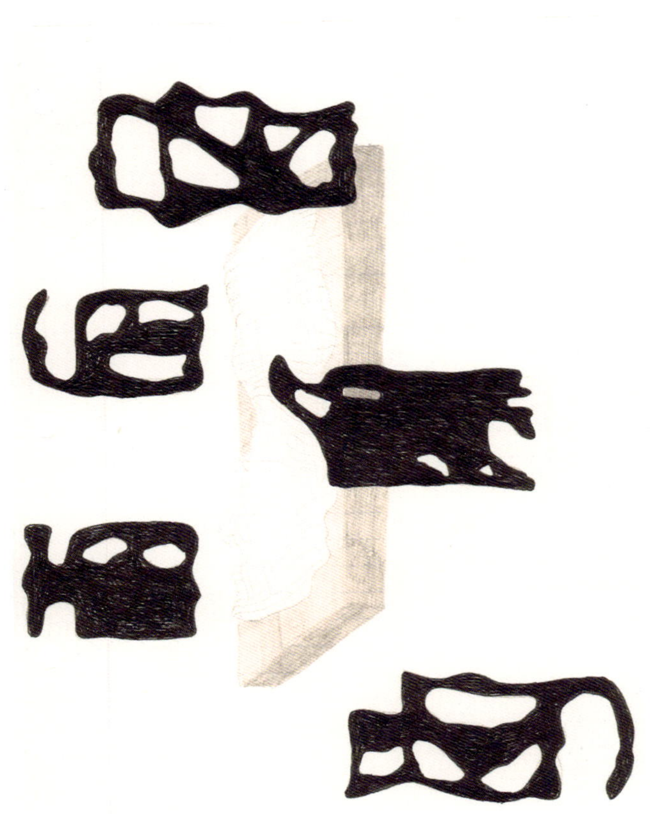